OFFICIAL HISTORY
OF
AUSTRALIA
IN THE WAR OF 1914-1918

ATLAS

Volume XIII –
Cartographic Record of the War

The Naval & Miltary Press

Published by

The Naval & Military Press Ltd
Unit 5 Riverside, Brambleside
Bellbrook Industrial Estate
Uckfield, East Sussex
TN22 1QQ England

Tel: +44 (0)1825 749494

www.naval-military-press.com
www.nmarchive.com

In reprinting in facsimile from the original, any imperfections are inevitably reproduced and the quality may fall short of modern type and cartographic standards.

CONTENTS

VOLUME I 1
THE STORY OF ANZAC
From the outbreak of war to the end of the first phase of the Gallipoli Campaign, May 4, 1915

VOLUME II 33
THE STORY OF ANZAC
From 4 May, 1915, to the evacuation of the Gallipoli peninsula

VOLUME III 69
THE AUSTRALIAN IMPERIAL FORCE IN FRANCE
1916

VOLUME IV 85
THE AUSTRALIAN IMPERIAL FORCE IN FRANCE
1917

VOLUME V 93
THE AUSTRALIAN IMPERIAL FORCE IN FRANCE
During the main German Offensive, 1918

VOLUME VI 101
THE AUSTRALIAN IMPERIAL FORCE IN FRANCE
During the Allied Offensive, 1918

VOLUME VII 107
THE AUSTRALIAN IMPERIAL FORCE IN SINAI AND PALESTINE
1914-1918

VOLUME VIII 175
THE AUSTRALIAN FLYING CORPS : 1914-1919
Operations on the Western Front, Sinai and Palestine

VOLUME IX 199
THE ROYAL AUSTRALIAN NAVY
1914-1918

VOLUME X 239
THE AUSTRALIANS AT RABAUL
The capture and administration of the German possessions in the Southern Pacific

VOLUME XI 253
AUSTRALIA DURING THE WAR

THE
STORY OF ANZAC

FROM THE OUTBREAK OF WAR TO THE END
OF THE FIRST PHASE OF THE GALLIPOLI
CAMPAIGN, MAY 4, 1915

VOLUME I

LIST OF MAPS

1. Position of the transports when the *Sydney* left the convoy in chase of the *Emden*, 7 a.m., 9th November, 1914
2. The Turkish advance against the Suez Canal, January-February, 1915
3. The Turkish attack on the Suez Canal between Tussum and Serapeum, 3rd-4th February, 1915
4. The Dardanelles, showing the known Turkish forts at the time of the Naval attack, February-March, 1915
5. Lemnos, Imbros, Tenedos and the Dardanelles
6. The Eastern Mediterranean traversed by the Expedition, showing Alexandretta and Gallipoli
7. Objectives for the 1st Australian Division, and for the A. and N.Z. Army Corps (Mal Tepe); and the position eventually gained by the Corps
8. Disposition of the Turkish forces on the Peninsula prior to the landing
9. Diagram showing the intended disposition of the warships and transports of the 1st Australian Division approaching Gaba Tepe
10. Ships off Ari Burnu at the time of landing of the 1st Australian Division, 4.30 a.m., 25th April, 1915
11. The rush of the Covering Force (3rd Australian Infantry Brigade) up the hills above its landing place, 4.30 to 5.30 a.m., 25th April, 1915
12. The Anzac position, showing the Turkish defences and some of the furthest points reached by the A. and N.Z. troops on 25th April, 1915; the position eventually held; and the "First," "Second" and "Third" ridges
13. Captain Tulloch's advance and the position on Baby 700 and MacLaurin's Hill, 9 to 10 a.m., 25th April, 1915
14. The Turkish counter-attack at the time of the loss of Baby 700, from 3.30 to 5 p.m., 25th April, 1915
15. The fighting at Fisherman's Hut, 25th April, 1915
16. The 400 Plateau at the time of Salisbury's advance, 9 to 10 a.m., 25th April, 1915
17. The position on the 400 Plateau during the retirement of the advanced parties of 3rd Brigade, and the advance of 2nd Brigade, between 10 a.m. and noon, 25th April, 1915
18. Position of the right of the 1st Australian Division about noon, 25th April, 1915
19. Turkish counter-attacks on the A. and N.Z. Army Corps at Ari Burnu on the day of the landing
20. The advance of the 4th Battalion, Saker, and McNicoll on the 400 Plateau, about 3 p.m., 26th April, 1915
21. The advance of Braund with the 2nd Battalion and New Zealanders on Russell's Top, 27th April, 1915
22. The Anzac position about 5th May, 1915, showing headquarters, gun positions, stores, etc.
23. Captain Leane's raid on Gaba Tepe at dawn, 4th May, 1915
24. Attack by the N.Z. and A. Division on Baby 700. The position at dawn, 3rd May, 1915

Map No. 1

DIAGRAM SHOWING THE POSITION OF THE TRANSPORTS WHEN THE *Sydney* LEFT THE CONVOY IN CHASE OF THE *Emden*, 7 A.M., 9TH Nov., 1914

Map No. 2

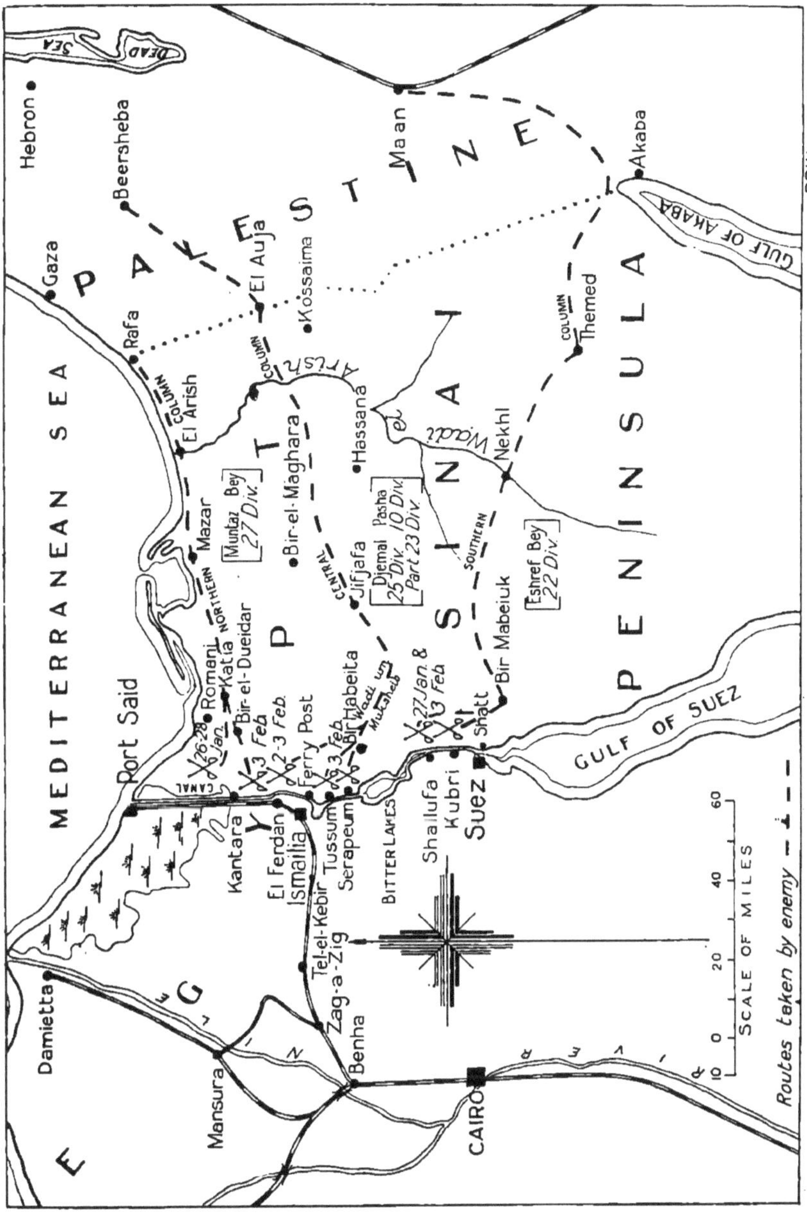

Map No. 3

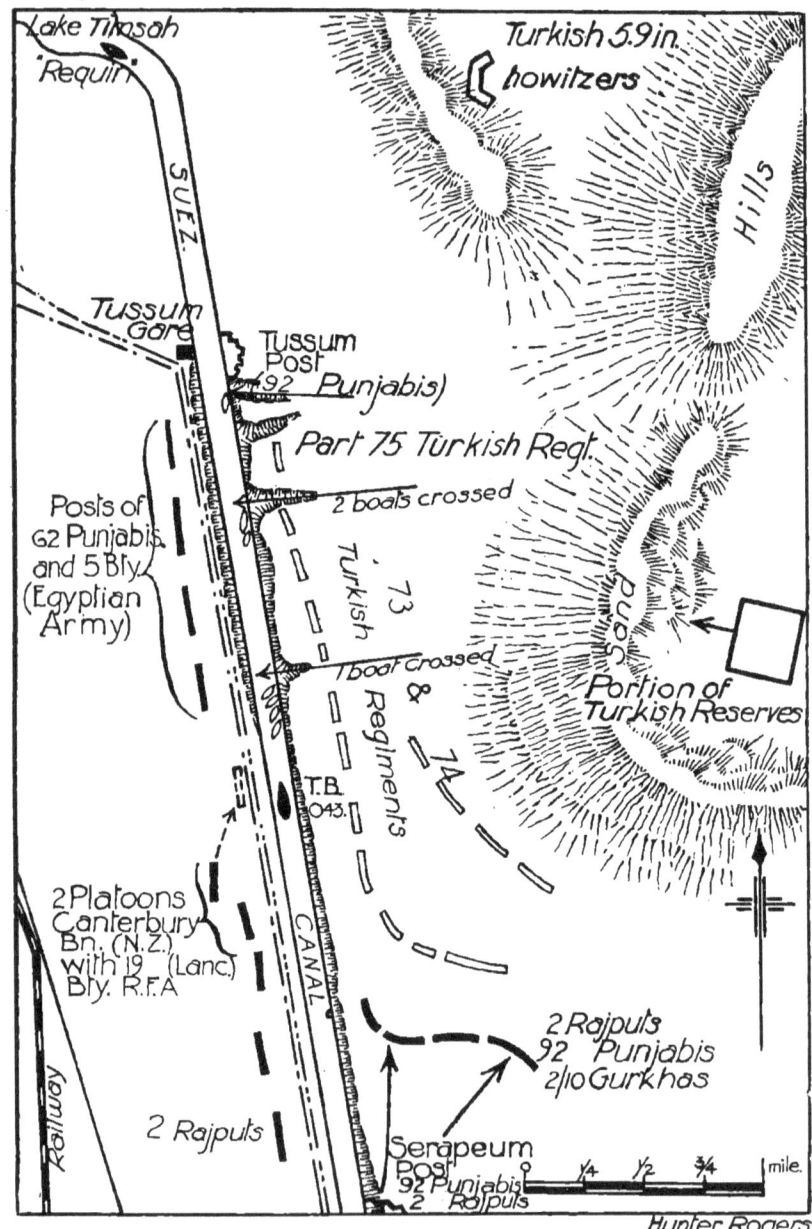

THE TURKISH ATTACK ON THE SUEZ CANAL BETWEEN TUSSUM AND SERAPEUM, 3RD-4TH FEBRUARY, 1915

Map No. 4

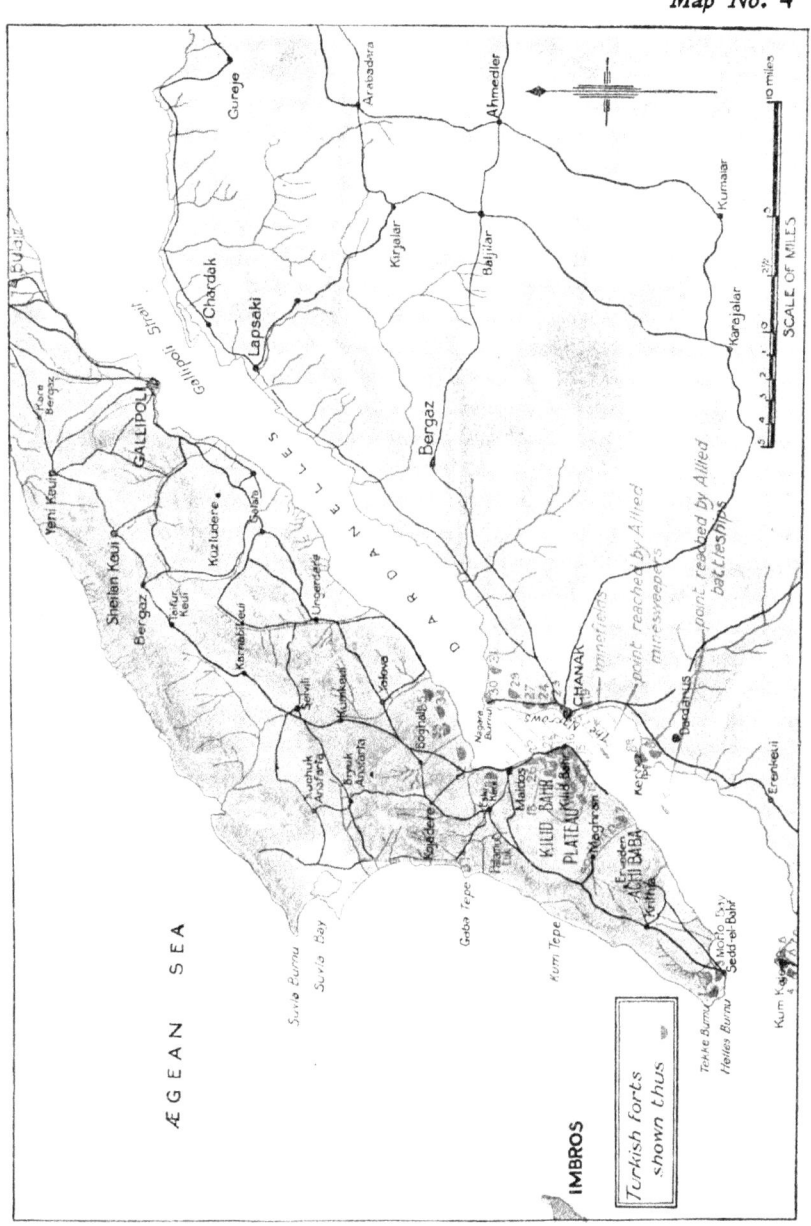

THE DARDANELLES, SHOWING THE KNOWN TURKISH FORTS AT THE TIME OF THE NAVAL ATTACK, FEBRUARY-MARCH, 1915

Map No. 5

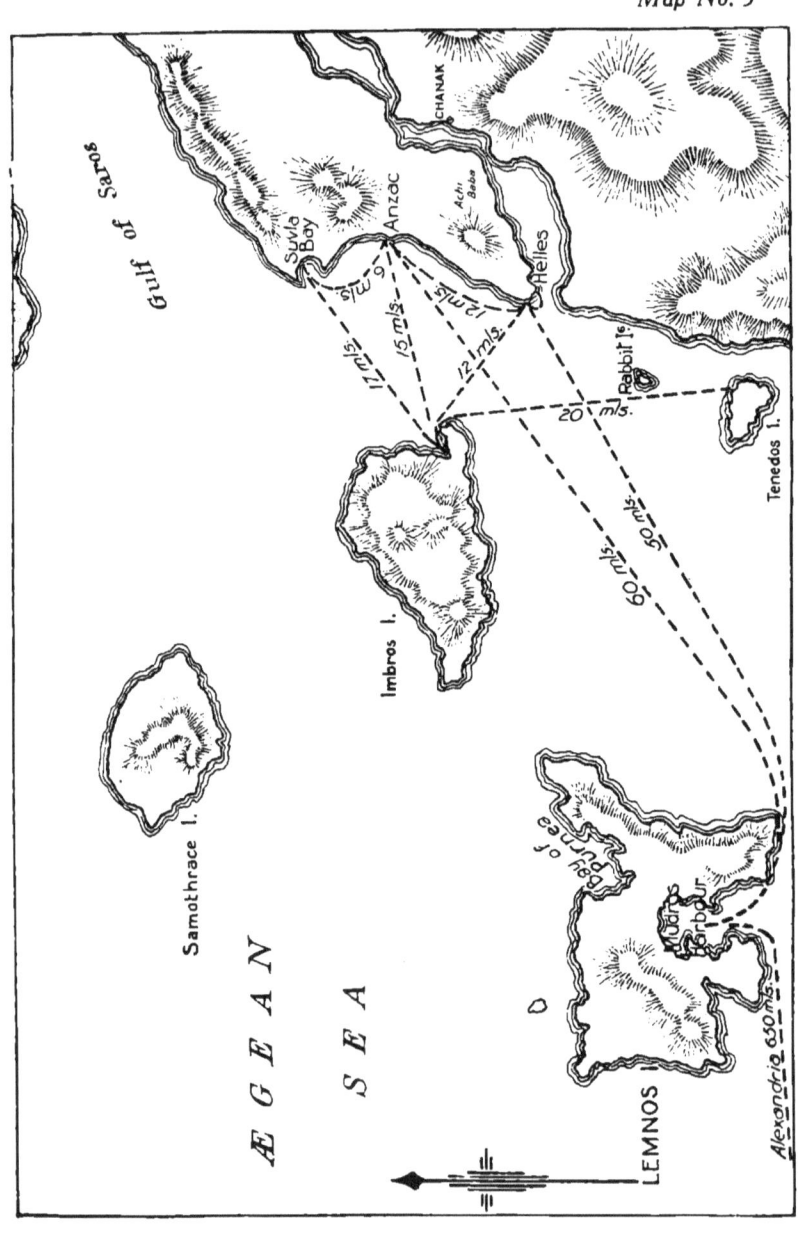

Lemnos, Imbros, Tenedos and the Dardanelles

Map No. 6

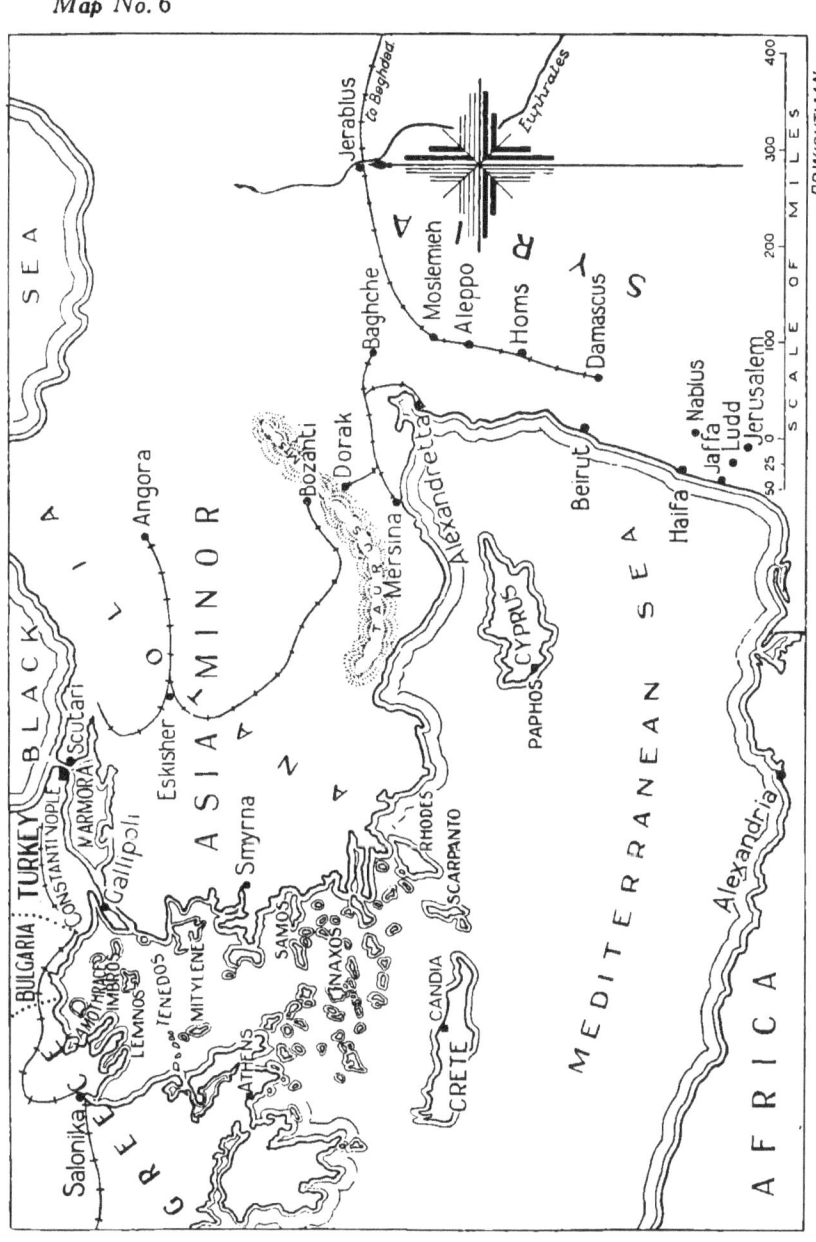

THE EASTERN MEDITERRANEAN TRAVERSED BY THE EXPEDITION, SHOWING ALEXANDRETTA AND GALLIPOLI

Map No. 7

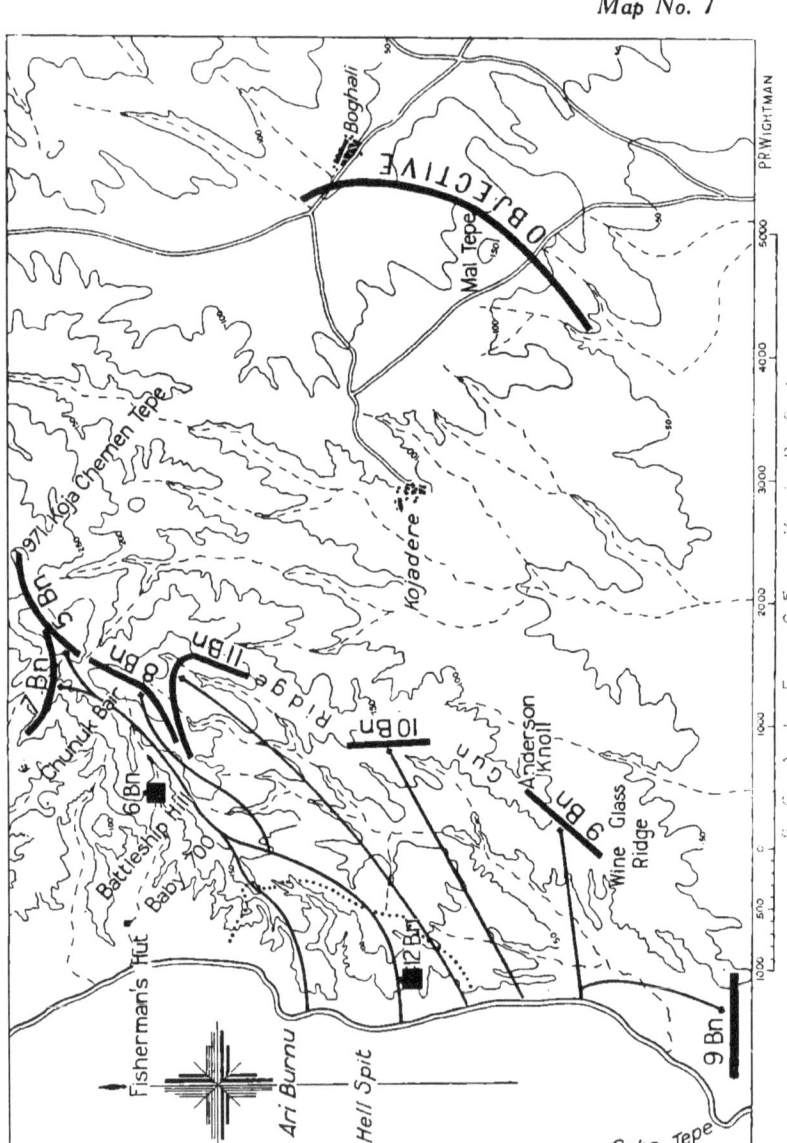

Objectives for the 1st Australian Division, and for the A. & N.Z. Army Corps (Mal Tepe). The small dotted line shows the position eventually gained by the Corps

Map No. 8

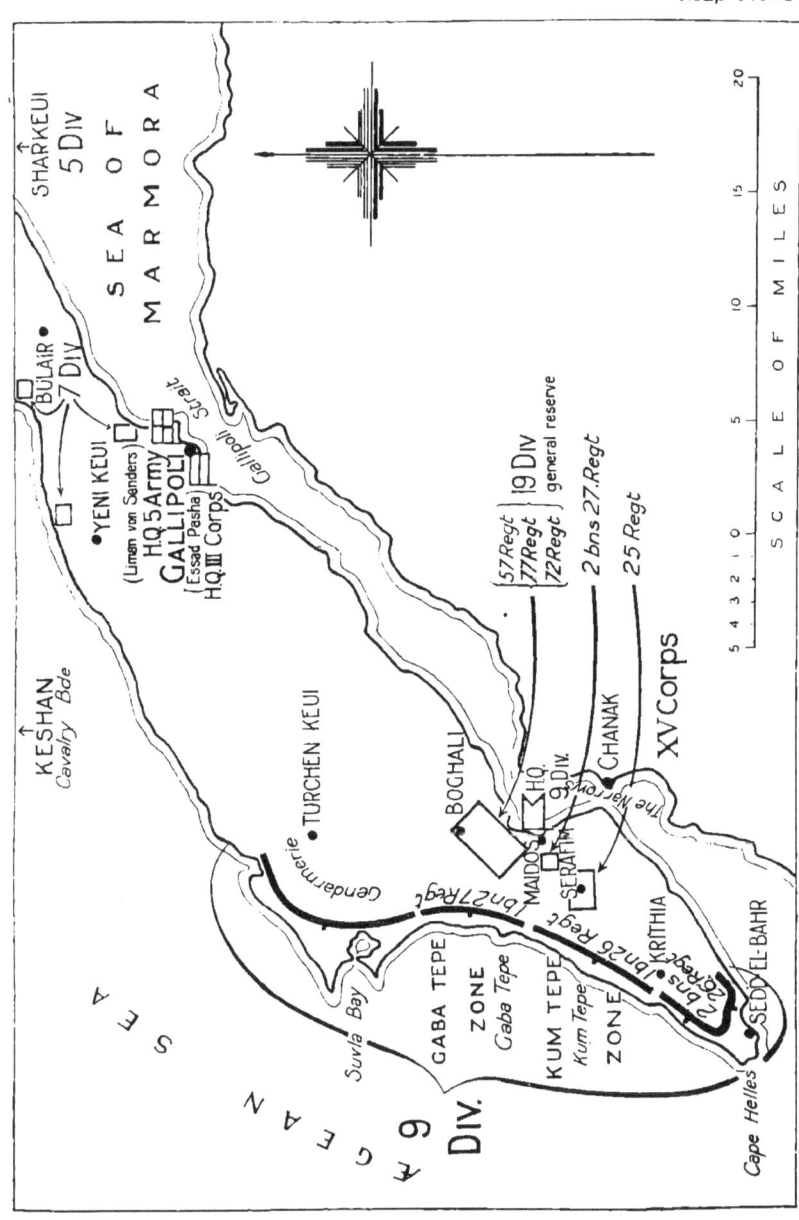

Map No. 9

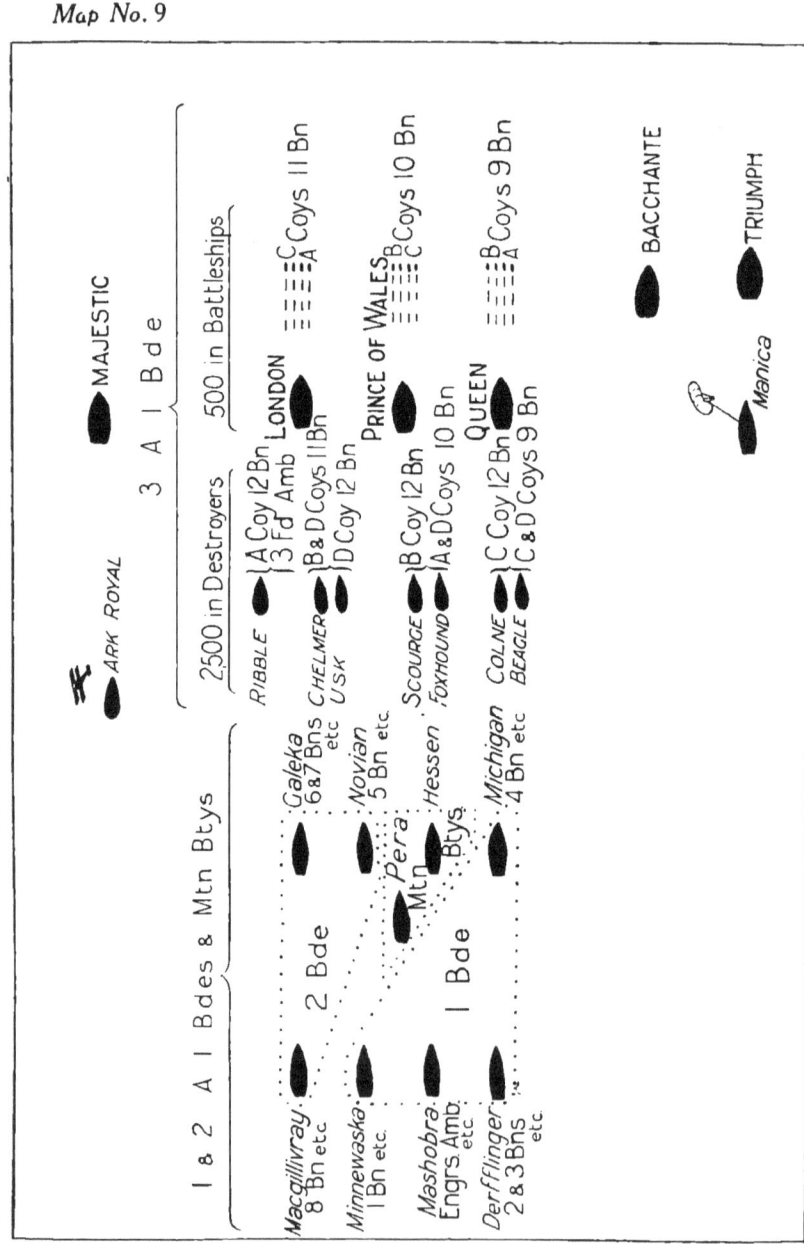

Diagram showing the intended disposition of the warships and transports of the 1st Australian Division approaching Gaba Tepe

Map No 10

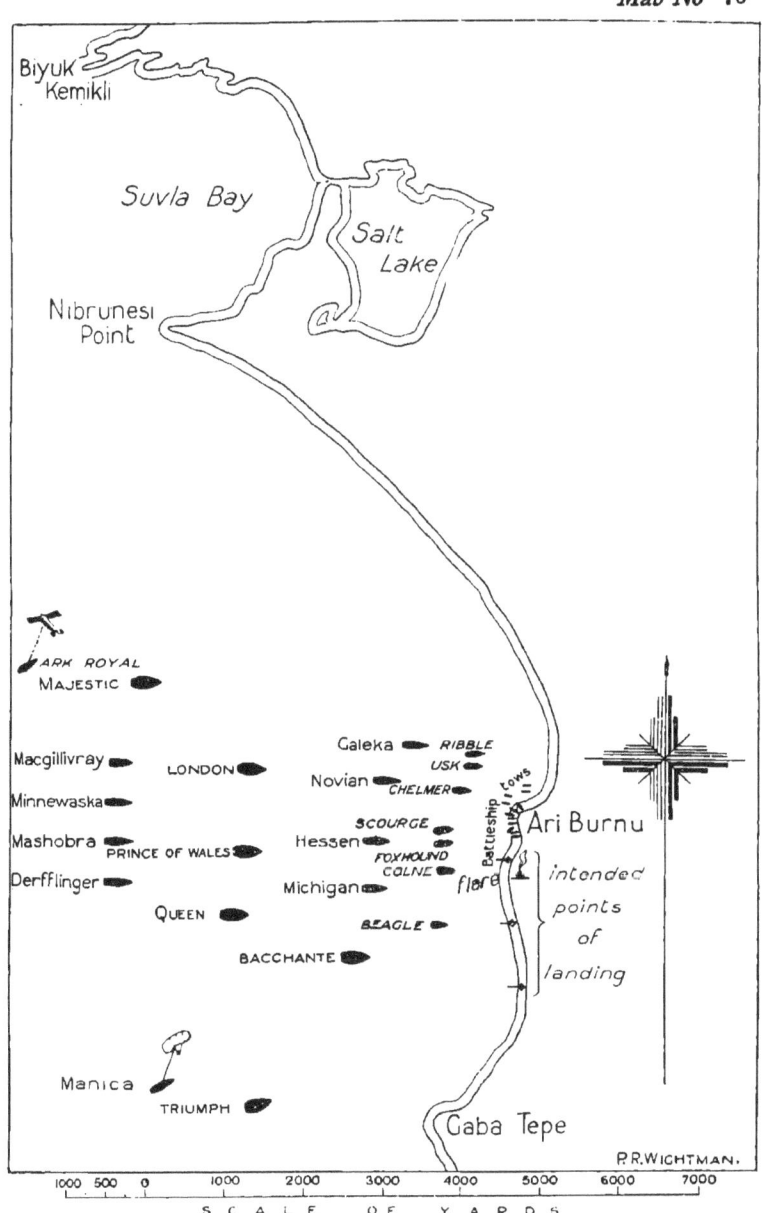

Ships off Ari Burnu at the time of landing of the 1st Australian Division, 4.30 a.m., 25th April, 1915

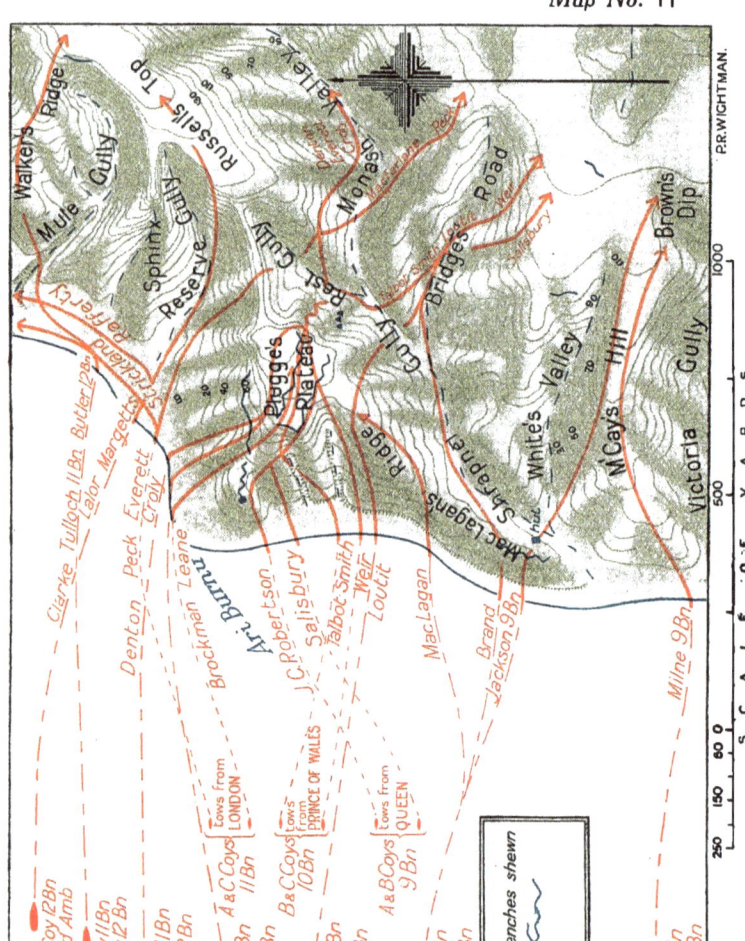

Map No. 11

The rush of the Covering Force (3rd Australian Infantry Brigade) up the hills above its landing place, 4.30 to 5.30 a.m., 25th April, 1915. British troops, etc., red; Turkish trenches, etc., blue. Height contours, 10 metres.

MAP

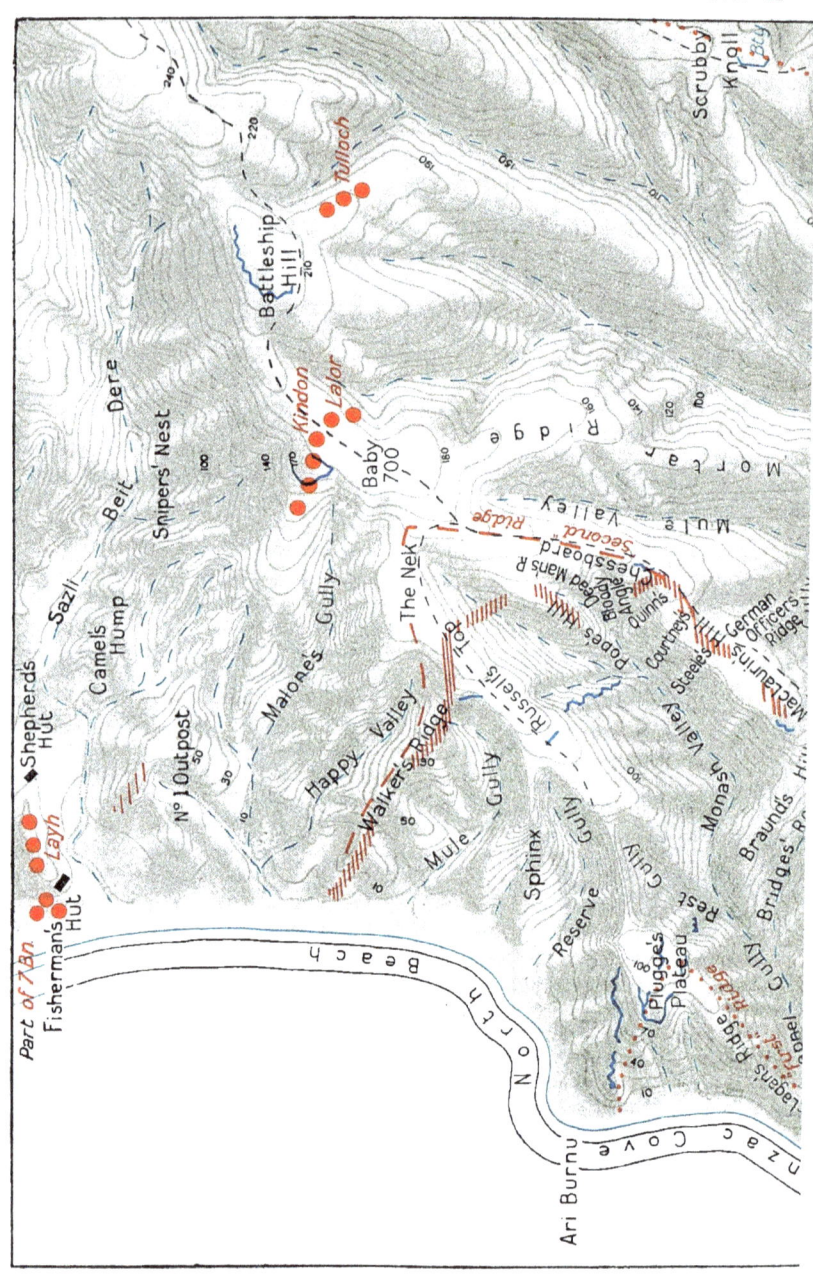

No. 12

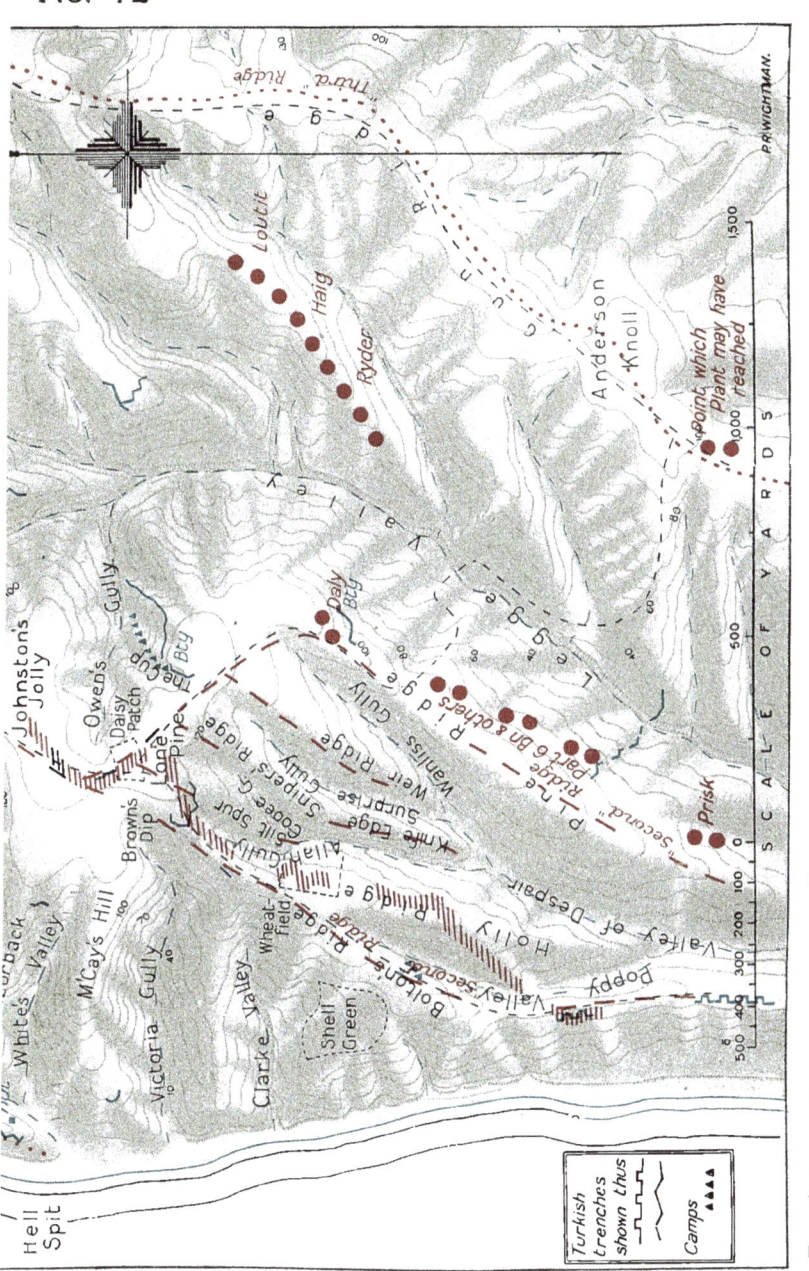

THE ANZAC POSITION, SHOWING THE TURKISH DEFENCES AND SOME OF THE FURTHEST POINTS REACHED BY THE A. & N.Z. TROOPS ON 25TH APRIL, 1915

The large red dots show the furthest positions attained. The hatched line shows the position eventually held. "First," "Second," and "Third" Ridges also red; Turkish trenches and camps, blue. Height contours, 10 metres.

Map No. 13

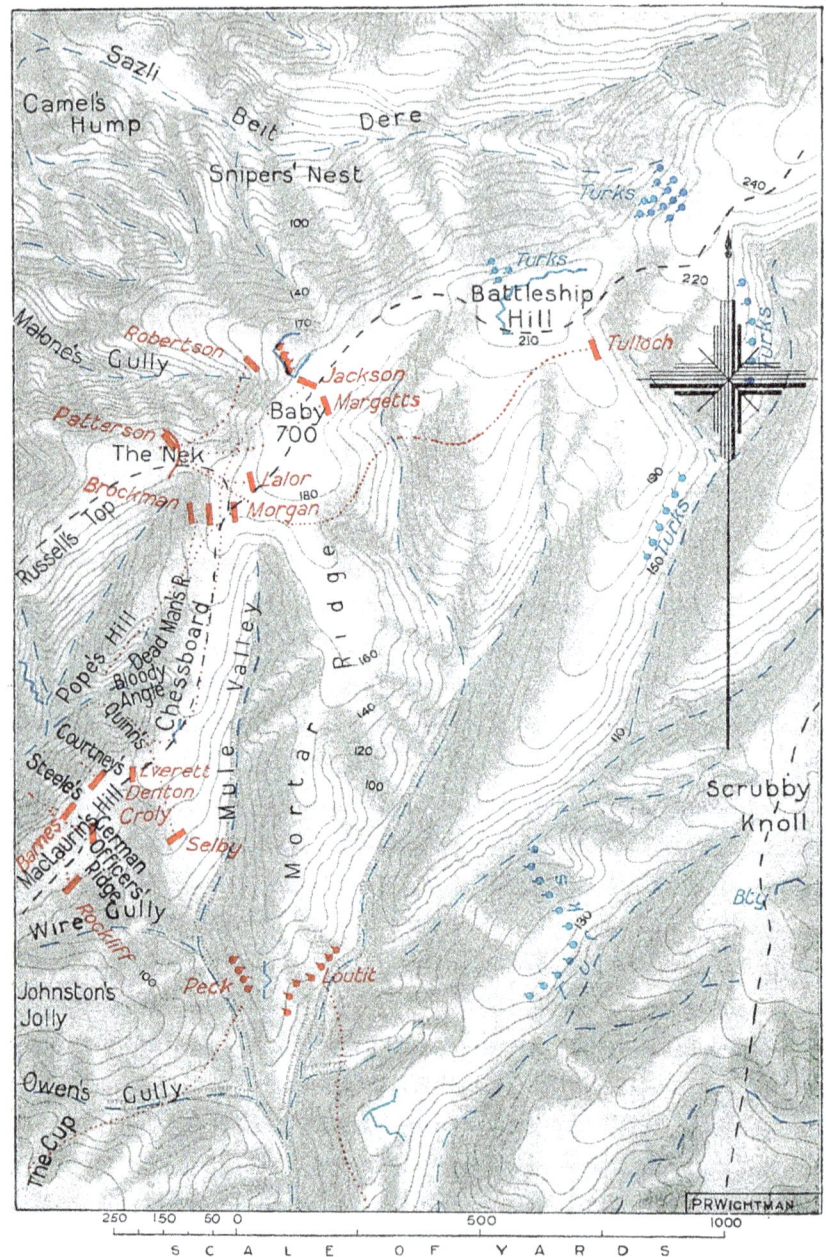

Captain Tulloch's advance and the position on Baby 700 and
MacLaurin's Hill, 9 to 10 a.m., 25th April, 1915

There is some evidence that another advanced party of Australians was at this time to the right rear of Capt. Tulloch.

British troops, etc., red: Turkish, blue. Height contours, 10 metres.

Map No. 14

THE TURKISH COUNTER-ATTACK AT THE TIME OF THE LOSS OF BABY 700
FROM 3.30 TO 5 P.M., 25TH APRIL, 1915
British troops and trenches, red; Turkish, blue. Height contours, 10 metres.

Map No. 15

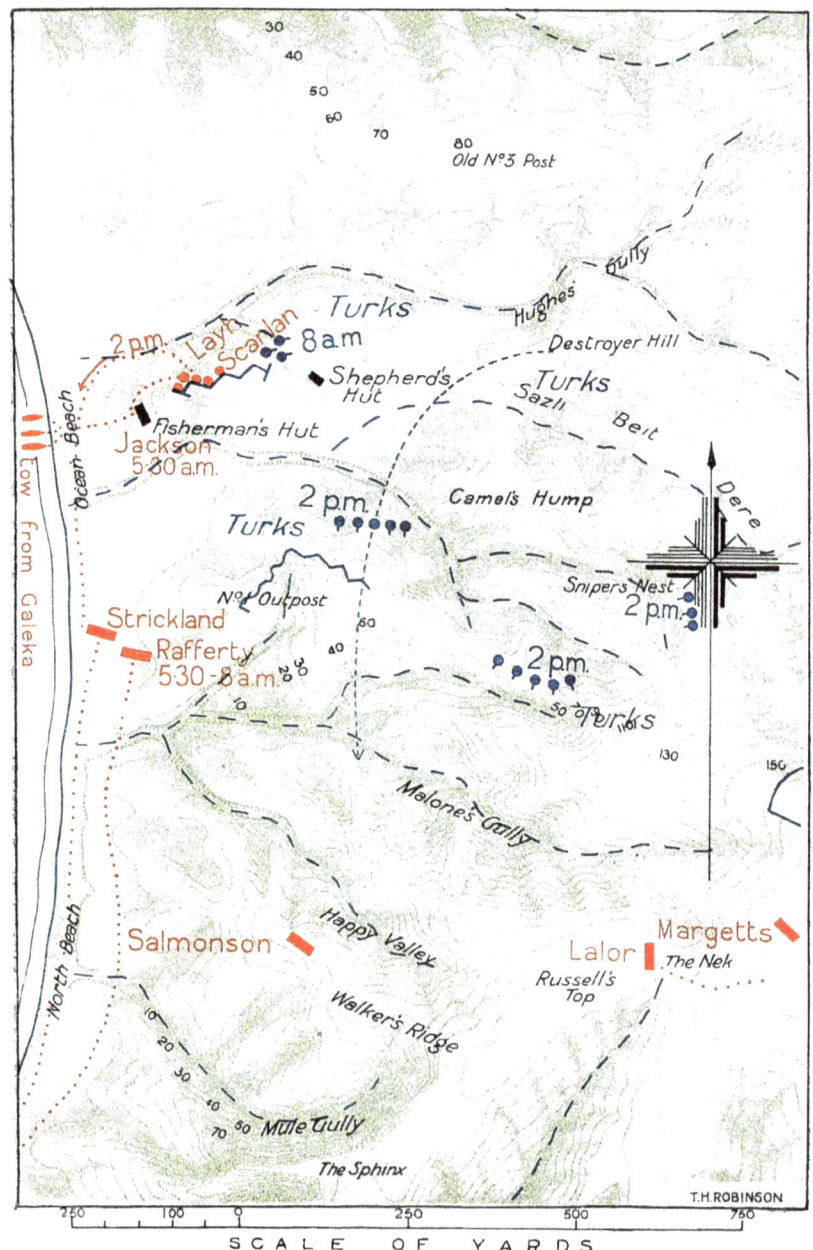

THE FIGHTING AT FISHERMAN'S HUT, 25TH APRIL, 1915
British works and troops, red; Turkish, blue. Height contours, 10 metres.

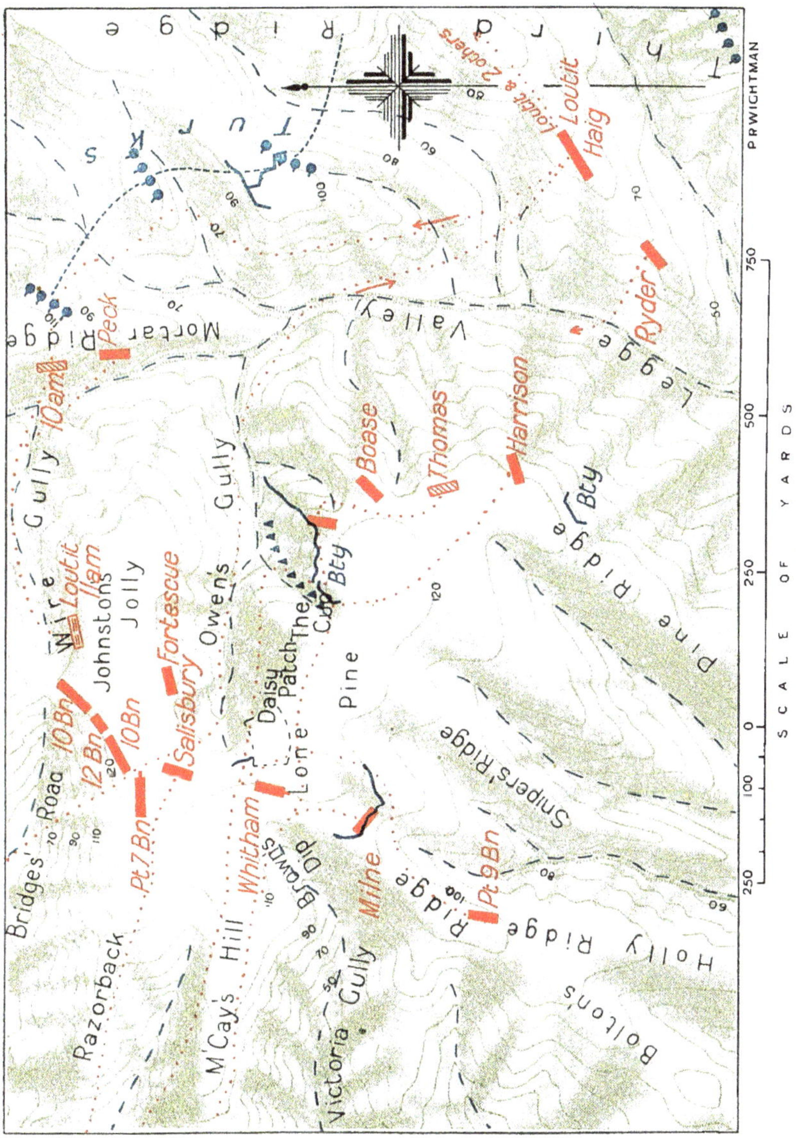

Map No. 17

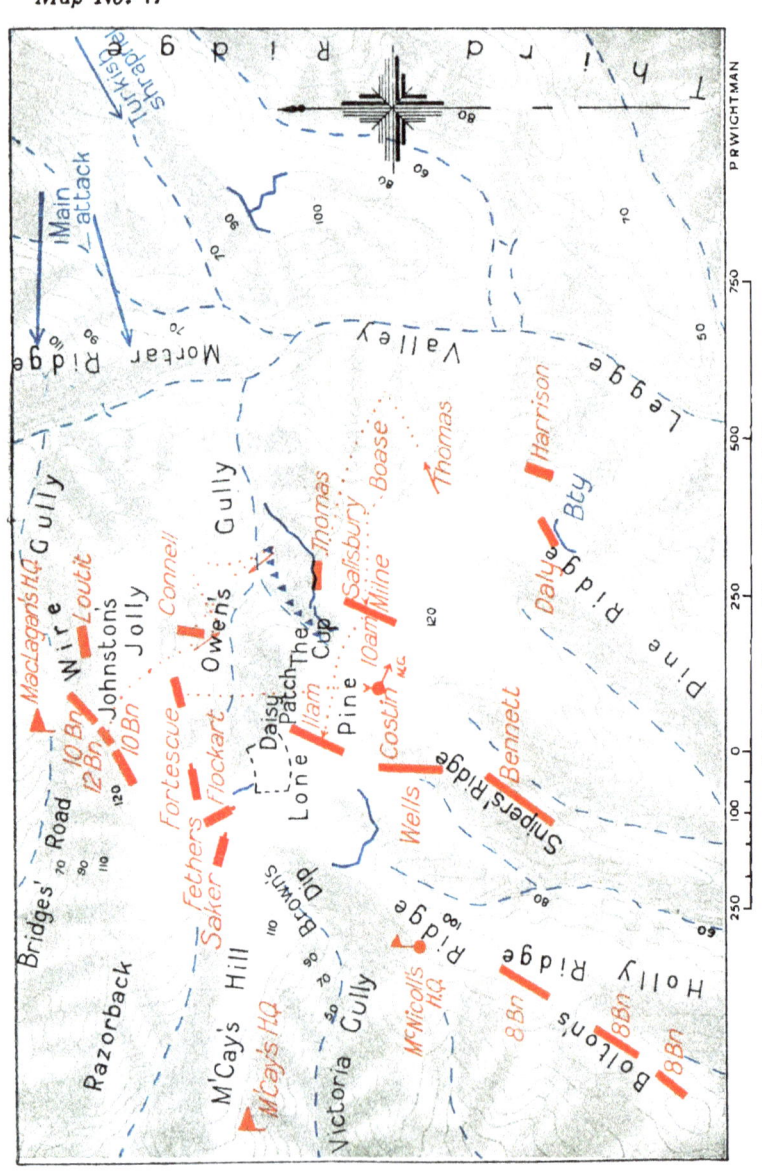

The position on the 400 Plateau during the retirement of the advanced parties of 3rd Brigade, and the advance of 2nd Brigade, between 10 a.m. and noon, 25th April, 1915. British troops, etc., red; Turkish, blue. Height contours, 10 metres.

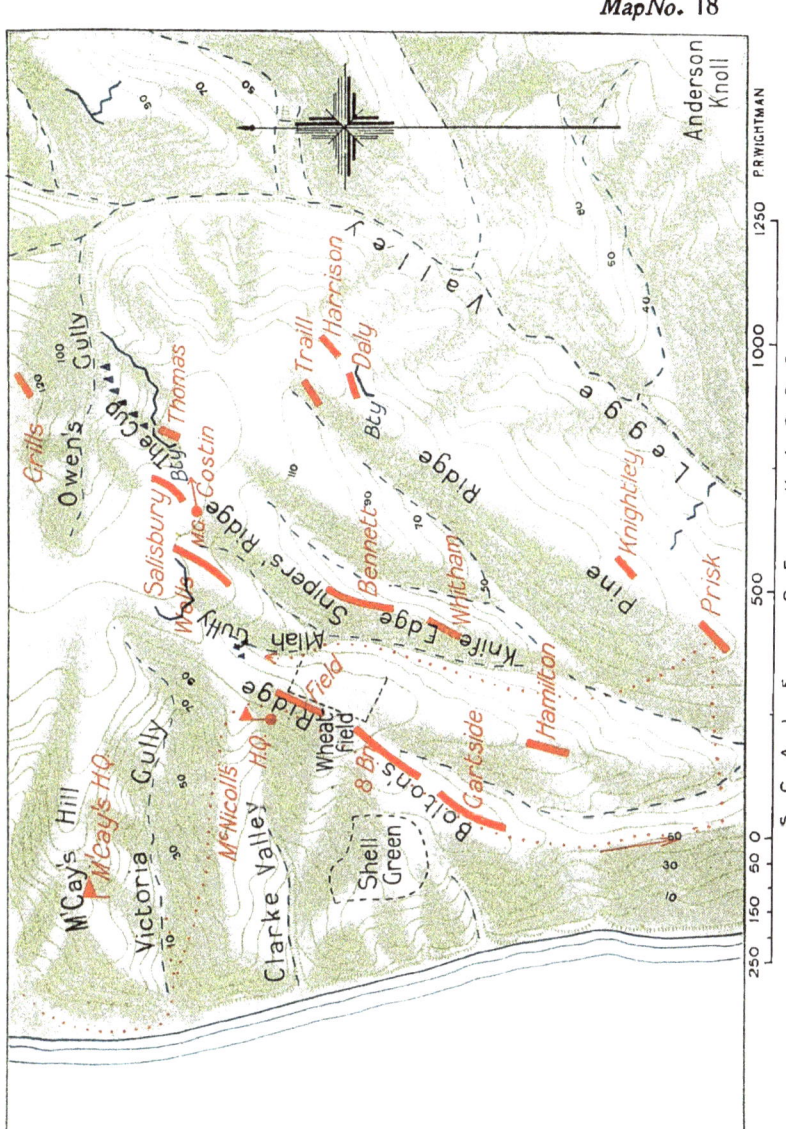

Map No. 19

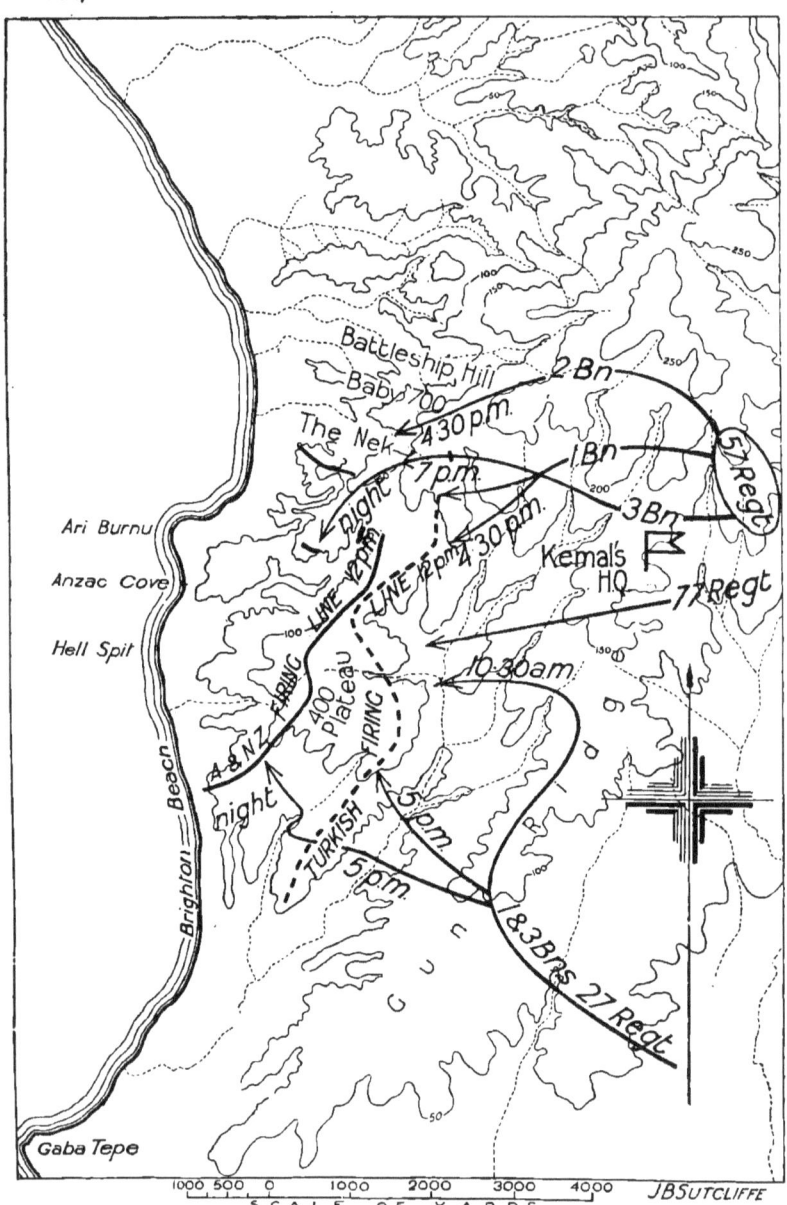

TURKISH COUNTER-ATTACKS ON THE A. & N.Z. ARMY CORPS AT
ARI BURNU ON THE DAY OF THE LANDING
Height contours, 50 metres.

Map No. 20

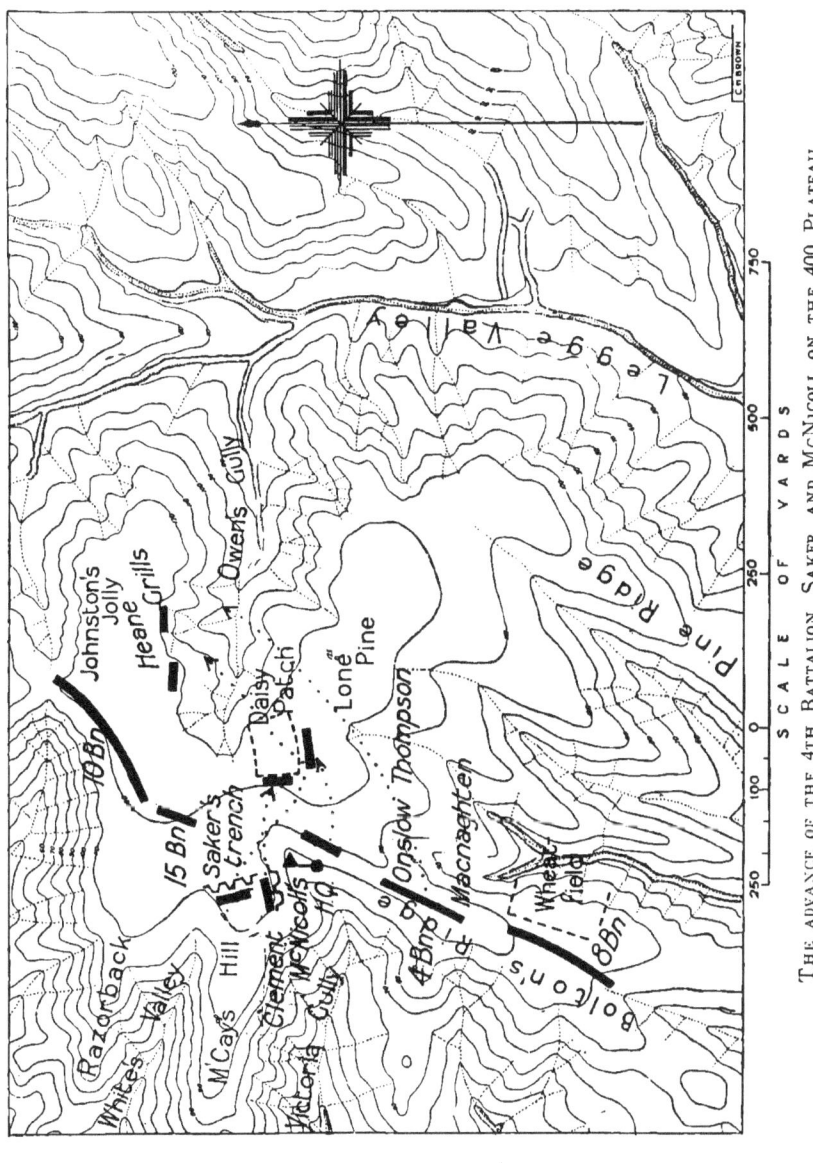

The advance of the 4th Battalion, Saker, and McNicoll on the 400 Plateau at 3.30 p.m, 26th April, 1915
Height contours, 10 metres.

Map No. 21

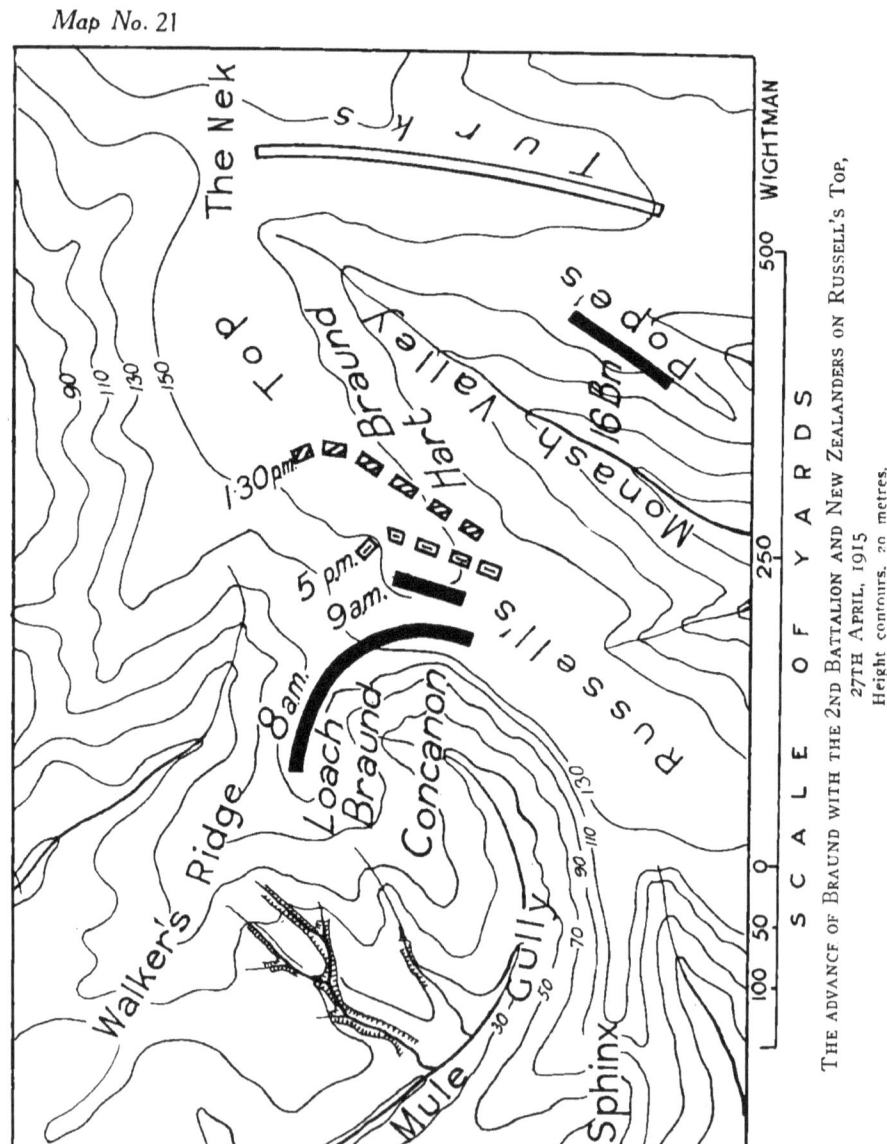

The advance of Braund with the 2nd Battalion and New Zealanders on Russell's Top, 27th April, 1915
Height contours, 20 metres.

MAP

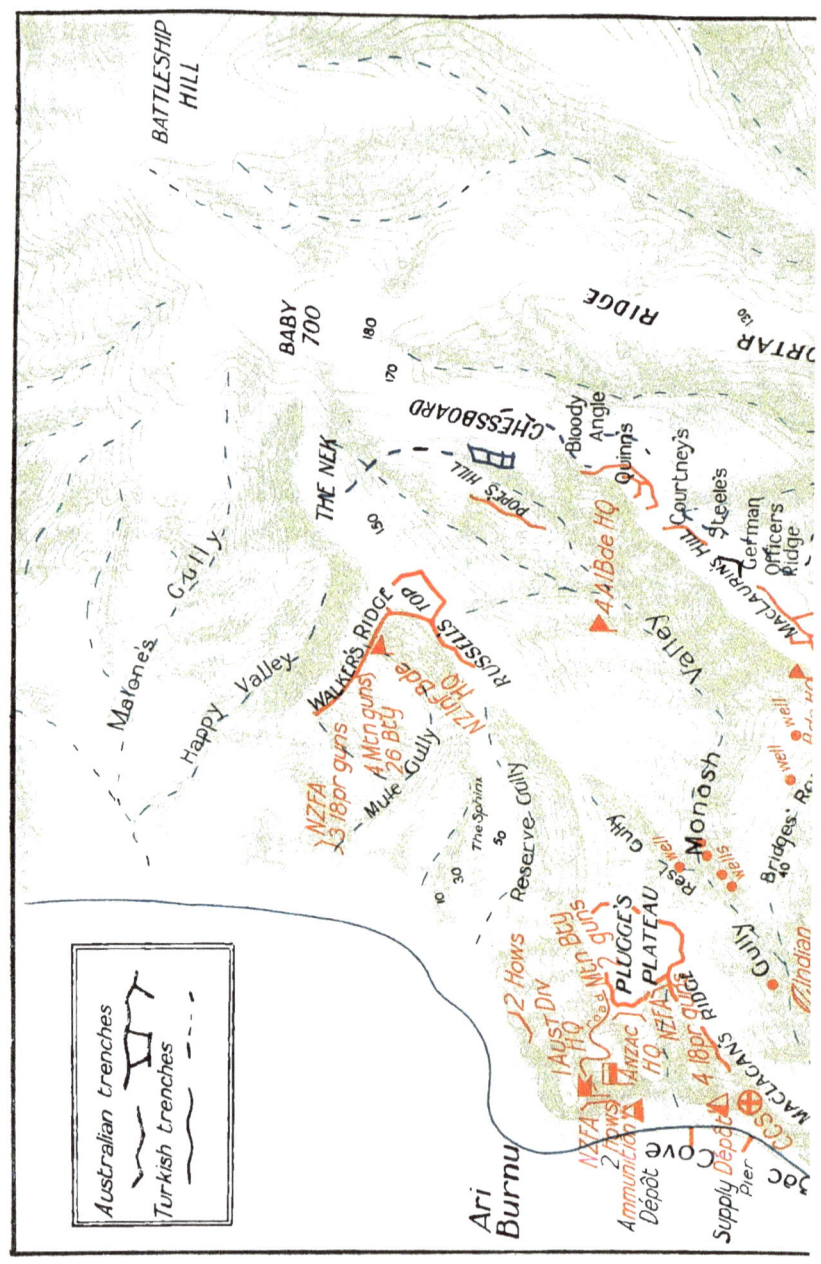

No. 22

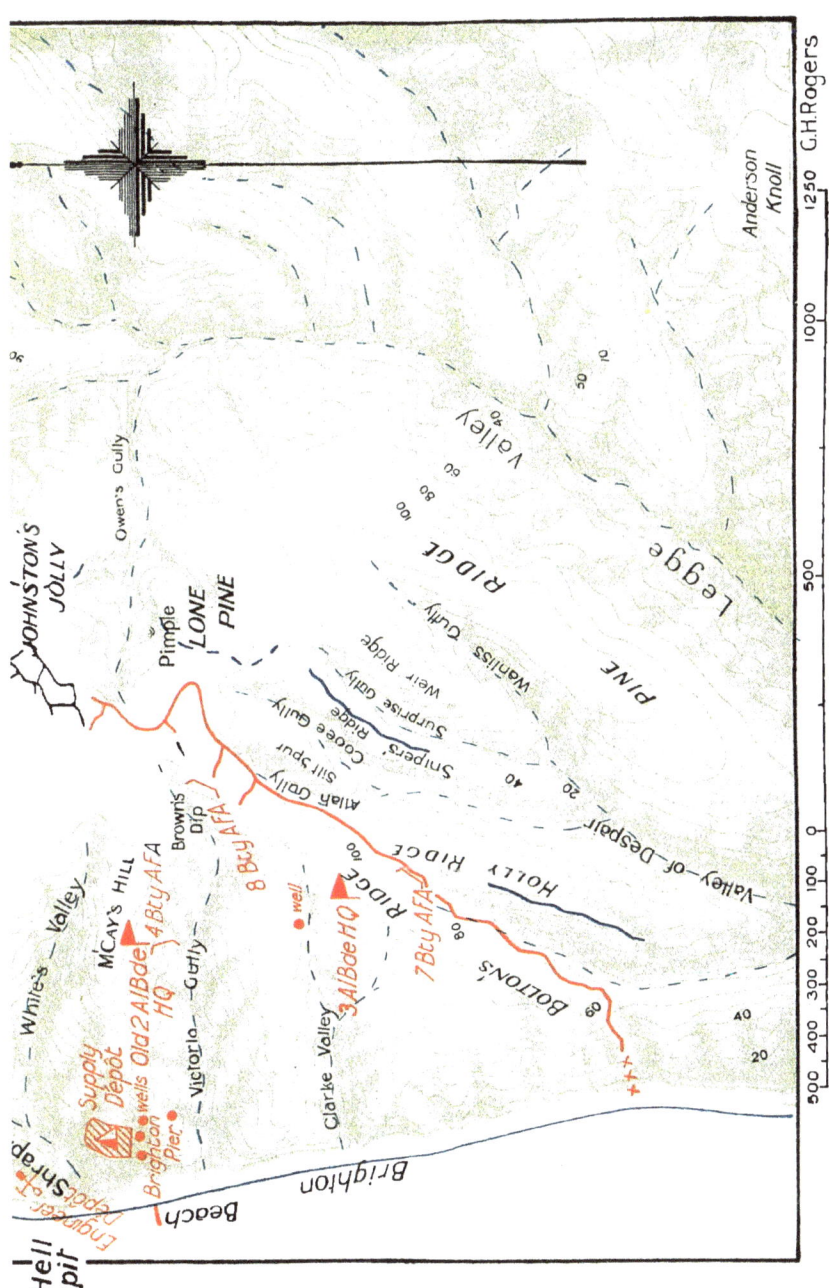

THE ANZAC POSITION ABOUT 5TH MAY, 1915, SHOWING HEADQUARTERS, GUN POSITIONS, STORES, ETC. C.C.S., Casualty Clearing Station; British troops and works, red; Turkish, blue. Height contours, 10 metres.

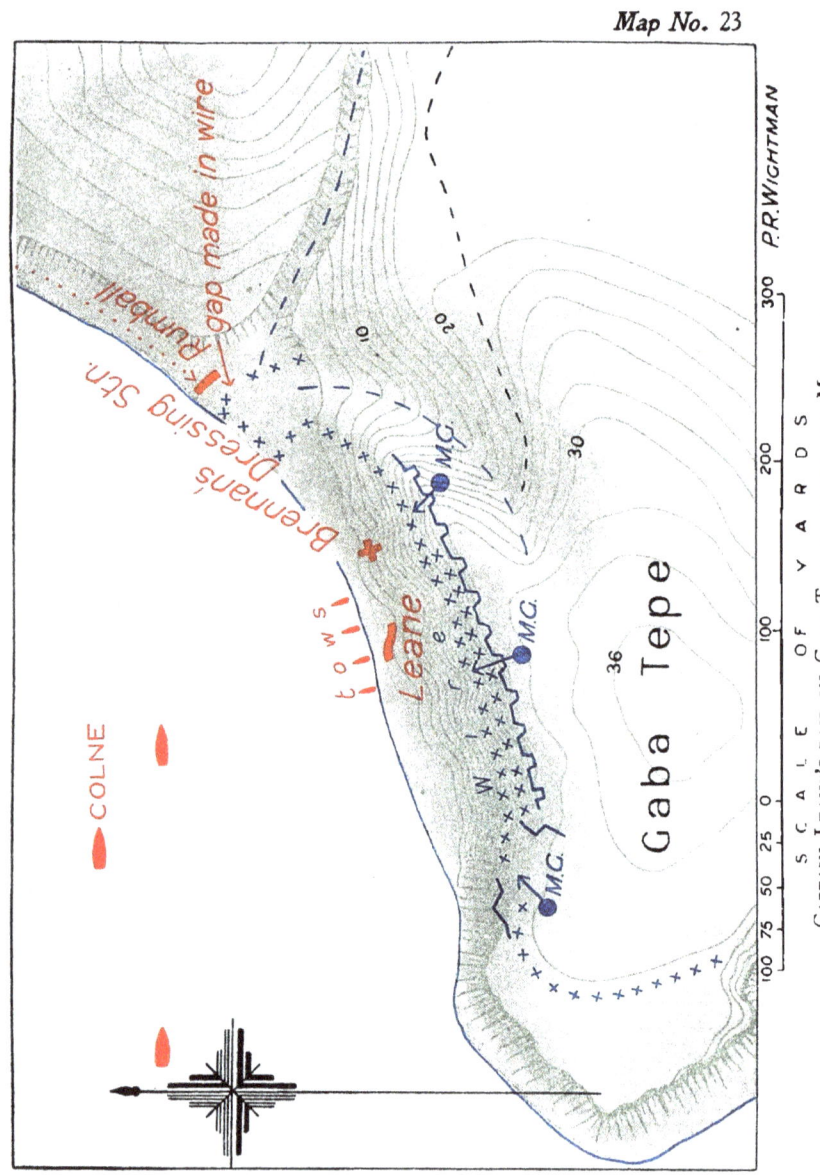

Map No. 23

Captain Leane's raid on Gaba Tepe at dawn, 4th May, 1915
British troops, etc., red; Turkish, blue. Height contours, 2 metres.

Map No. 24

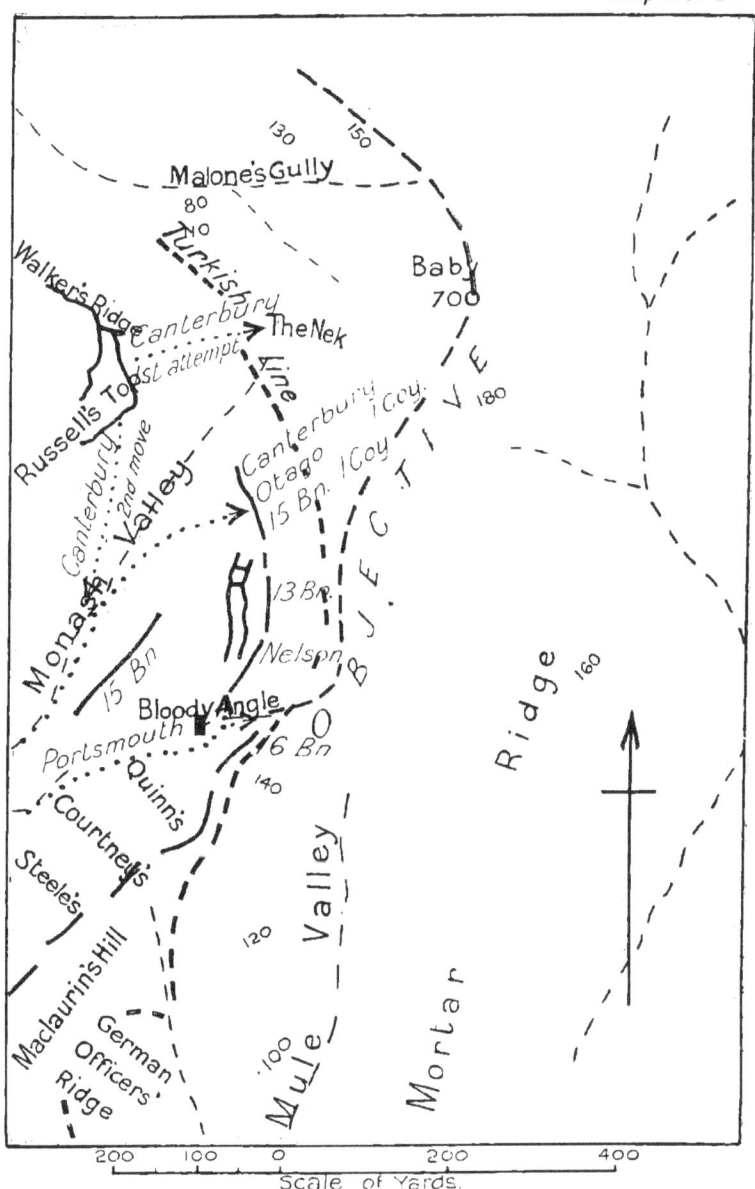

ATTACK BY THE N.Z. & A. DIVISION ON BABY 700.
THE POSITION AT DAWN, 3RD MAY, 1915
British troops and trenches, red; Turkish, blue. Height contours, 10 metres.

THE
STORY OF ANZAC

FROM 4 MAY, 1915, TO THE EVACUATION
OF THE GALLIPOLI PENINSULA

VOLUME II

LIST OF MAPS

1 The Cape Helles area, showing the advance of the Allied army in the Second Battle of Krithia, 6th, 7th, and 8th May, 1915
2 Advance of the 2nd Australian Infantry Brigade at Helles on 8th May, 1915
3 Positions of the Anzac artillery at the end of May, 1915
4 The Turkish battery-positions at the Olive Grove
5 Quinn's Post, showing the situation shortly before dawn on 10th May, 1915
6 The Turkish attack upon Anzac, 19th May, 1915
7 The central sub-sections of Quinn's Post at the time of the Turkish attack of 29th May, 1915
8 Four stages in the growth of the trenches at the Pimple salient, Anzac
9 Quinn's Post, showing the trenches, shelters, and mine-galleries eventually constructed
10 The Anzac line near the Pimple, showing the old trenches and underground firing line
11 The Anzac-Suvla area, showing the objectives of the projected offensive
12 Portion of the line on the southern flank of Anzac, showing the position (Leane's Trench) established by the enemy on Holly Ridge prior to 31st July, 1915
13 Lone Pine and the Australian lines at the Pimple, from which the attack started
14 Lone Pine after the battle of 6th-10th August, 1915
15 The foot-hills north of Anzac, showing the points occupied by the mounted rifles about midnight on August 6th
16 The opposing lines on MacLaurin's Hill at the time of the attack by the 6th Battalion on German Officers' Trench, 7th August, 1915
17 The attack by the 3rd Light Horse Brigade on The Nek, 7th August, 1915
18 The assaults made by the 1st and 2nd Light Horse Regiments and Royal Welch Fusiliers, 7th August, 1915
19 Positions of General Godley's columns north of Anzac at day-break, 7th August, 1915
20 Position on the evening of 7th August, 1915, after the attempt by the Auckland Battalion to reach Chunuk Bair

MAPS

21 The attempt by the 4th Australian Infantry Brigade to reach Hill 971 by way of Abdel Rahman Bair, 8th August, 1915

22 The capture of the crest-line at Chunuk Bair by Wellington Battalion and 7th Gloucester at day-break on 8th August, 1915

23 Position on Sari Bair at 5.30 a.m. on 9th August, 1915—the climax of the campaign in Gallipoli

24 The counter-attack by Mustafa Kemal Pasha on Sari Bair at day-break, 10th August, 1915

25 Anzac-Suvla position, 12th August, 1915

26 Hill 60, showing the position on the night of 27th August, 1915

27 The trenches and mining system on Russell's Top at the beginning of December, 1915

28 The Evacuation of Anzac—position at 1.30 a.m., 20th December, 1915

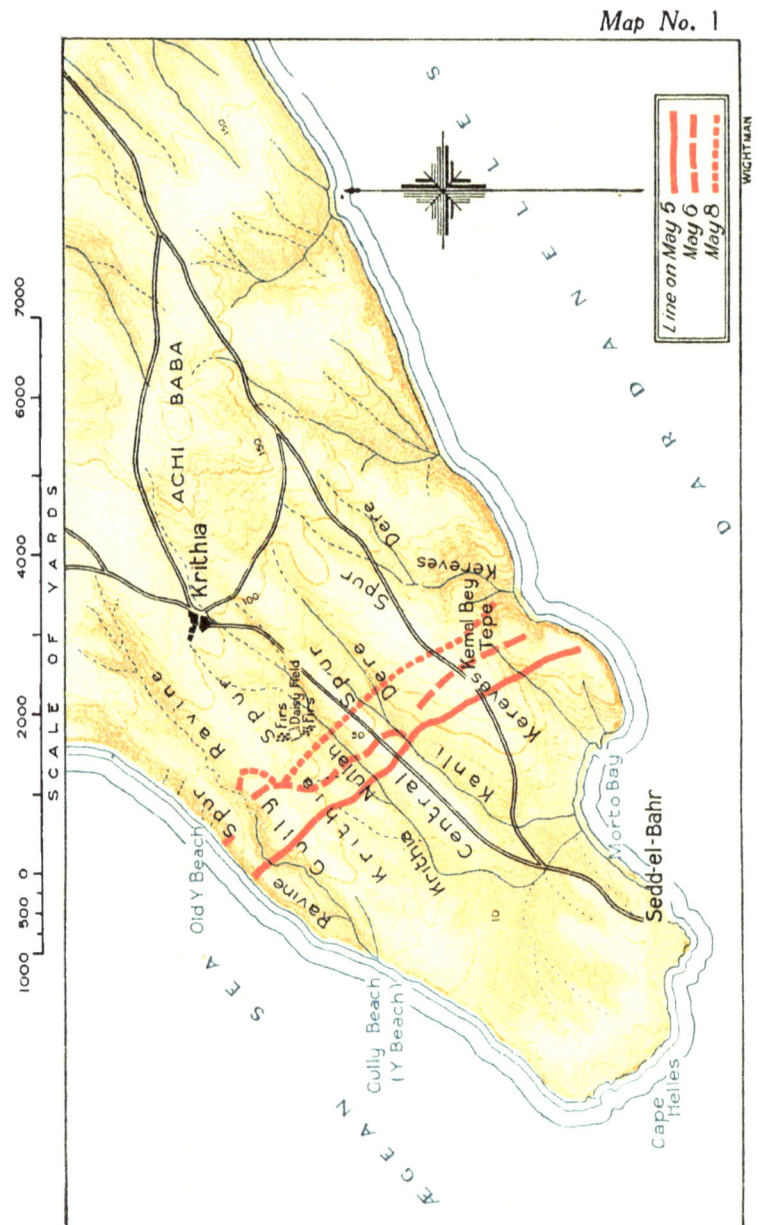

Map No. 1

The Cape Helles area, showing the advance of the Allied army towards Achi Baba in the Second Battle of Krithia, 6th, 7th, and 8th May, 1915. Allied line, red. Height contours, 10 metres.

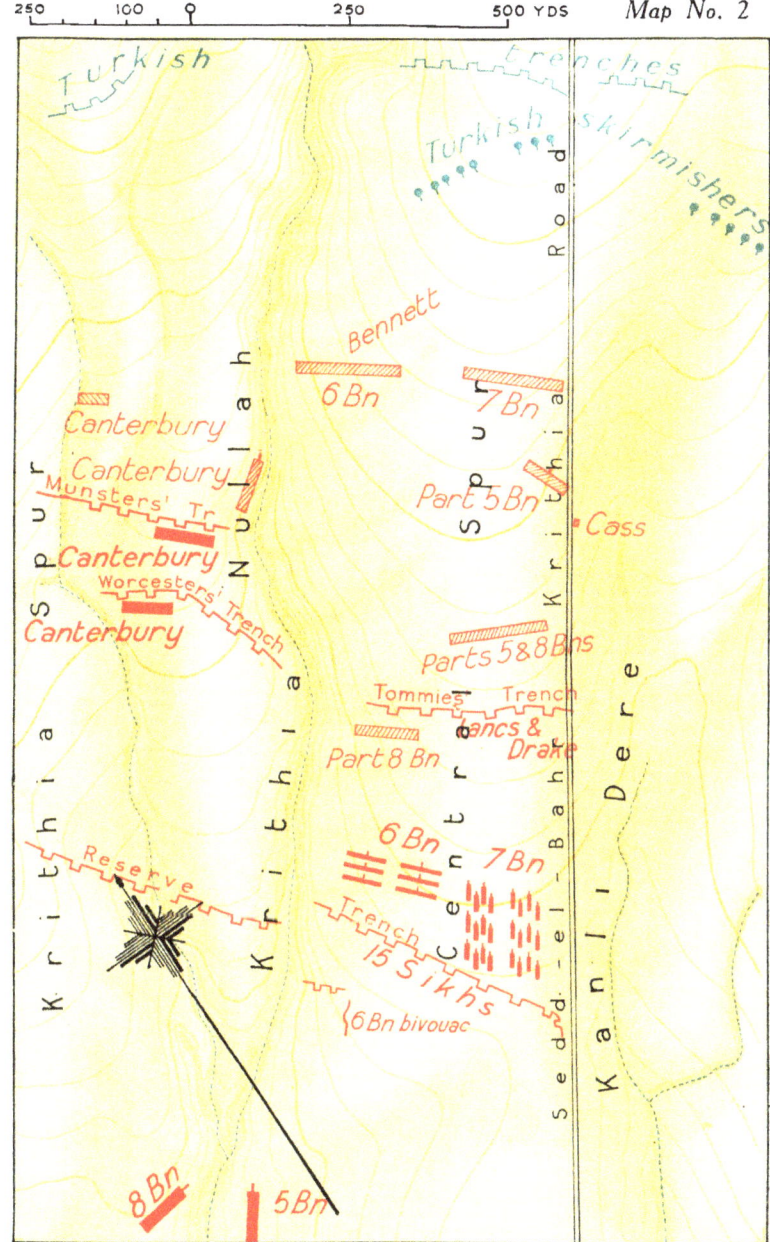

Map No. 2

Advance of the 2nd Australian Infantry Brigade at Helles on
8th May, 1915

The approximate position of units at 5.30 p.m. is shown in full red; that at 6.30 is shown by *hachuring*. (British troops and trenches, red; Turkish, blue. Height contours, 10 metres.)

Map No. 3

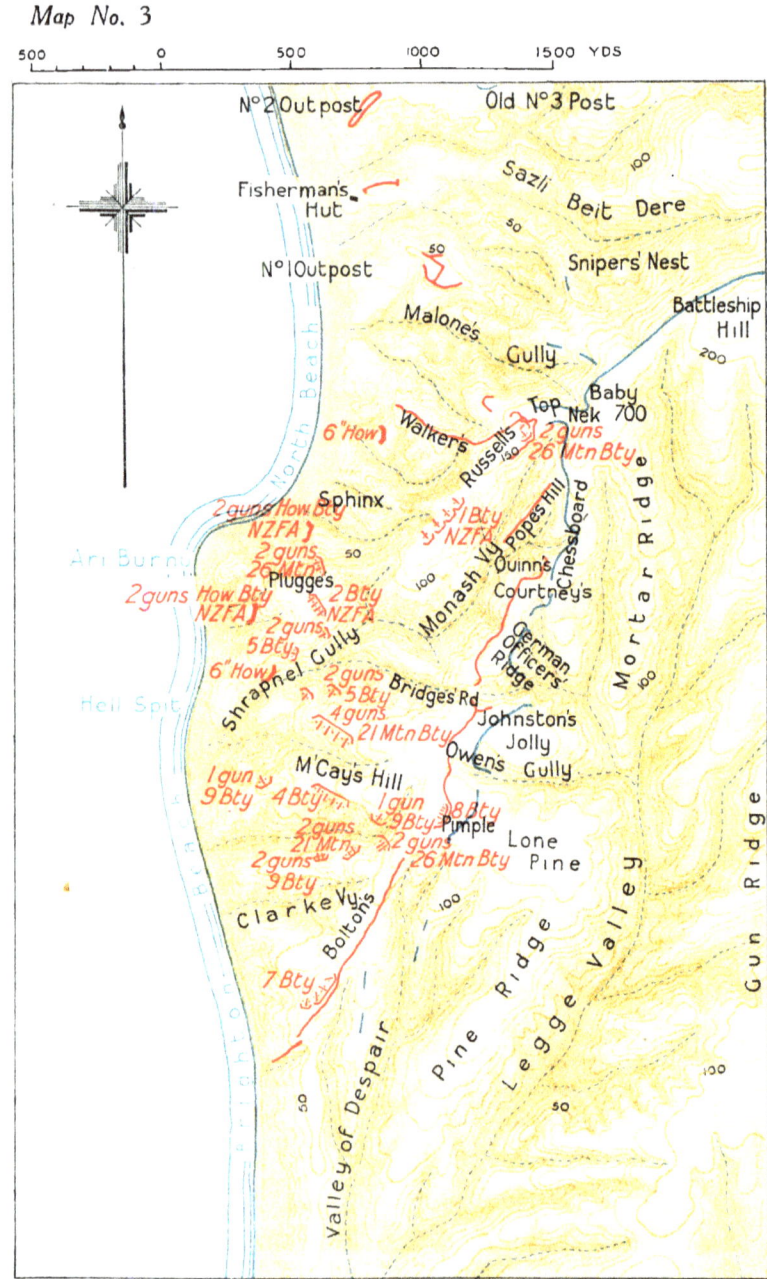

POSITIONS OF THE ANZAC ARTILLERY AT THE END OF MAY, 1915
British guns and line, red; Turkish, blue. Height contours, 10 metres.

Map No. 4

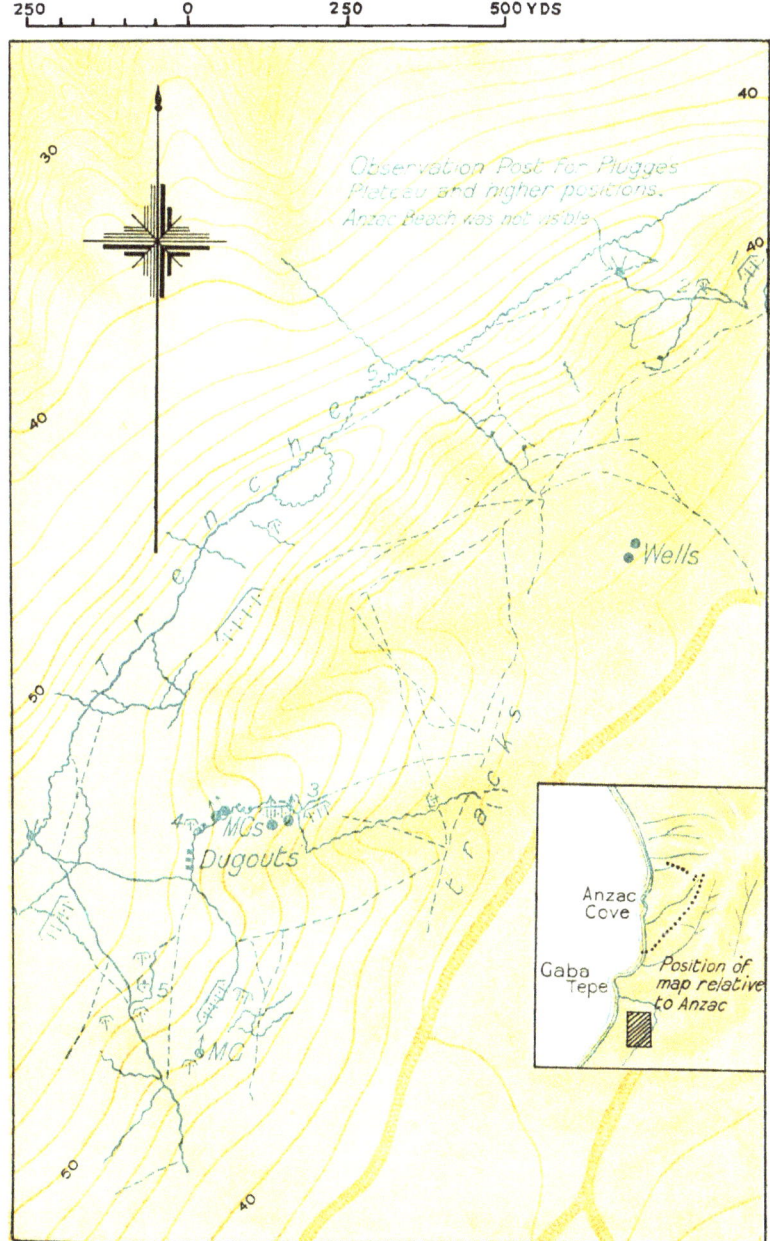

Hunter Rogers

THE TURKISH BATTERY-POSITIONS AT THE OLIVE GROVE.

Some of the emplacements here shown are alternative. The positions of the old 5.9-inch howitzers are marked 1 and 2. At 3 and 4 were guns which fired at Anzac. Some of those at 5 usually fired at the shipping. (Turkish trenches and positions, blue. Height contours, 2 metres.)

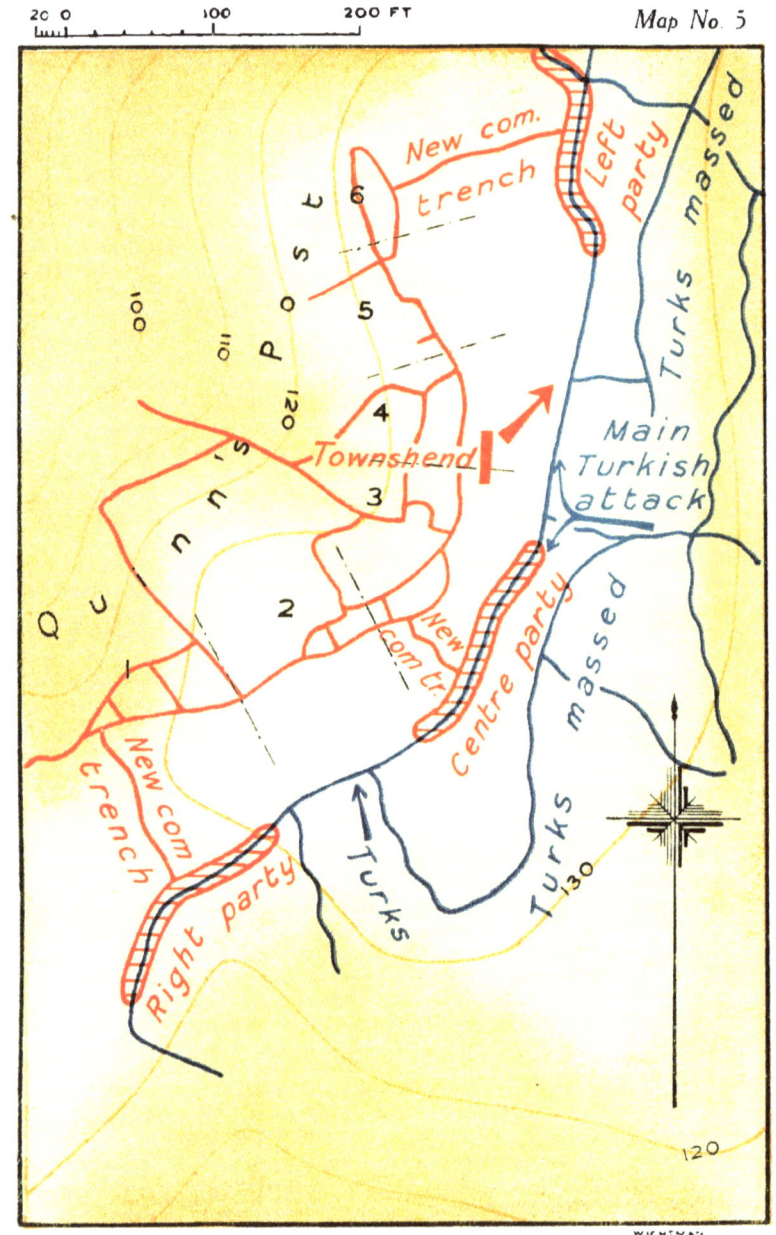

'QUINN'S POST, SHOWING THE SITUATION SHORTLY BEFORE DAWN ON 10TH MAY, 1915
British troops and trenches, red; Turkish, blue. Height contours, 10 metres.

MAP

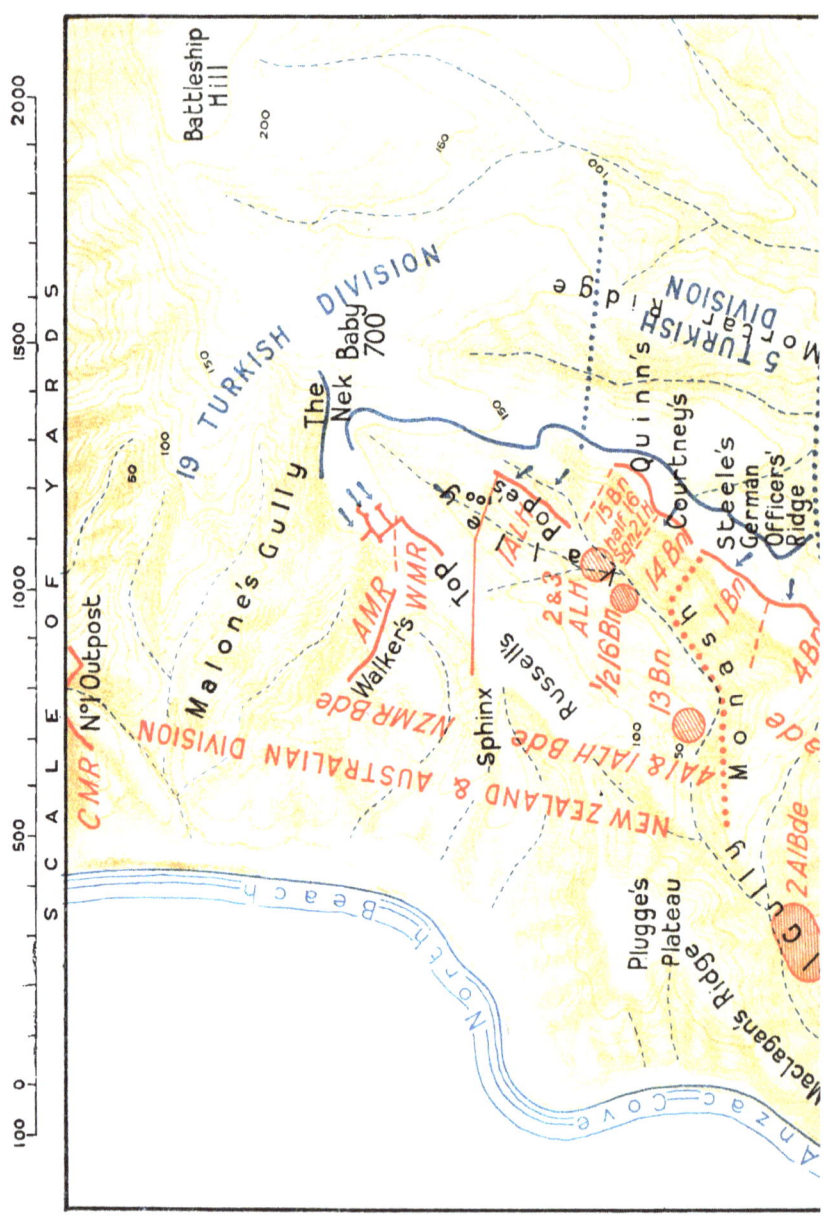

No. 6

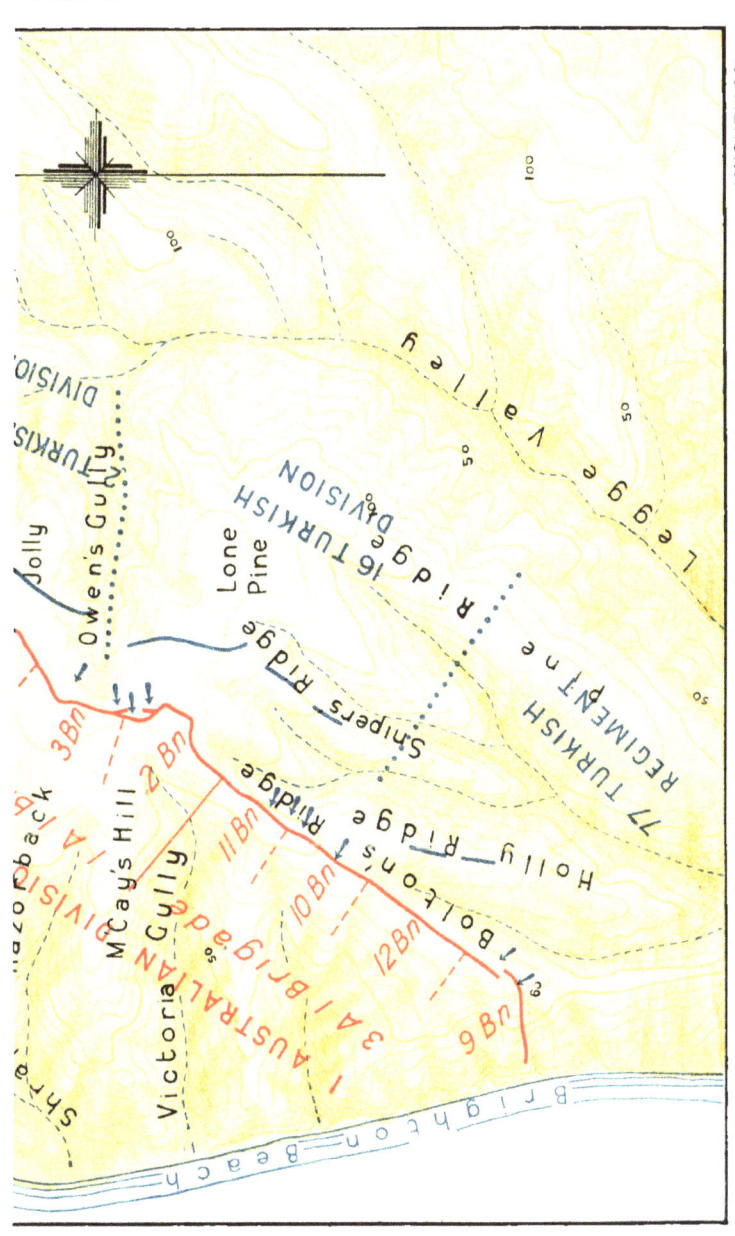

Map No. 7

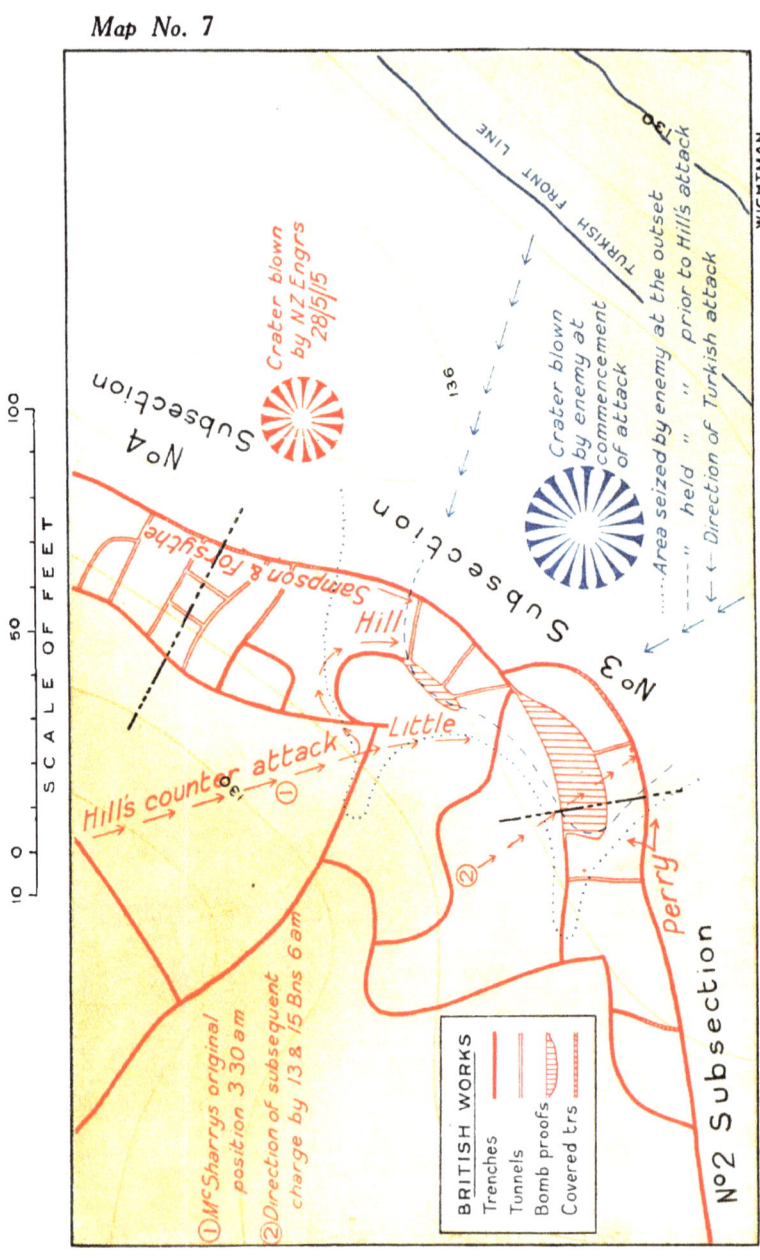

Map No. 8

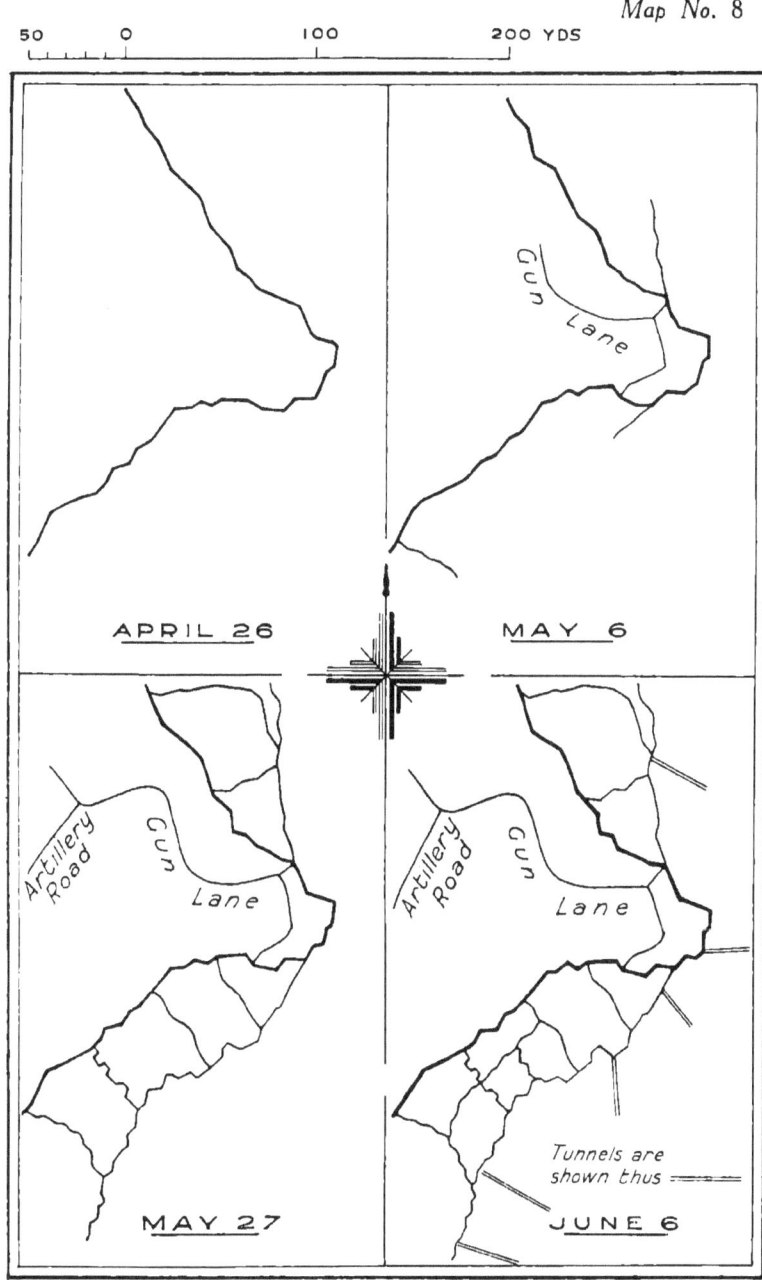

FOUR STAGES IN THE GROWTH OF THE TRENCHES AT THE PIMPLE SALIENT, ANZAC

Map No. 9

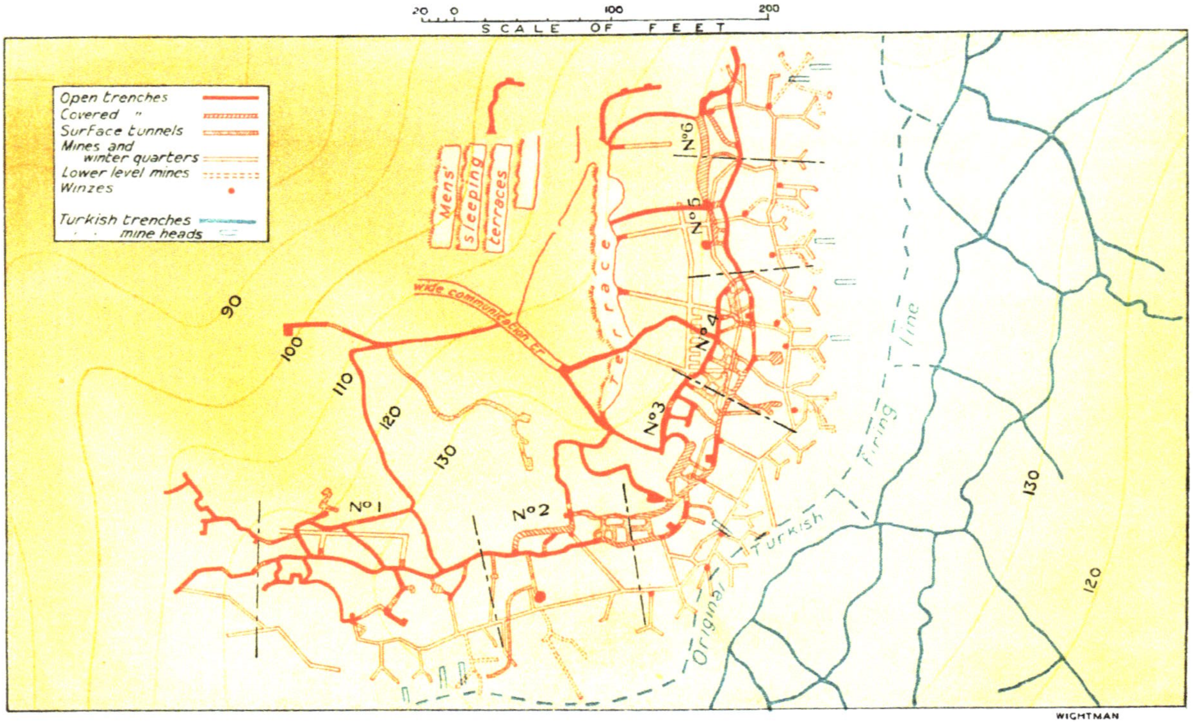

QUINN'S POST, ANZAC, SHOWING THE TRENCHES, SHELTERS, AND MINE-GALLERIES EVENTUALLY CONSTRUCTED

Based on a plan by Sapper R. A. McInnis, 8th Fld. Coy., Engrs. (British trenches and works, red; Turkish, blue. Height contours, 10 metres.)

Map No. 10

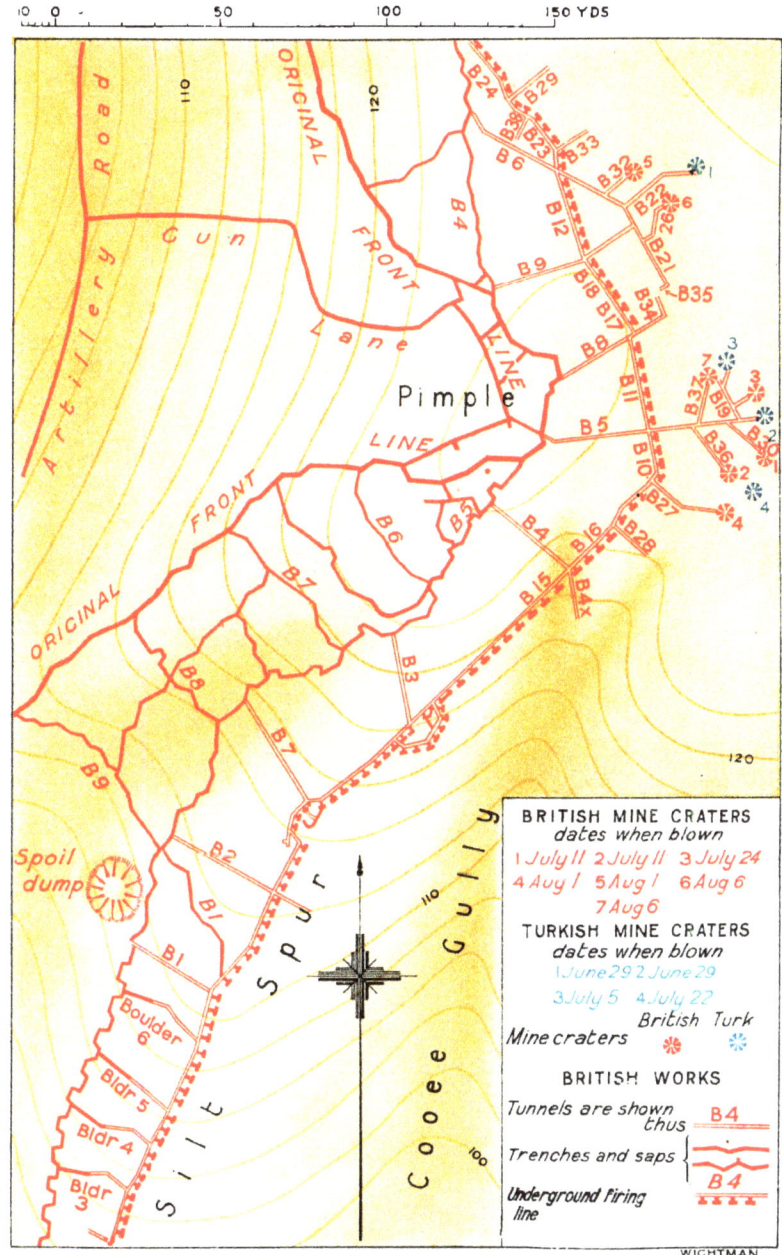

THE ANZAC LINE NEAR THE PIMPLE, SHOWING THE OLD TRENCHES AND
UNDERGROUND FIRING LINE
Height contours, 2 metres.

Map No. 11

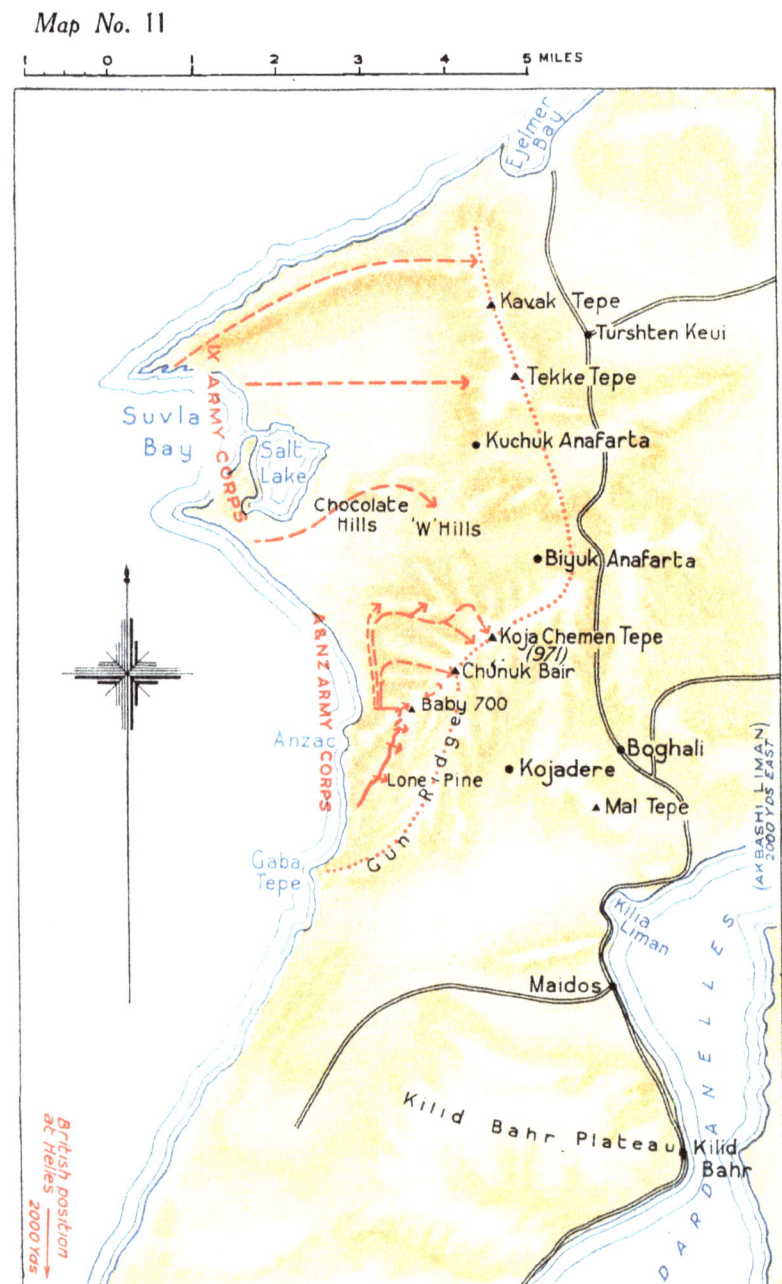

THE ANZAC-SUVLA AREA, SHOWING THE OBJECTIVES OF THE PROJECTED OFFENSIVE

The front proposed to be occupied at the end of the main operations is shown by a red dotted line.

Map No. 12

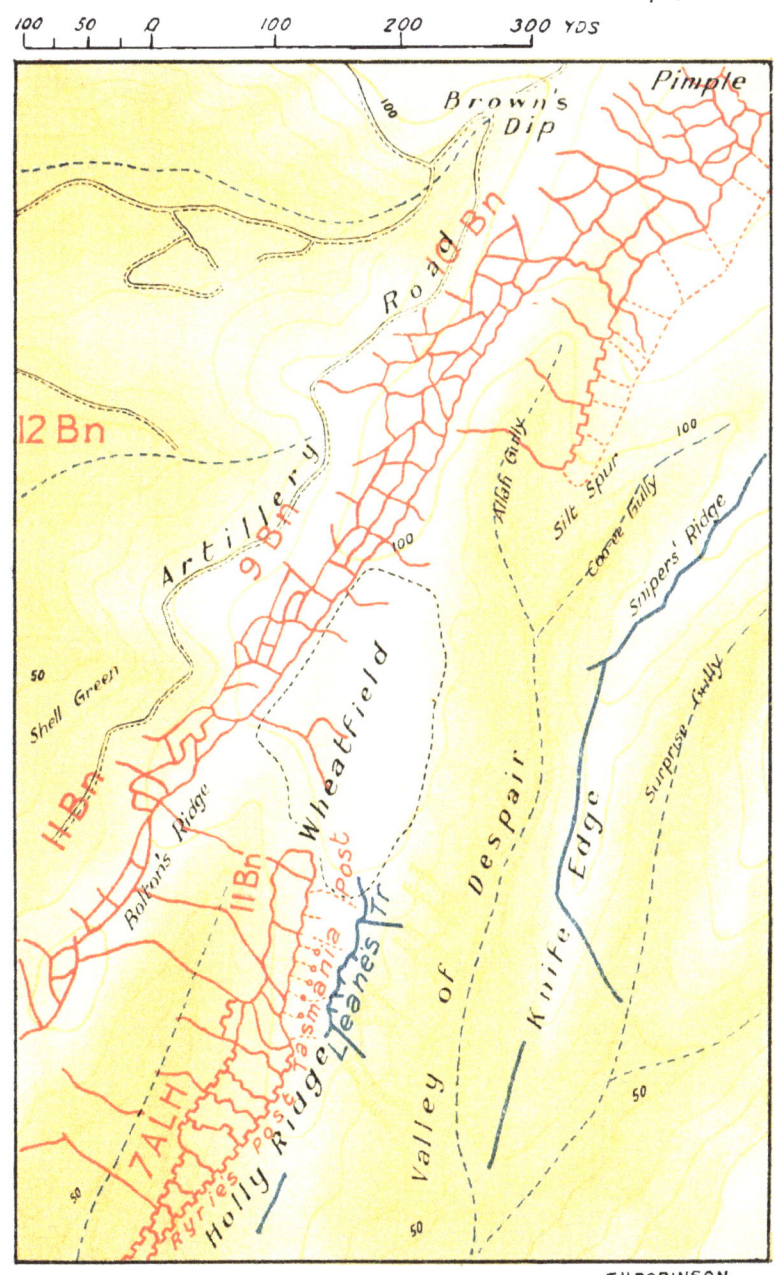

PORTION OF THE LINE ON THE SOUTHERN FLANK OF ANZAC, SHOWING THE POSITION (LEANE'S TRENCH) ESTABLISHED BY THE ENEMY ON HOLLY RIDGE PRIOR TO 31ST JULY, 1915

British trenches, red; Turkish, blue. Height contours, 10 metres.

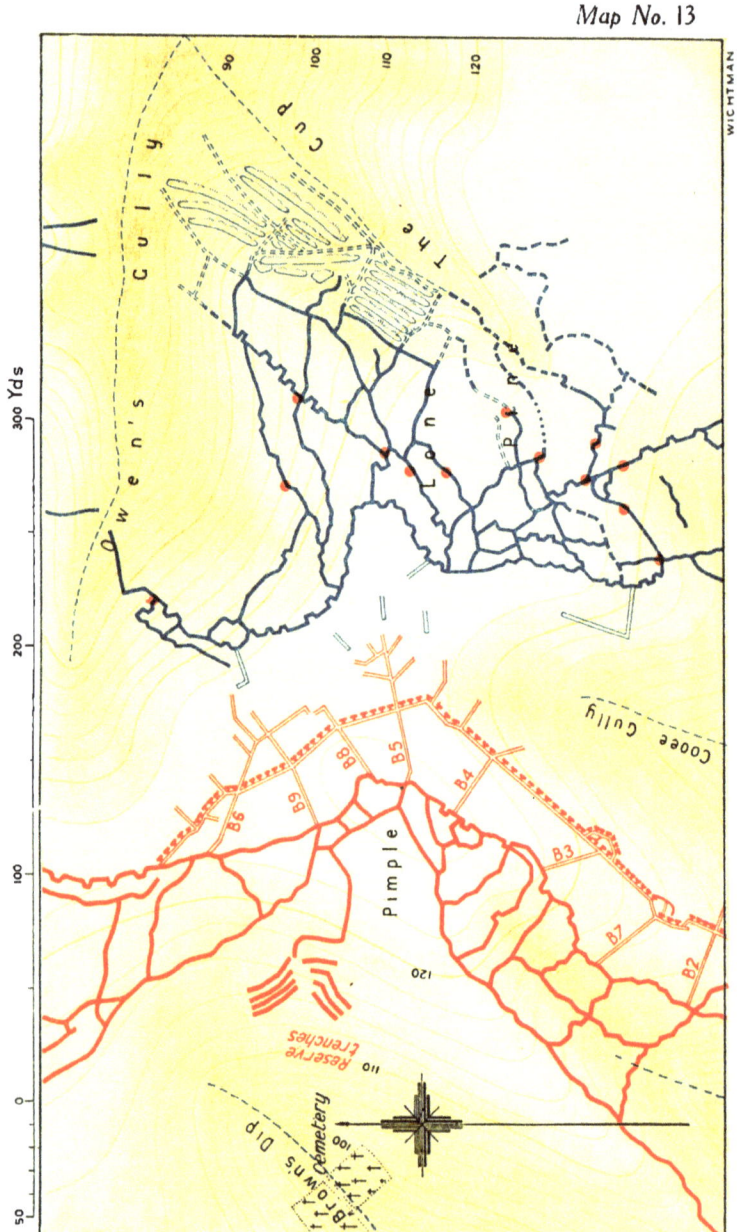

Map No. 13

LONE PINE AND THE AUSTRALIAN LINES AT THE PIMPLE, FROM WHICH THE ATTACK STARTED
The posts established by the Australian infantry in the Turkish trenches before midnight on 6th August, 1915, are shown by red dots. (British trenches, red; Turkish, blue. Height contours, 10 metres.)

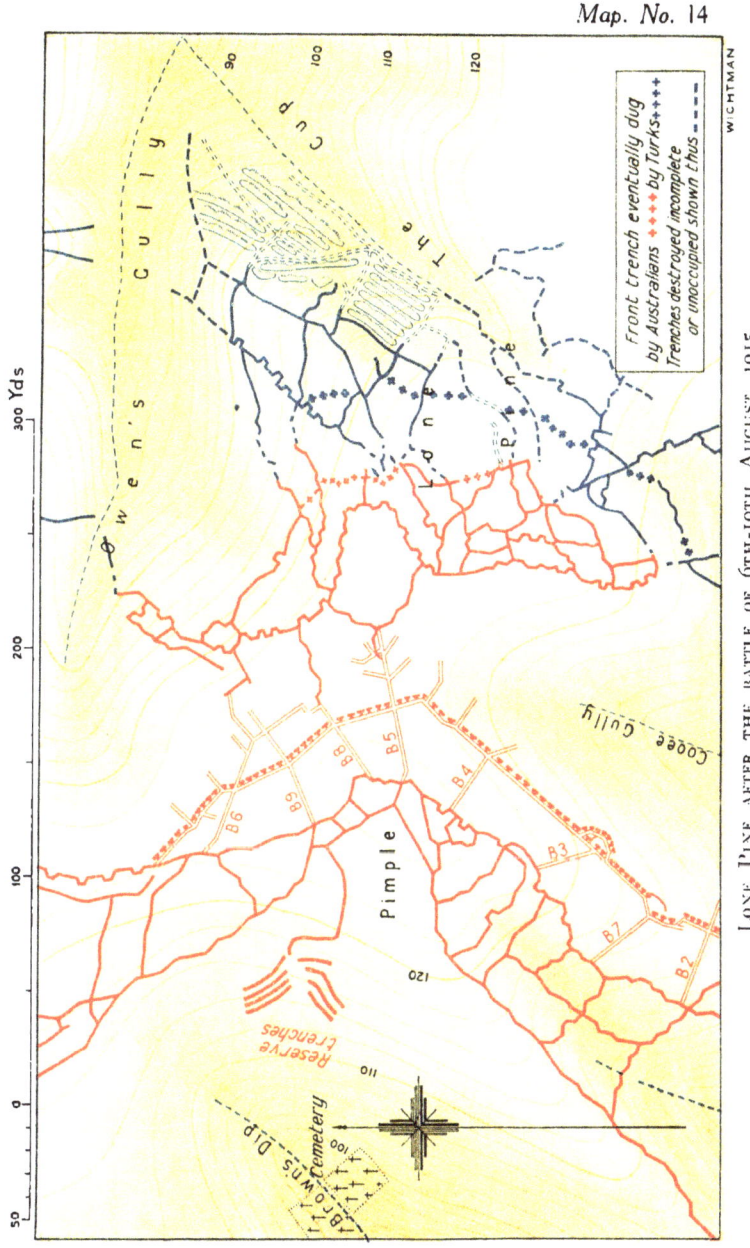

Map. No. 14

Lone Pine after the battle of 6th-10th August, 1915
British trenches, red; Turkish, blue. Height contours, 10 metres.

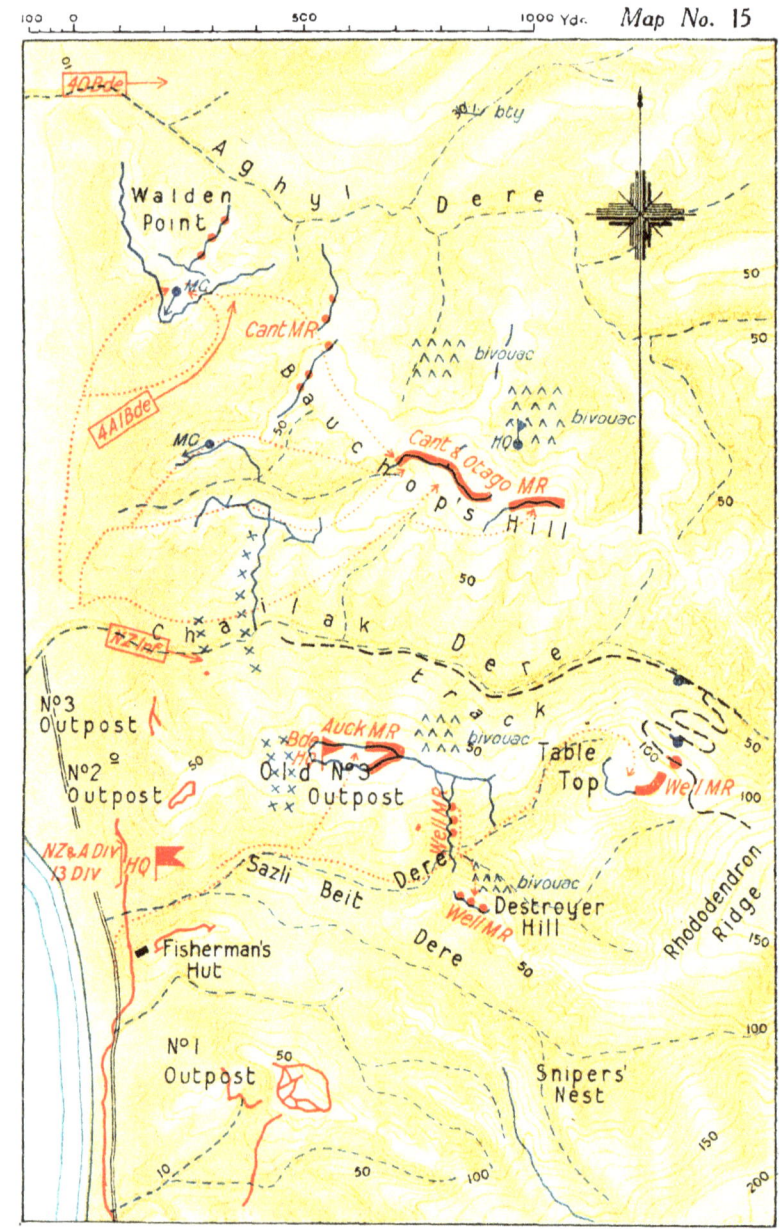

THE FOOT-HILLS NORTH OF ANZAC, SHOWING THE POINTS OCCUPIED BY
THE MOUNTED RIFLES ABOUT MIDNIGHT ON AUGUST 6TH
British troops and trenches, red; Turkish, blue. Height contours, 10 metres.

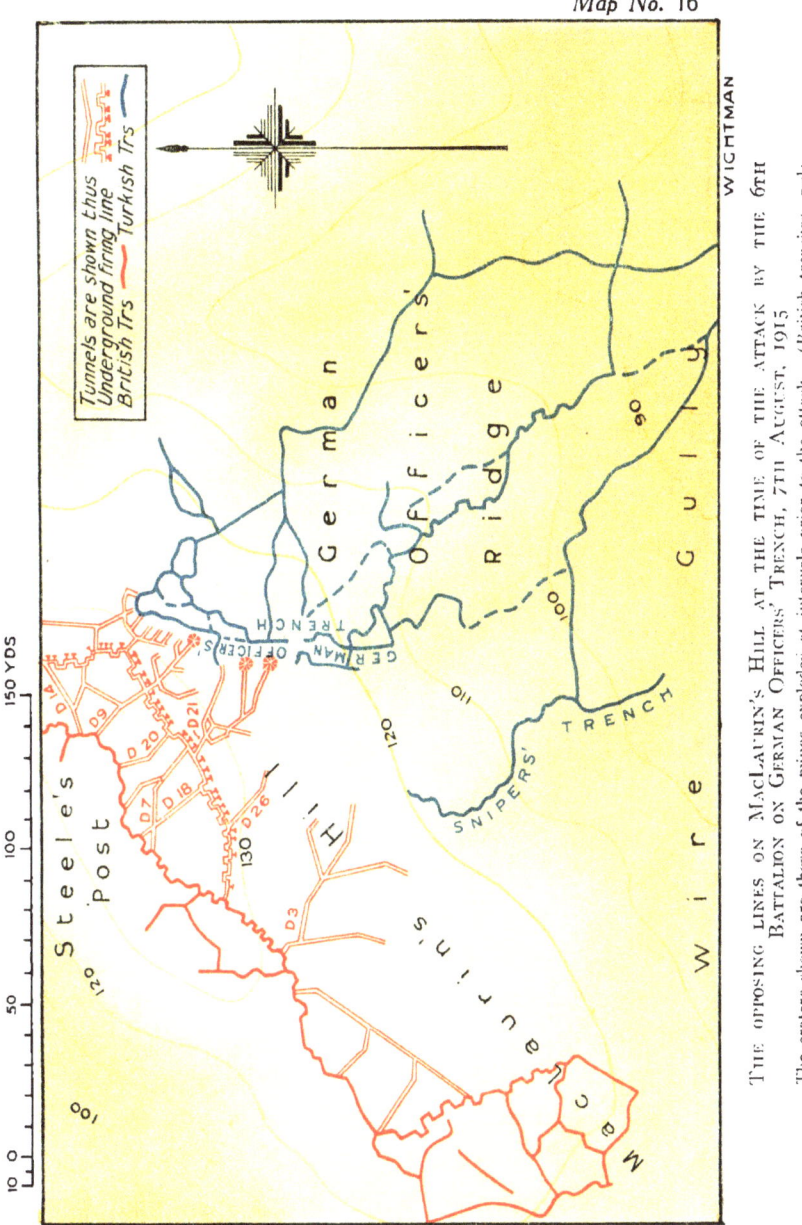

Map No. 16

The opposing lines on MacLaurin's Hill at the time of the attack by the 6th Battalion on German Officers' Trench, 7th August, 1915

The craters shown are those of the mines exploded at intervals prior to the attack. (British trenches, red; Turkish, blue. Height contours, 10 metres.)

Map No. 17

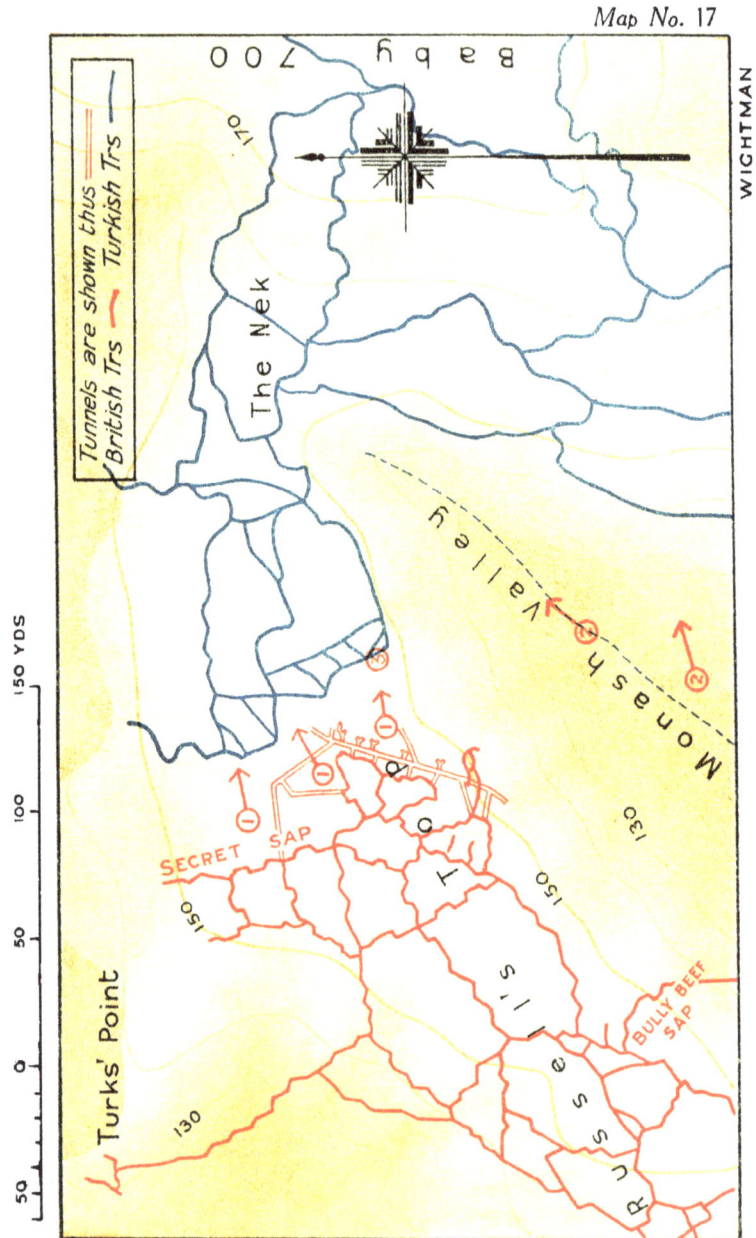

THE ATTACK BY THE 3RD LIGHT HORSE BRIGADE ON THE NEK, 7TH AUGUST, 1915

(1) Direction of light horse attack. (2) Attempt by Royal Welch Fusiliers. (3) Point where flag was raised. (British troops and trenches, red; Turkish trenches, blue. Height contours, to metres.)

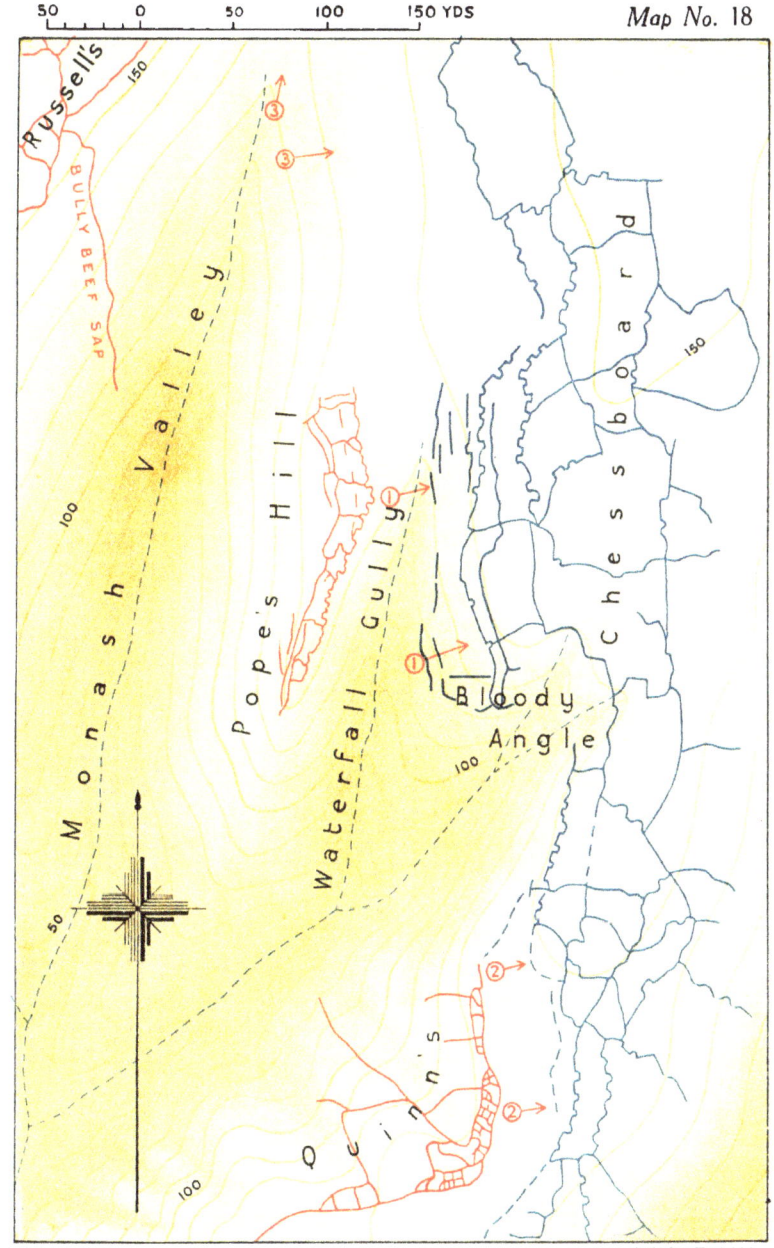

THE ASSAULTS MADE BY THE 1ST AND 2ND LIGHT HORSE REGIMENTS AND ROYAL WELCH FUSILIERS, 7TH AUGUST, 1915

(1) 1st Light Horse Regiment. (2) 2nd Light Horse Regiment. (3) Royal Welch Fusiliers. (British troops and trenches, red; Turkish trenches, blue. Height contours, 10 metres.)

Map No. 19

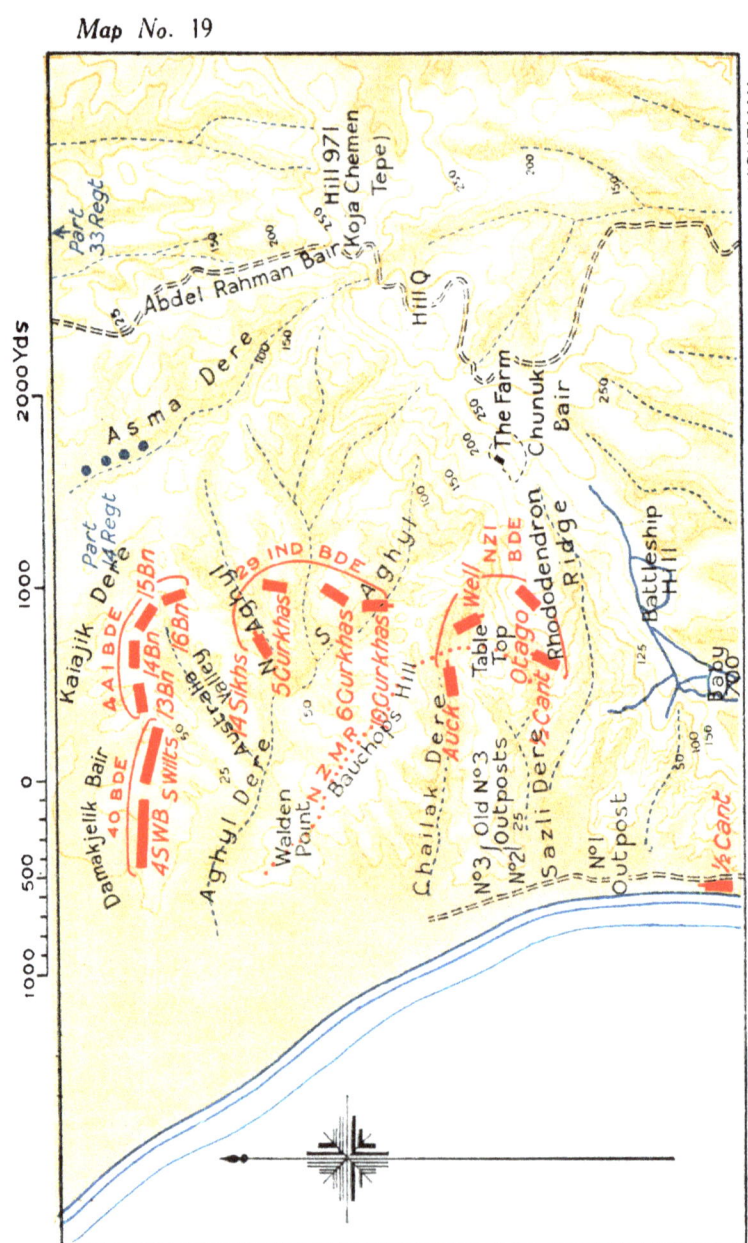

Positions of General Godley's Columns North of Anzac, at day-break, 7th August, 1915. British troops, red; Turkish troops and trenches, blue. Height contours, 25 metres.

Map No. 20

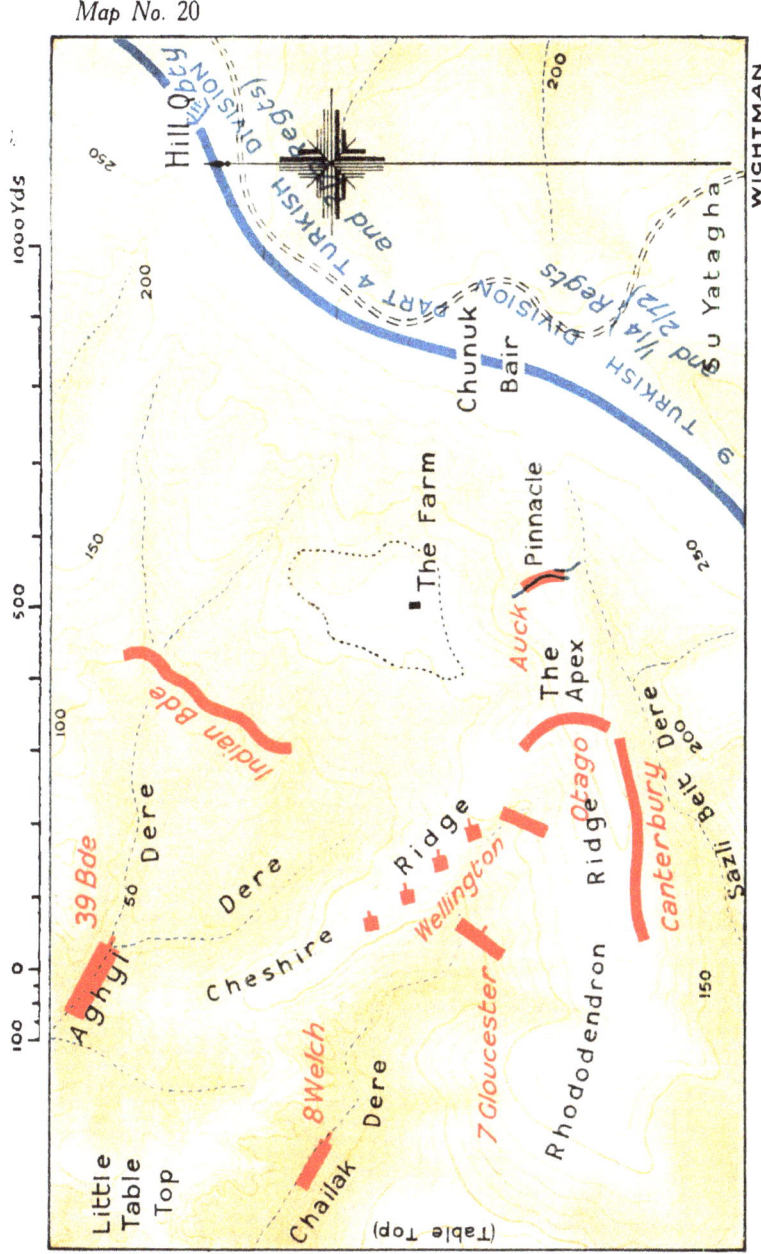

Position on the evening of 7th August, 1915, after the attempt by the Auckland Battalion to reach Chunuk Bair

British troops and trenches, red; Turkish troops and trenches, blue. Height contours, in metres.

Map No. 21

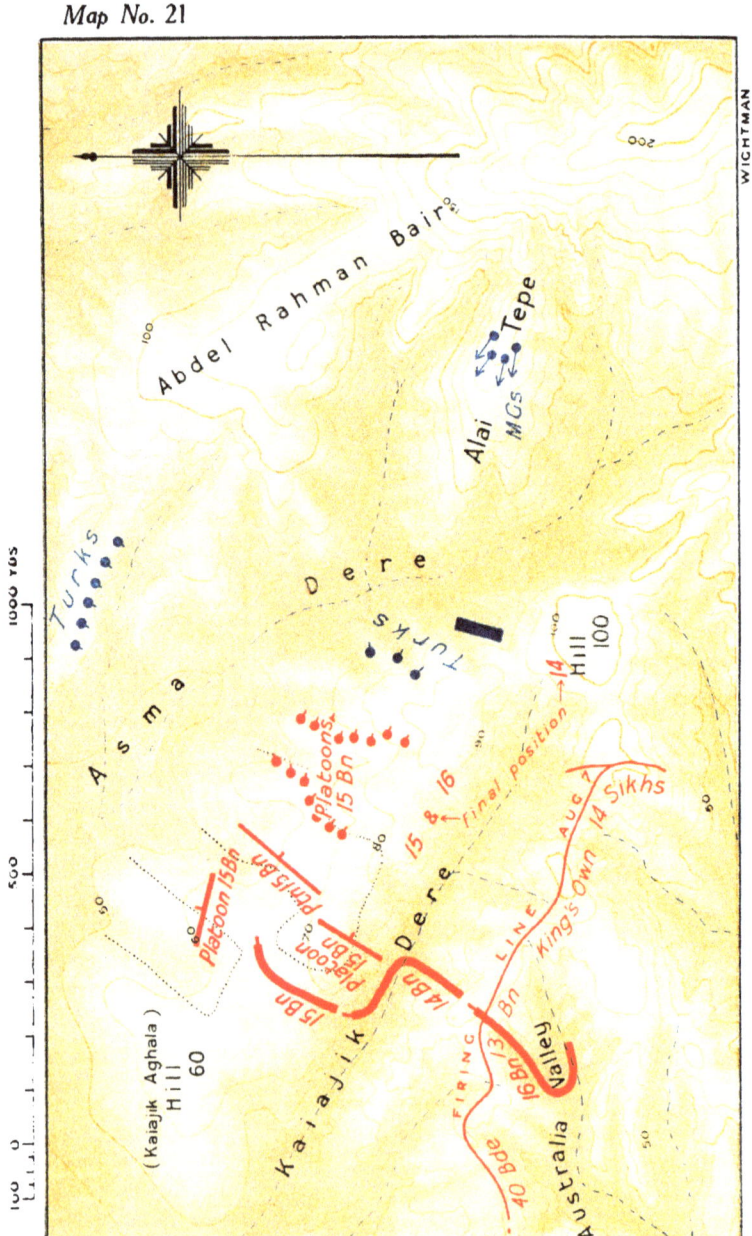

The attempt by the 4th Australian Infantry Brigade to reach Hill 971 by way of Abdel Rahman Bair, 8th August, 1915
British troops and trenches, red; Turkish, blue. Height contours, 10 metres.

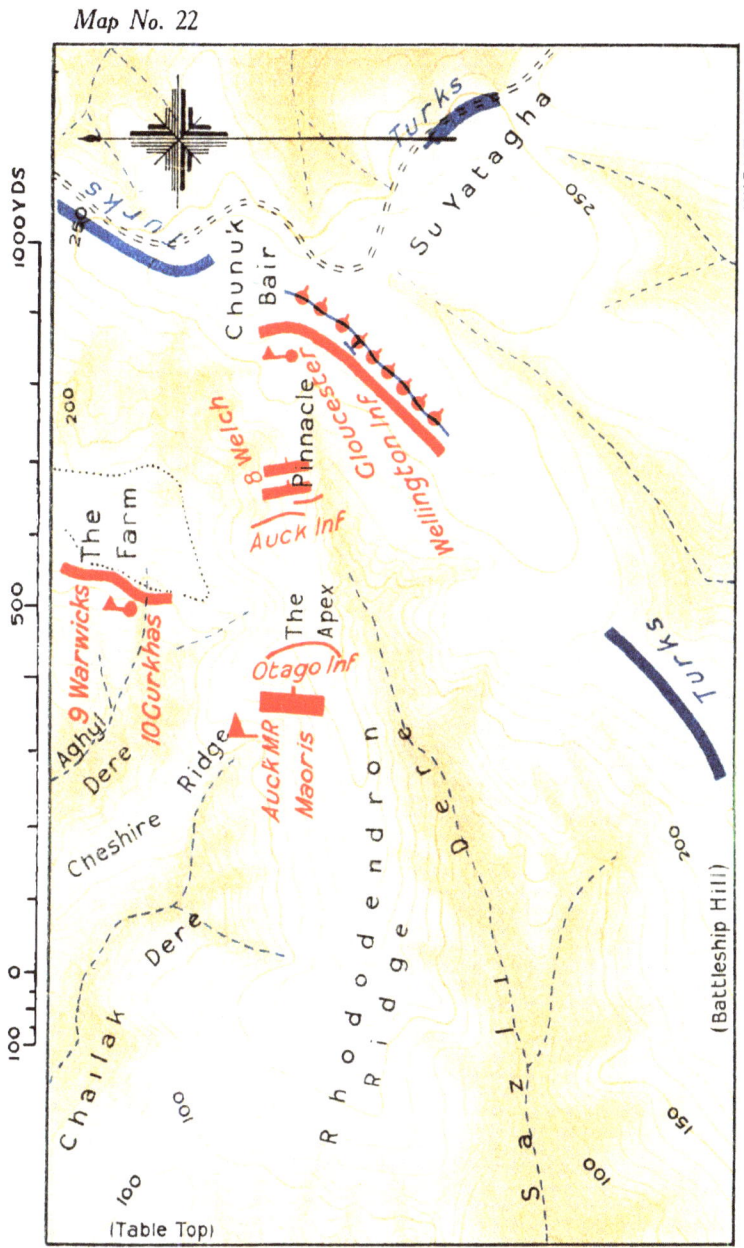

Map No. 22

THE CAPTURE OF THE CREST-LINE AT CHUNUK BAIR BY WELLINGTON BATTALION AND 7TH GLOUCESTER AT DAY-BREAK ON 8TH AUGUST, 1915

British troops and trenches, red; Turkish, blue. Height contours, 10 metres.

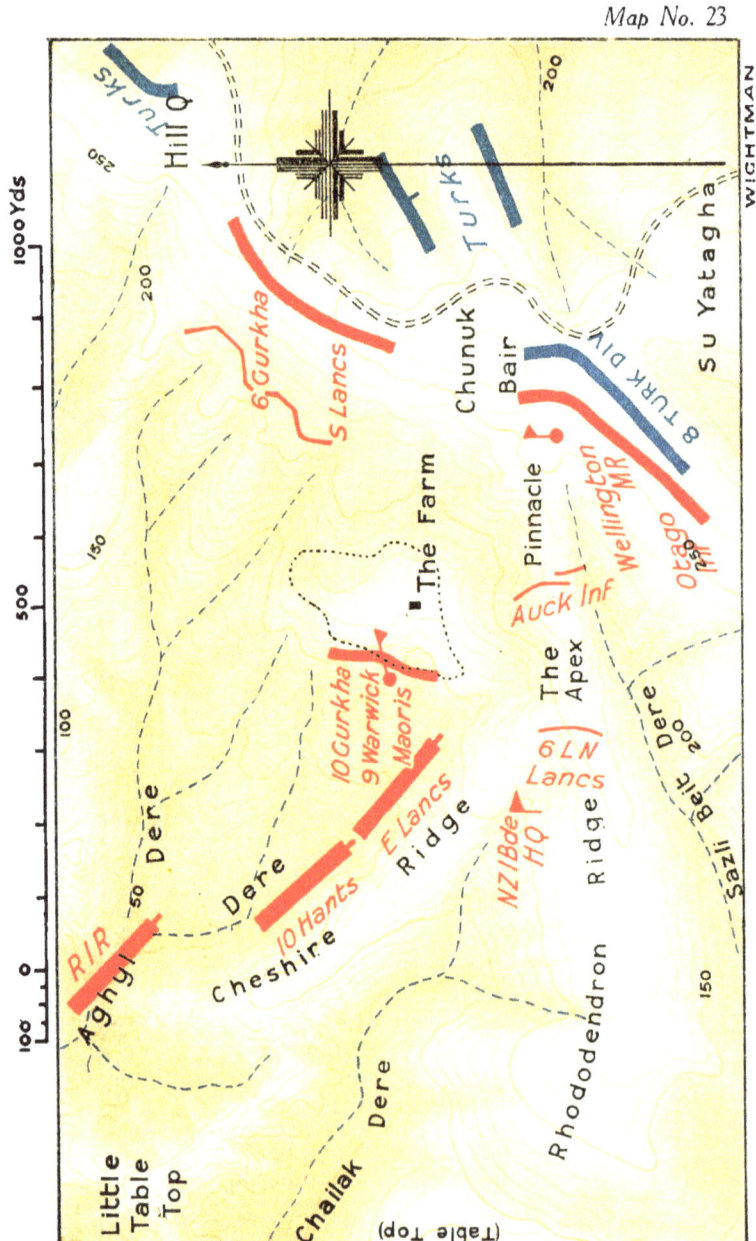

Map No. 23

Position on Sari Bair at 5.30 a.m. on 9th August, 1915—The Climax of the Campaign in Gallipoli

British troops and trenches, red; Turkish troops, blue. Height contours, to metres.

Map No. 24

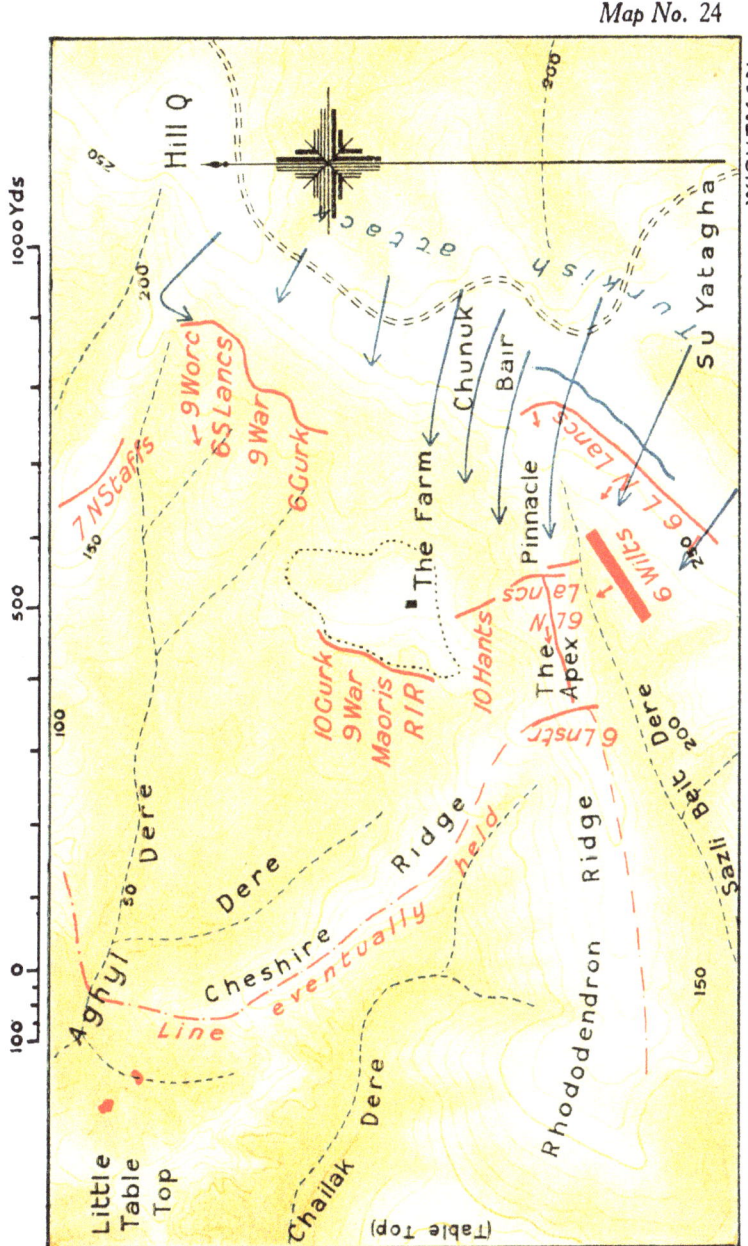

The counter-attack by Mustafa Kemal Pasha on Sari Bair, at day-break, 10th August, 1915

British troops and trenches, red; Turkish, blue. Height contours, 10 metres.

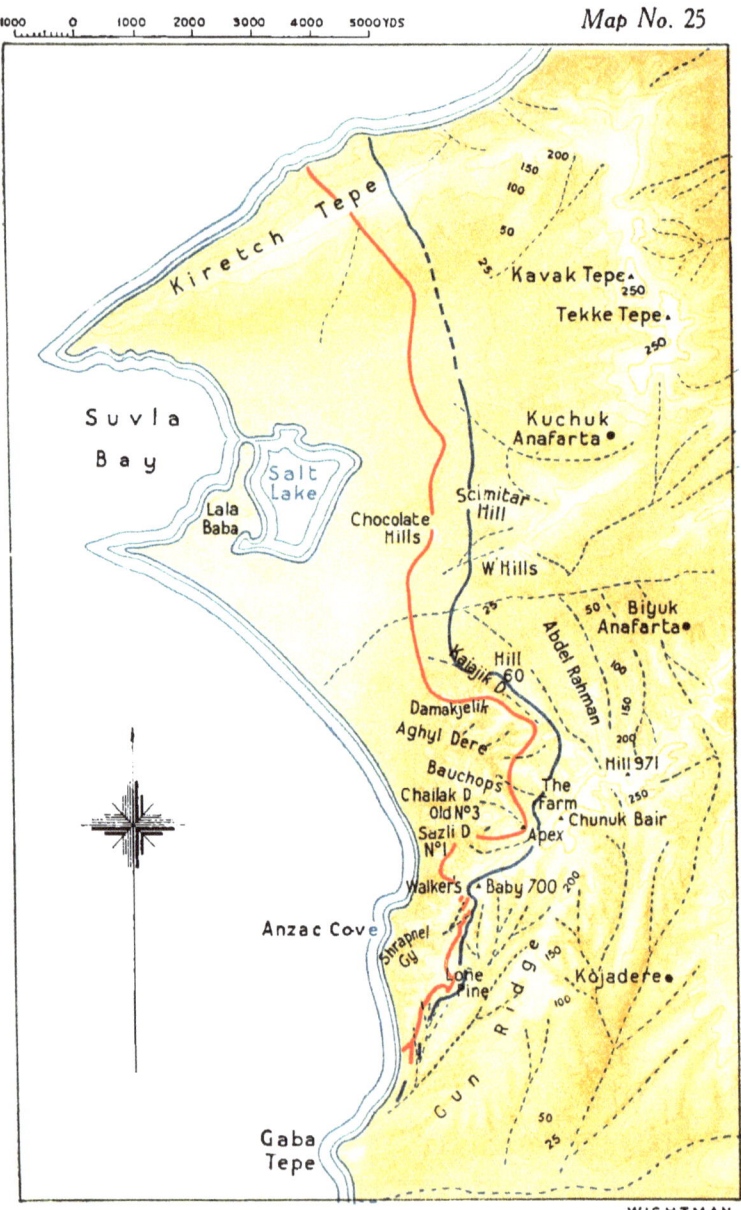

Anzac-Suvla position, 12th August, 1915
British line, red; Turkish, blue. Height contours, 50 metres.

Map No. 26

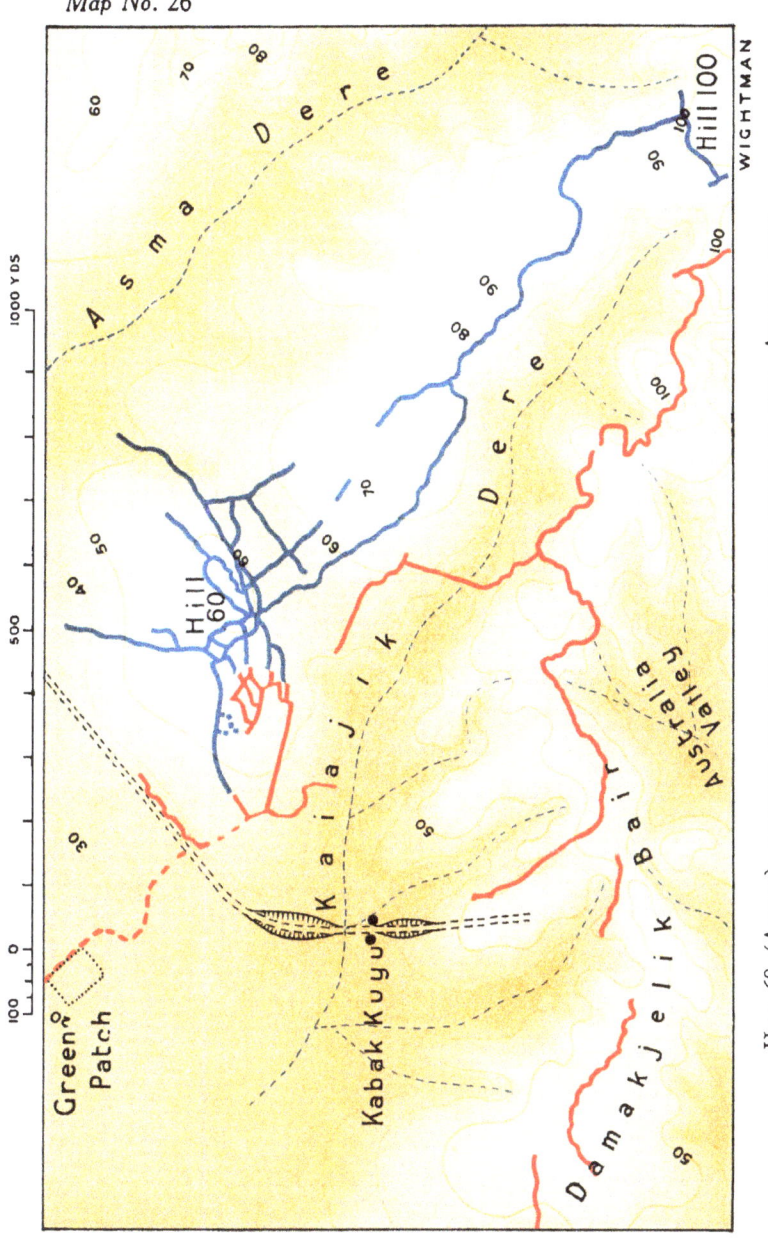

HILL 60 (ANZAC): SHOWING THE POSITION ON THE NIGHT OF 27TH AUGUST, 1915
British trenches, red; Turkish, blue. Height contours, 10 metres.

Map No. 27

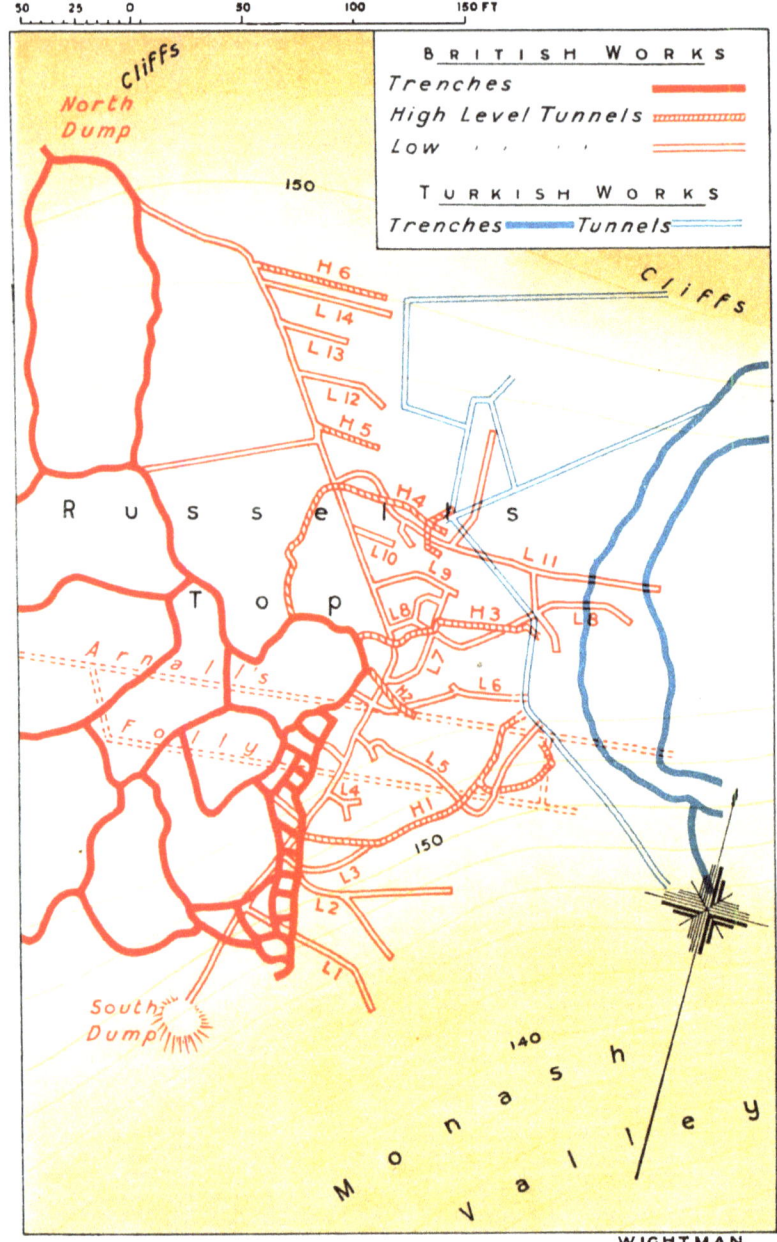

THE TRENCHES AND MINING SYSTEM ON RUSSELL'S TOP AT THE
BEGINNING OF DECEMBER, 1915
British works, red; Turkish, blue. Height contours, 2 metres.

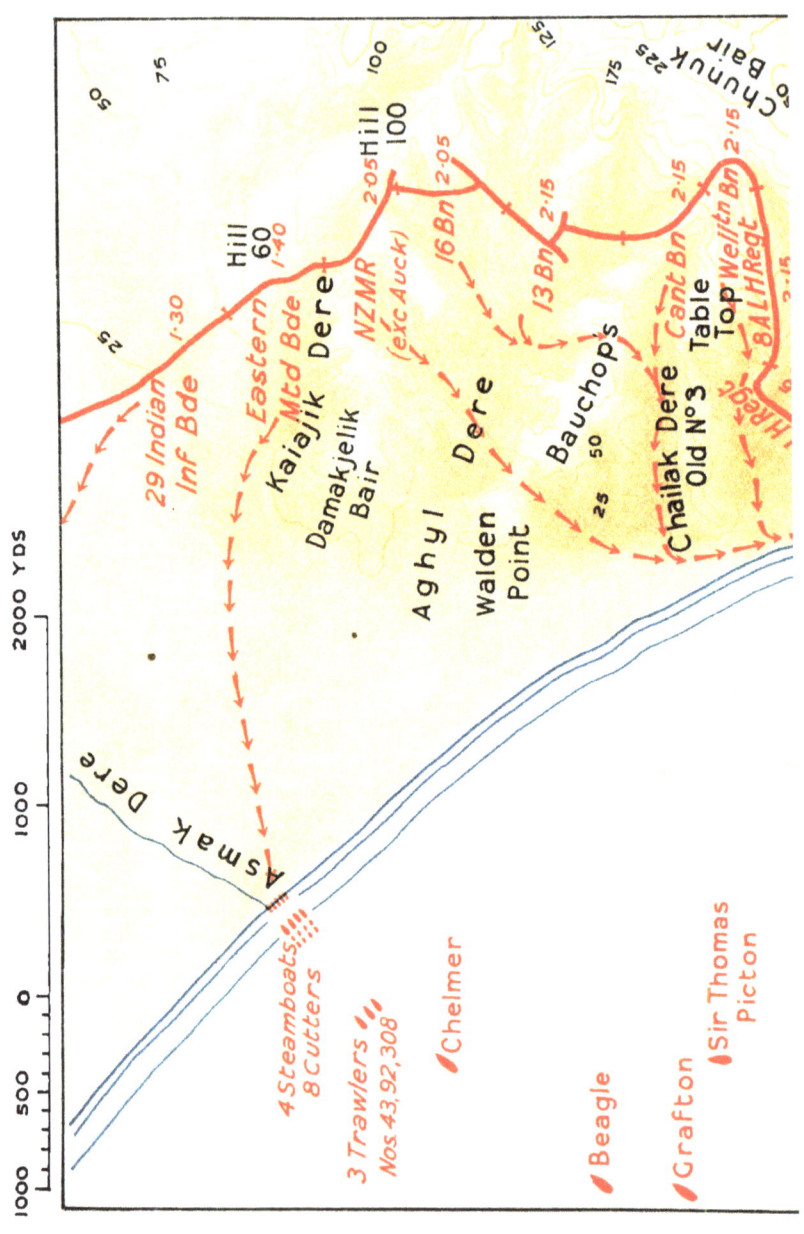

No. 28

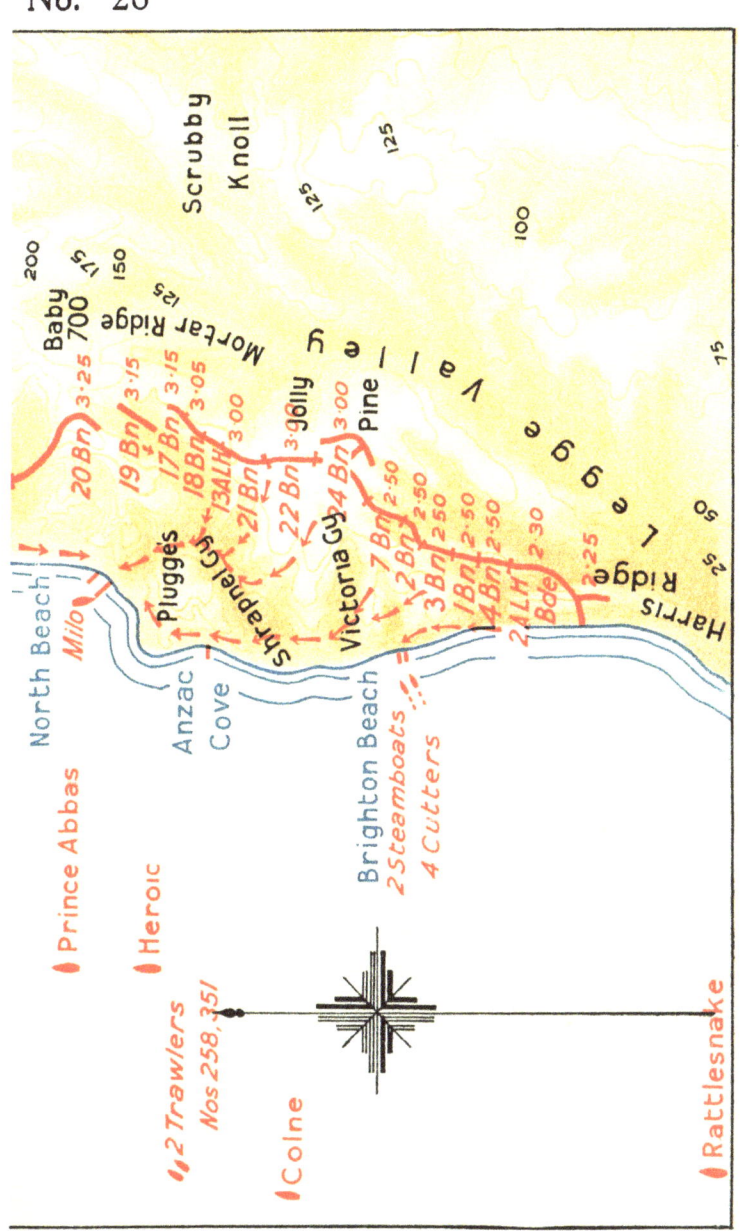

THE EVACUATION OF ANZAC—POSITION AT 1.30 A.M., 20TH DECEMBER, 1915, IMMEDIATELY BEFORE THE DEPARTURE OF THE "C" PARTIES

The times shown are those at which the last of the "C" parties were to leave. (British troops, &c., red. Height contours, 25 metres.)

THE
AUSTRALIAN IMPERIAL FORCE IN FRANCE
1916

VOLUME III

LIST OF MAPS

1 No. 2 (Central) Section of the Suez Canal Defences, 1916
2 The concentration area of the I Anzac Corps in Flanders, April 1916
3 The Western Front, April 1916
4 British and German trench systems near Bois Grenier, summer of 1916
5 Typical artillery barrage for a trench raid
6 The battlefield of Fromelles
7 The back area allotted to the I Anzac Corps on the Somme, July-August 1916
8 The battlefield of Pozières and Mouquet Farm
9 The I Anzac sector of the Somme battlefield on 5th November, 1916

Map No. 1

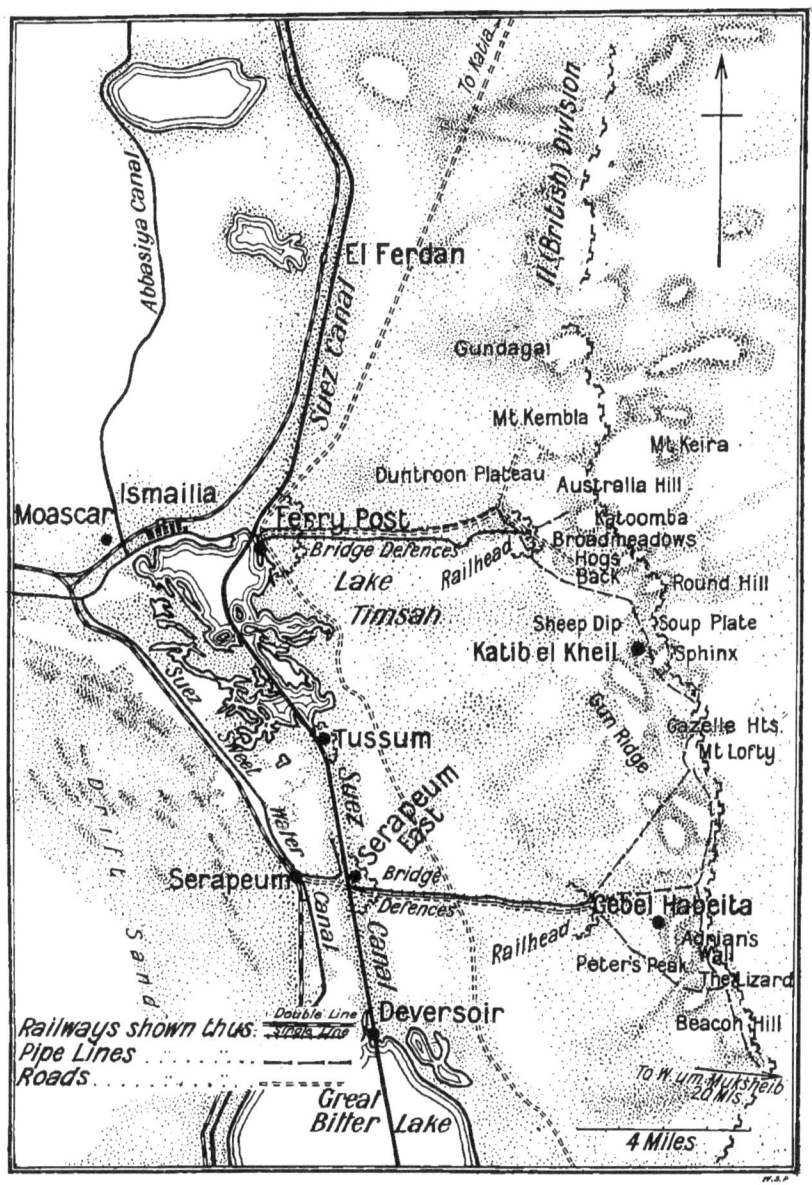

No. 2 (Central) Section of the Suez Canal Defences, dug by Australian divisions, January-March 1916

Map No. 2

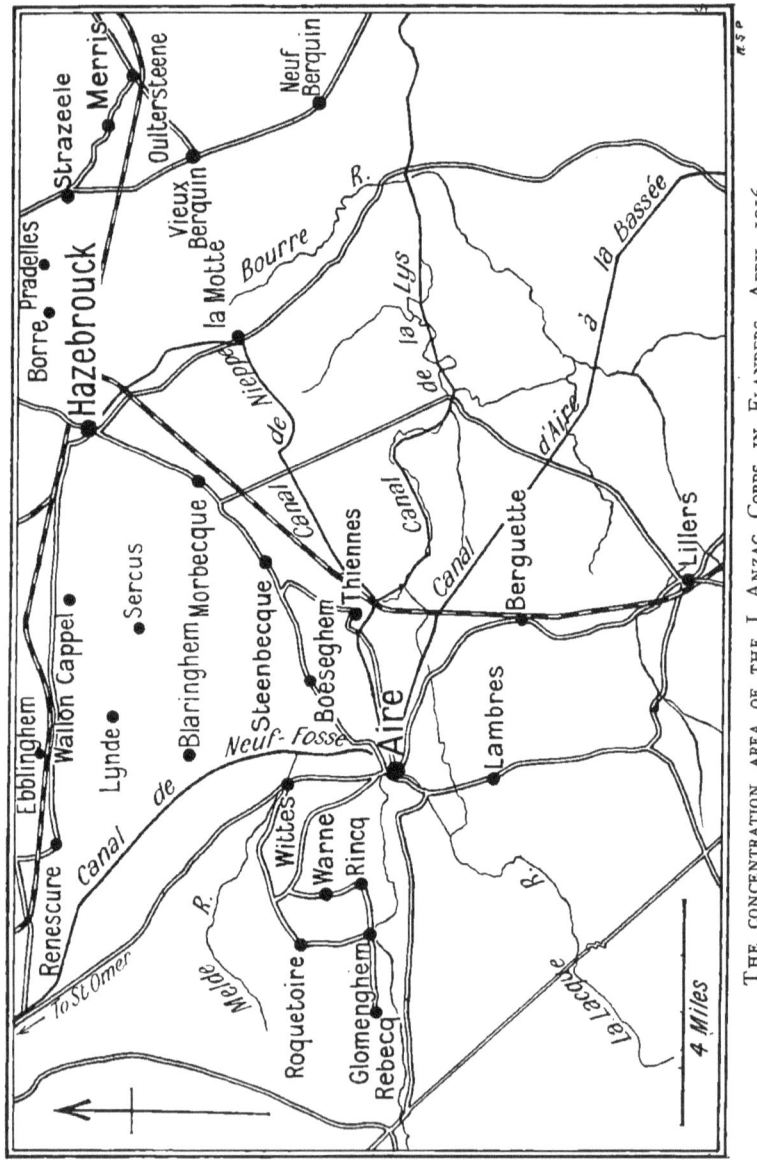

The concentration area of the I Anzac Corps in Flanders, April 1916

Map No. 3

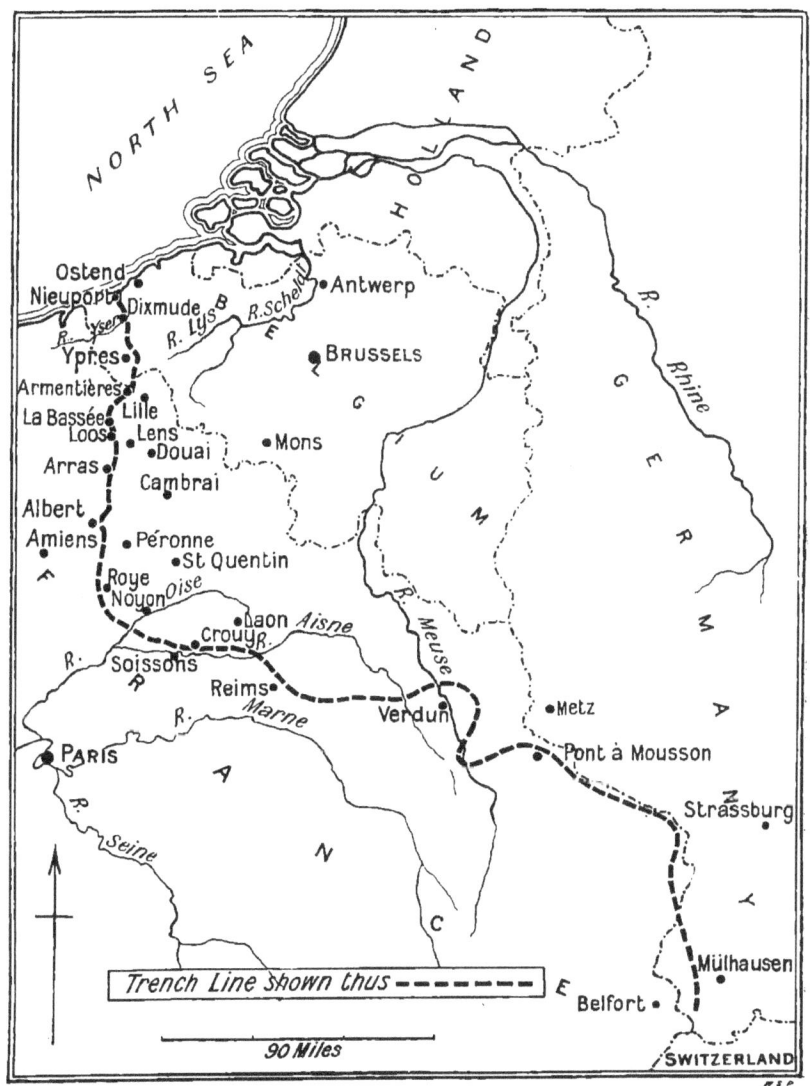

THE WESTERN FRONT, APRIL 1916

MAP

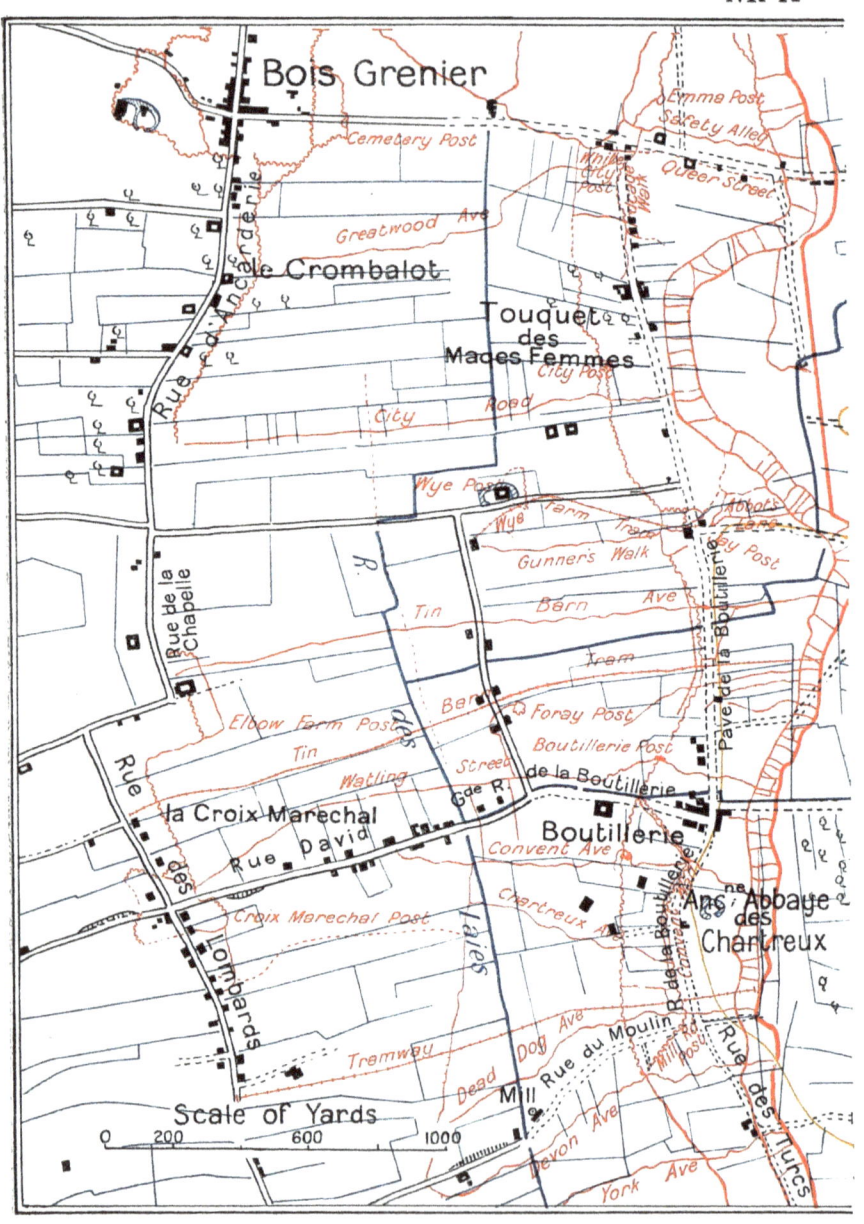

British and German trench systems

No. 4

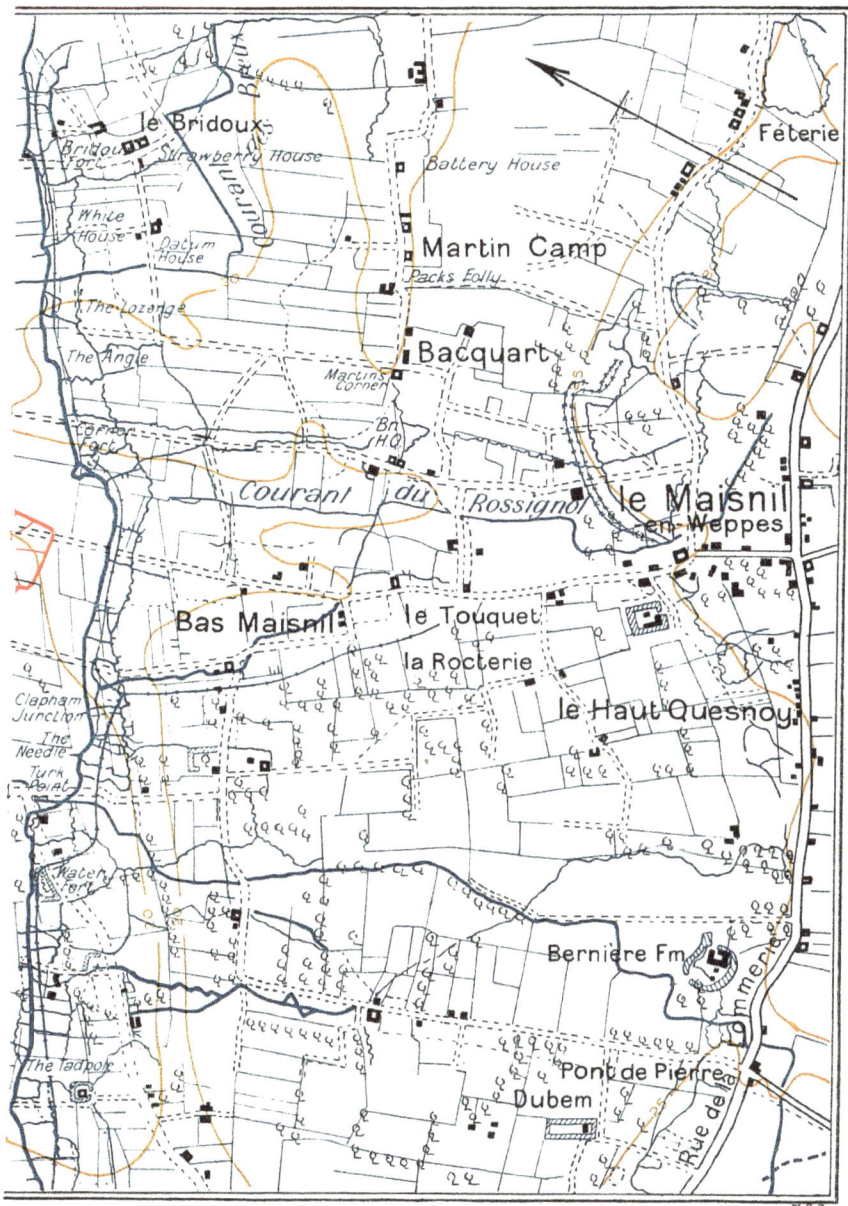

NEAR BOIS GRENIER, SUMMER OF 1916

Map No. 5

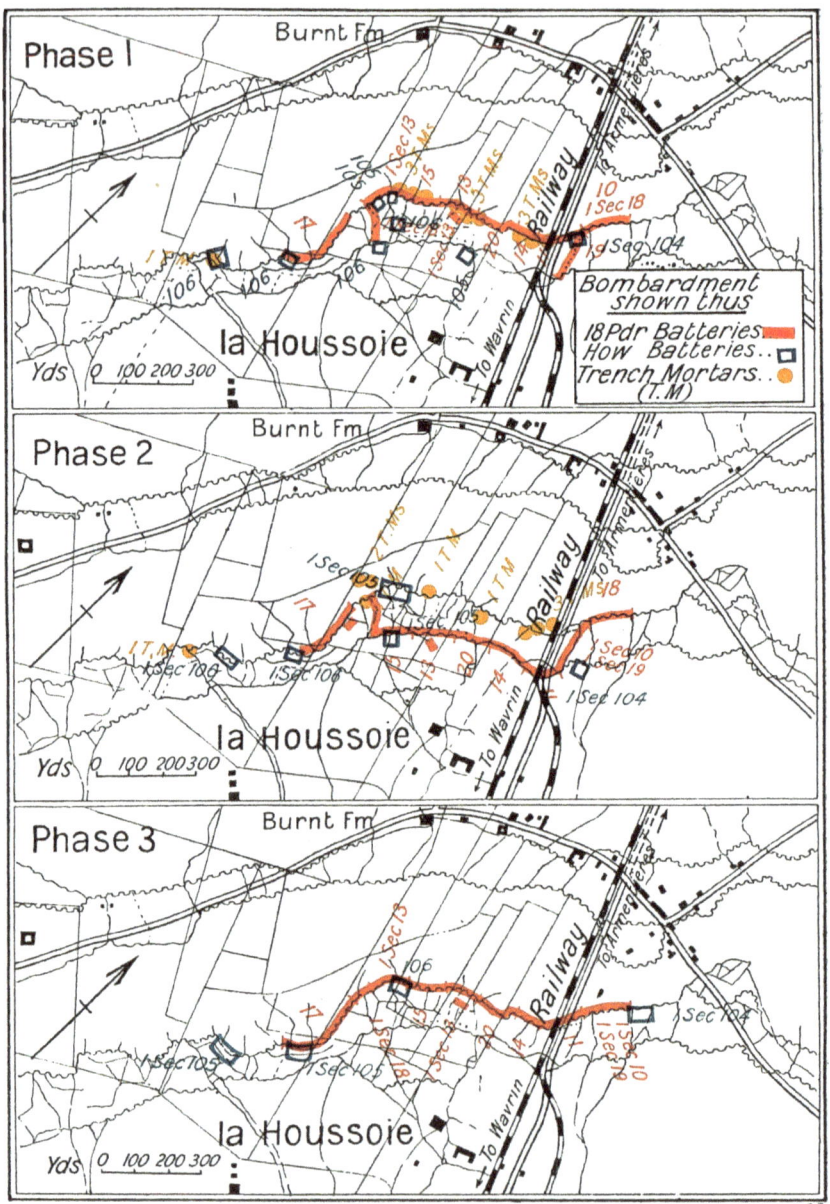

TYPICAL ARTILLERY BARRAGE FOR A TRENCH RAID

The barrage here shown is that covering the triple raid by the 6th Brigade south-west of Armentières on the night of 29-30 June 1916. The trenches at the top of each map are the British; those below are the German. The map of Phase 1 shows the trench-mortars cutting wire opposite the three points of entry. In Phase 2 the "box" is formed, and the infantry enters in the three spaces between the trench-mortar bursts. Phase 3 is after the withdrawal of the raiders. The batteries or sections firing are shown by the numbers (in colour); thus "1 sec. 10" means "one section (two guns) of the 10th Battery"; "3 T.M's" means "3 medium trench-mortars."

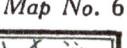

Map No. 6

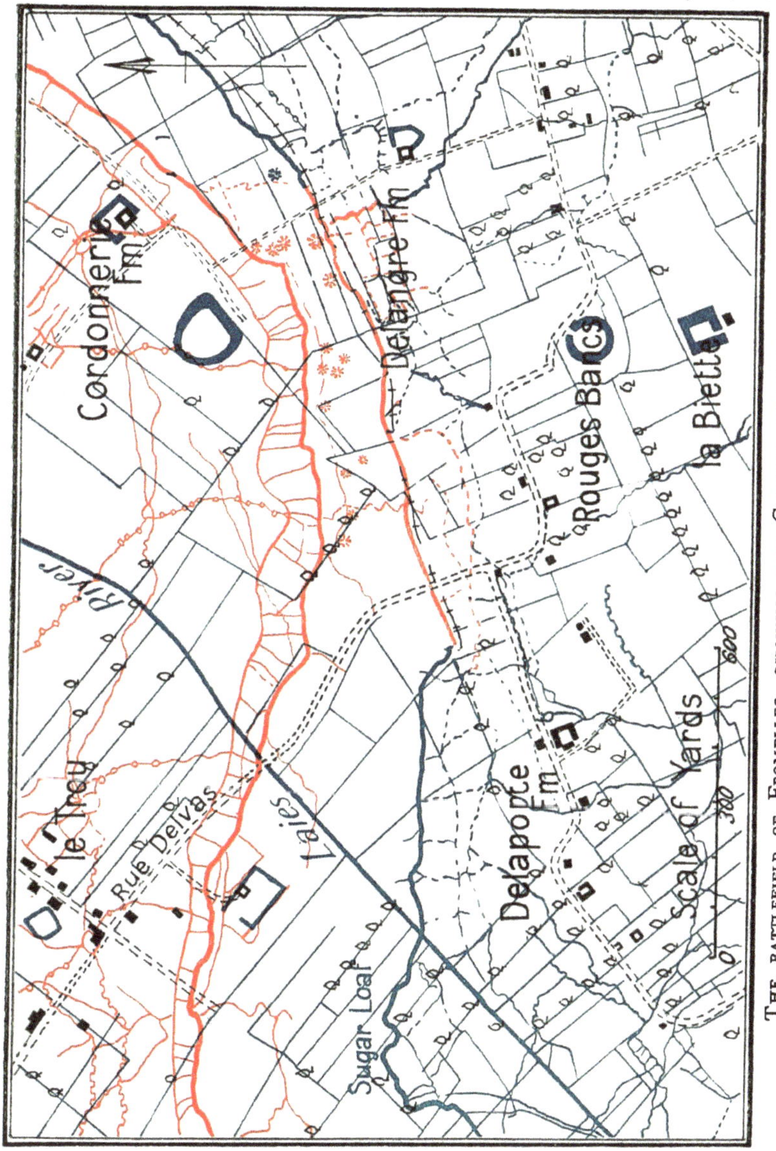

The battlefield of Fromelles, showing the German trenches captured by the 5th Australian Division on 19th July, 1916

Map No. 7

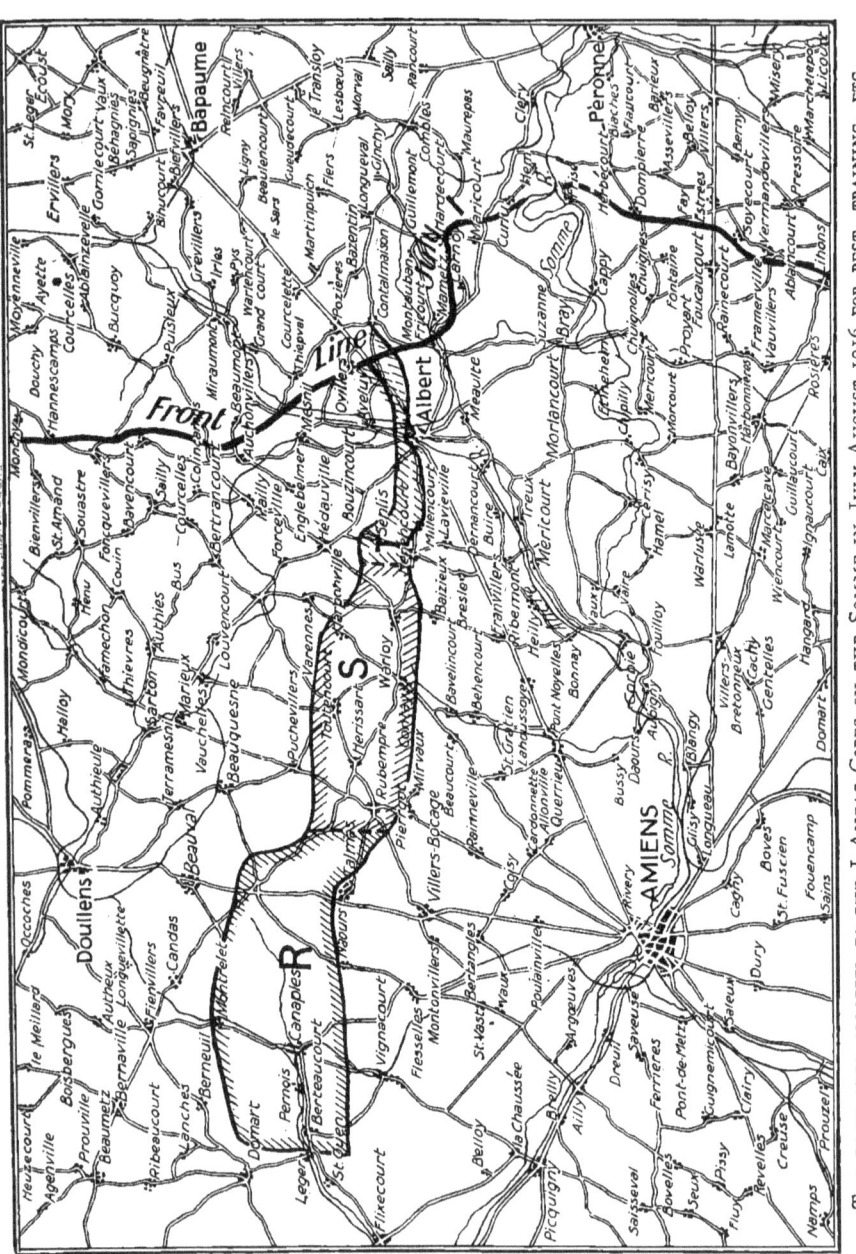

The back area allotted to the I Anzac Corps on the Somme in July-August 1916 for rest, training, etc. The area of the above map is 38 miles by 25.

MAP

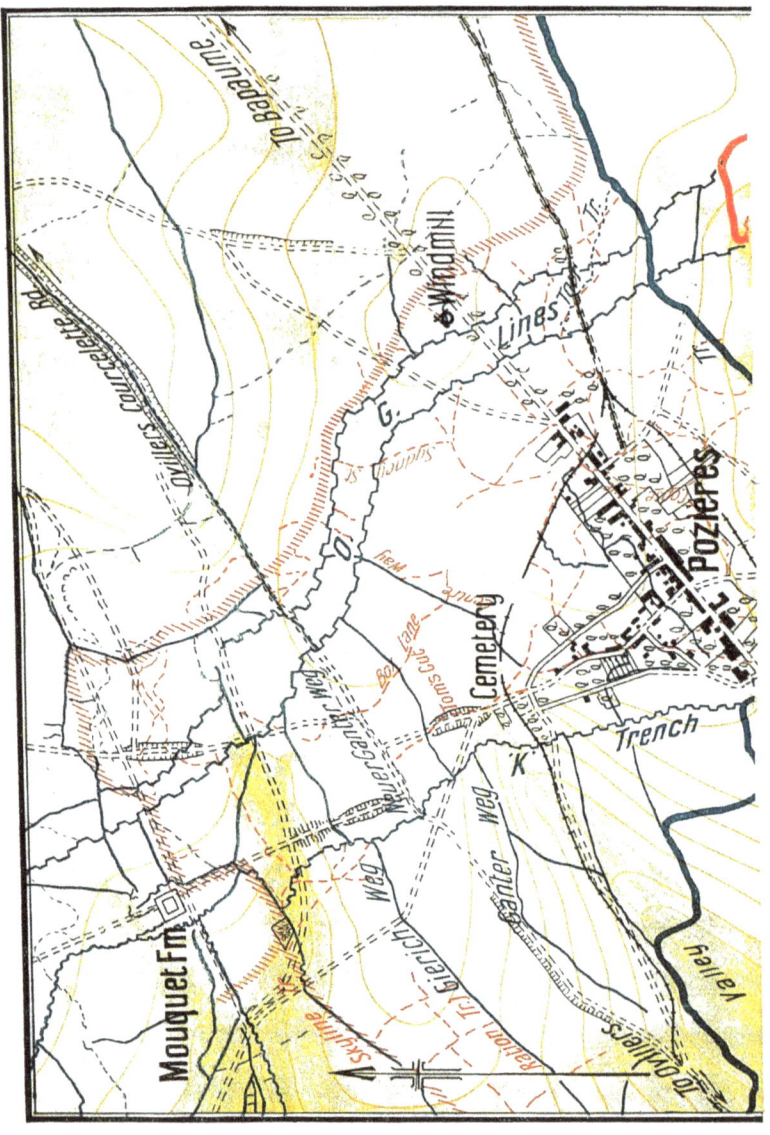

No. 8

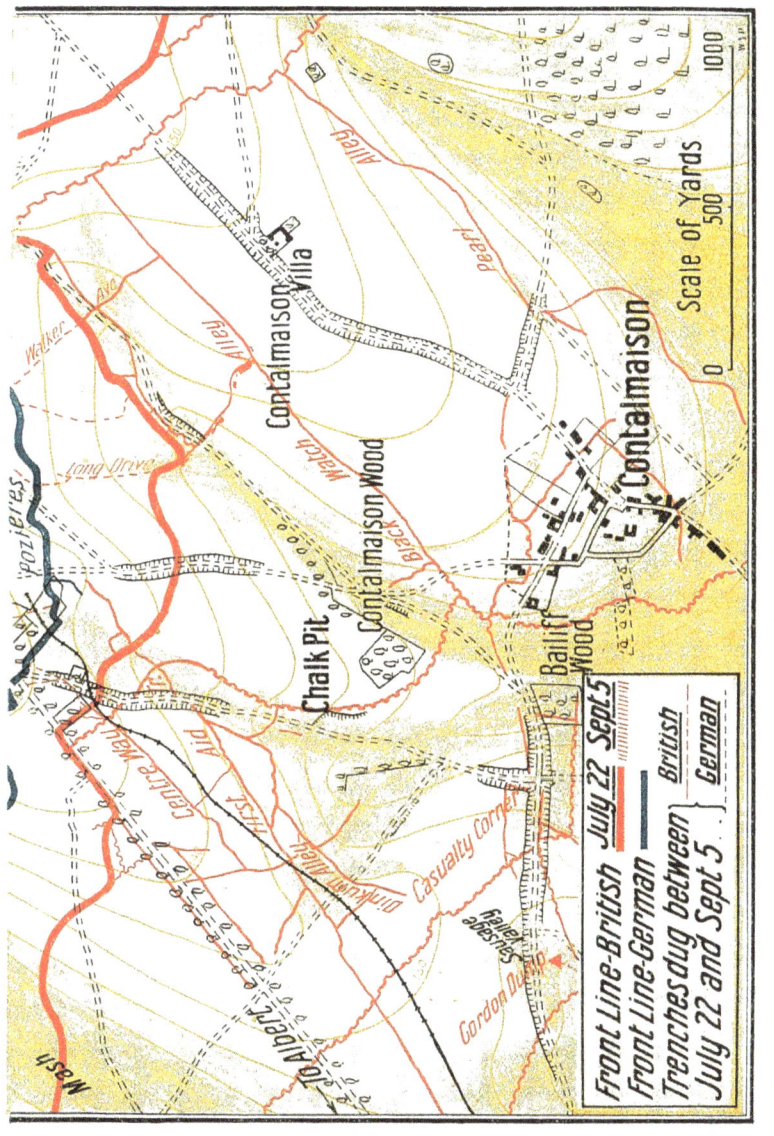

The battlefield of Pozières and Mouquet Farm, July–September 1916, showing the total advance of the I Anzac Corps

Map No. 9

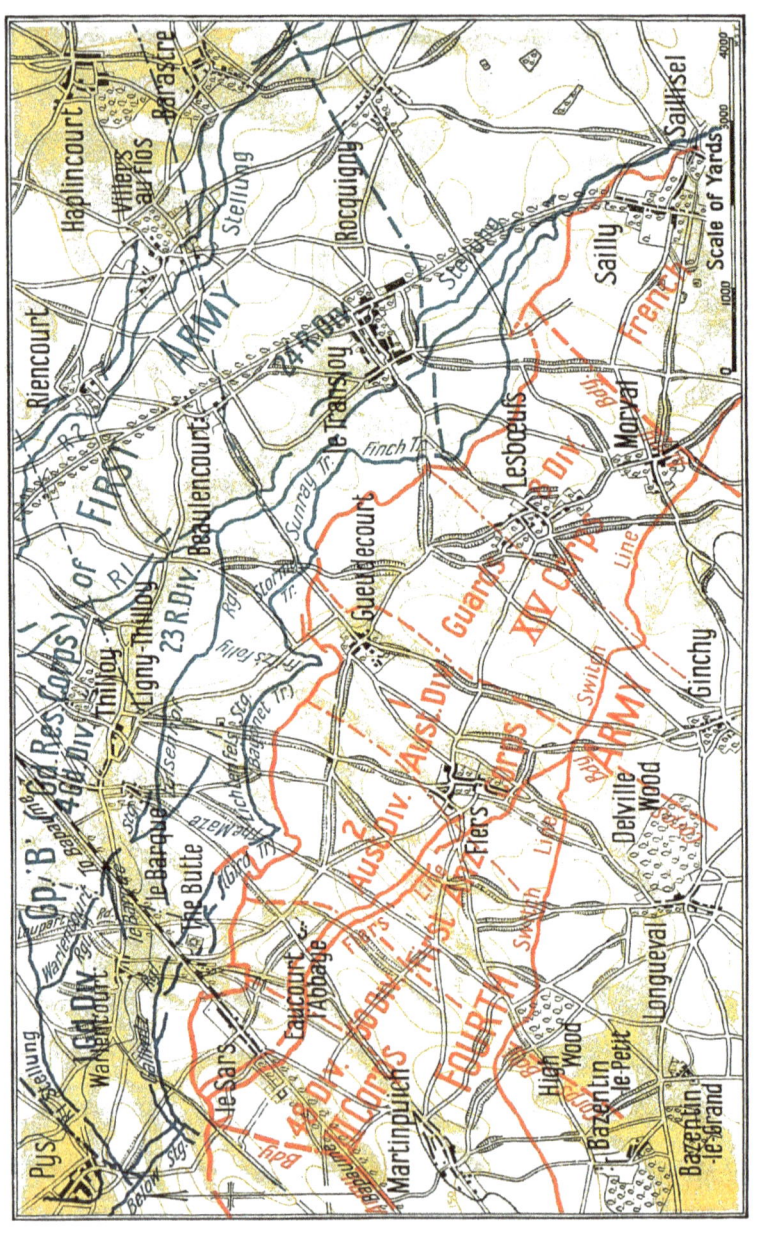

The I Anzac Corps sector of the Somme battlefield on 5th November, 1916

THE
AUSTRALIAN IMPERIAL FORCE IN FRANCE
1917

VOLUME IV

LIST OF MAPS

1 The area from Bapaume to the Hindenburg Line
2 The battlefield of Bullecourt, 11th April, 1917
3 The situation at Messines at 11.30 a.m., 7th June, 1917
4 The battlefield east of Ypres, 19th September, 1917

Map No. 1

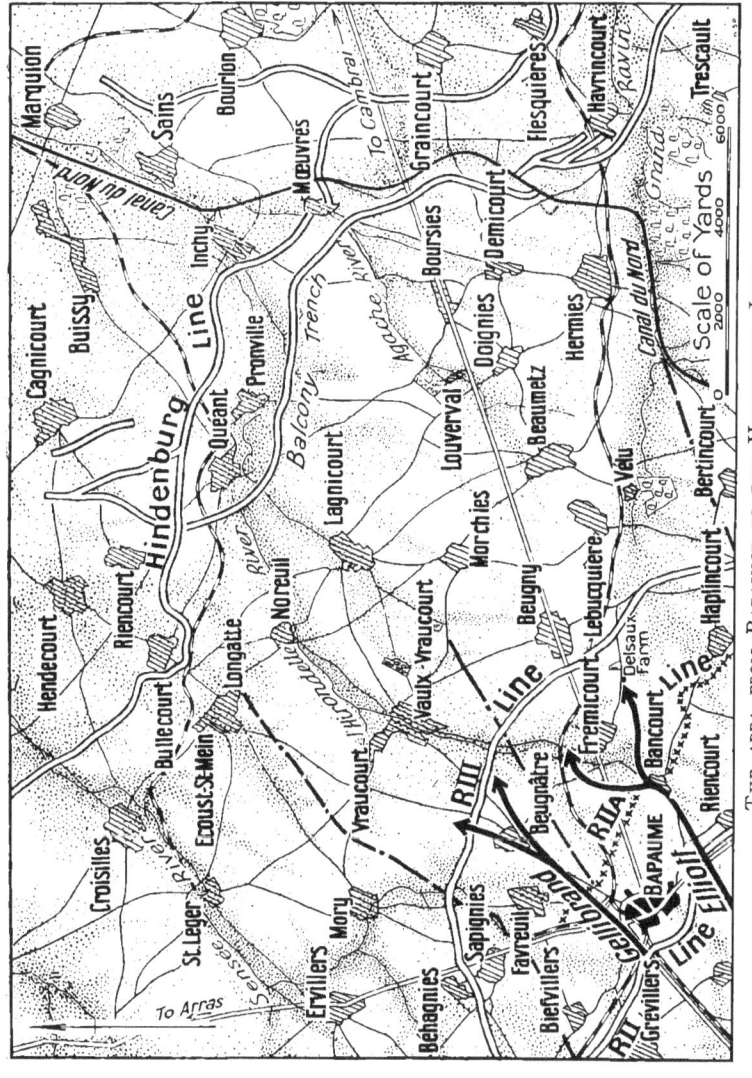

The area from Bapaume to the Hindenburg Line.

This shows the boundaries and sphere of operations of the two advanced guards of the I Anzac Corps when following the German withdrawal in March 1917.

Map No. 2

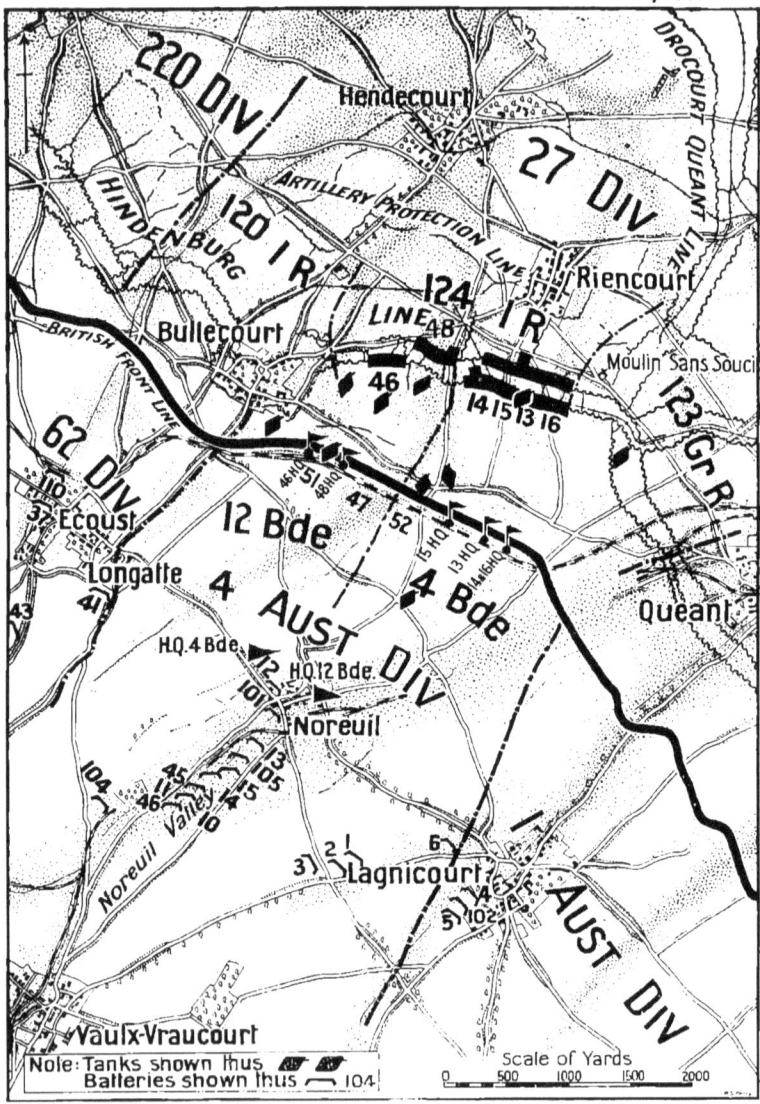

THE BATTLEFIELD OF BULLECOURT, SHOWING THE SITUATION AT ABOUT
9.30 A.M. ON 11TH APRIL, 1917, AFTER THE CAPTURE OF PORTION OF THE
HINDENBURG LINE BY THE 4TH AUSTRALIAN DIVISION
The tanks are shown in the positions in which they were put out of action.

Map No. 3

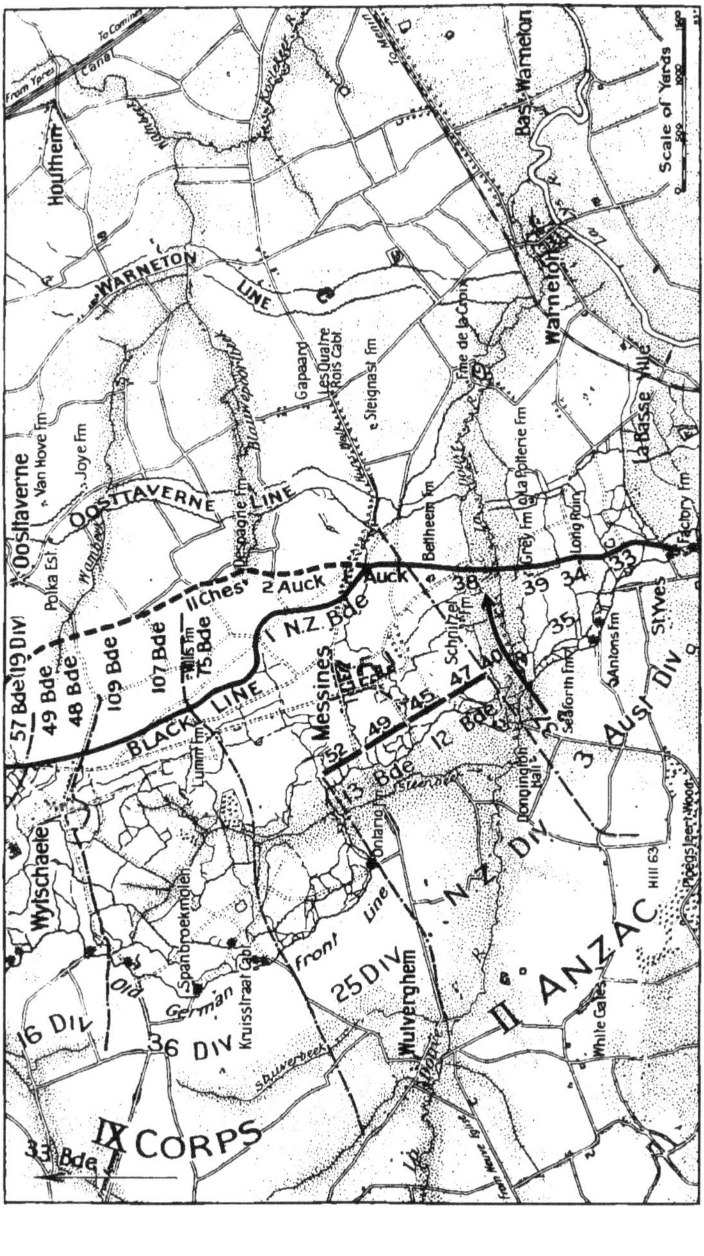

THE SITUATION AT MESSINES AT 11.30 A.M. ON 7TH JUNE, 1917

The black and black dotted lines had been captured, and in the II Anzac sector the assembly for the afternoon attack was beginning. The 12th and 13th Brigades (4th Division) were ready to move forward, and the 37th Battalion (3rd Division) was moving.

Map No. 4

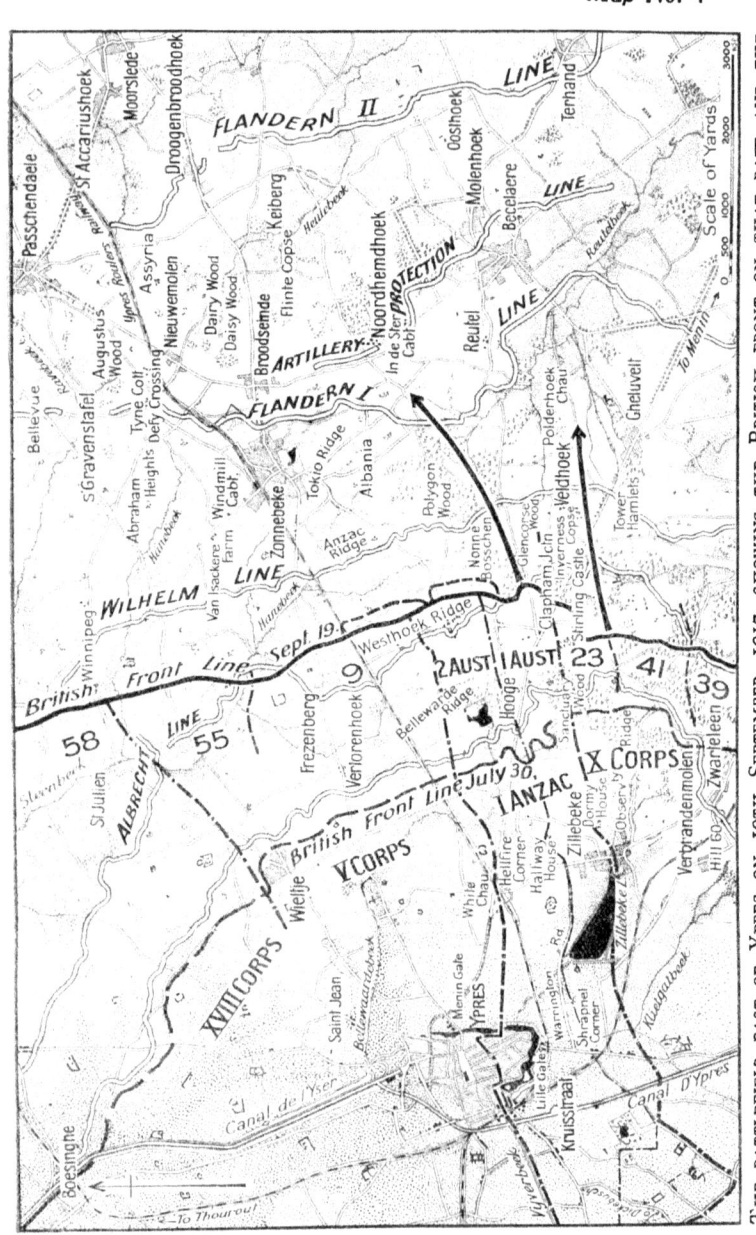

The battlefield east of Ypres on 19th September, 1917, showing the British front on that date and the main German defence lines

The arrows indicate the direction of the impending thrusts by the I Anzac and X Corps. (On this map and in the sketches the thick white lines indicate the successive German defence lines, including the old front held before the Battle of Messines.)

THE
AUSTRALIAN IMPERIAL FORCE IN FRANCE
DURING THE MAIN GERMAN OFFENSIVE, 1918

VOLUME V

LIST OF MAPS

1 First Villers-Bretonneux, 4th April, 1918
2 Second Dernancourt, 5th April, 1918
3 Second Villers-Bretonneux, 24th-25th April, 1918
4 The region of the British operations in Mesopotamia and North-West Persia

Map No. 1.

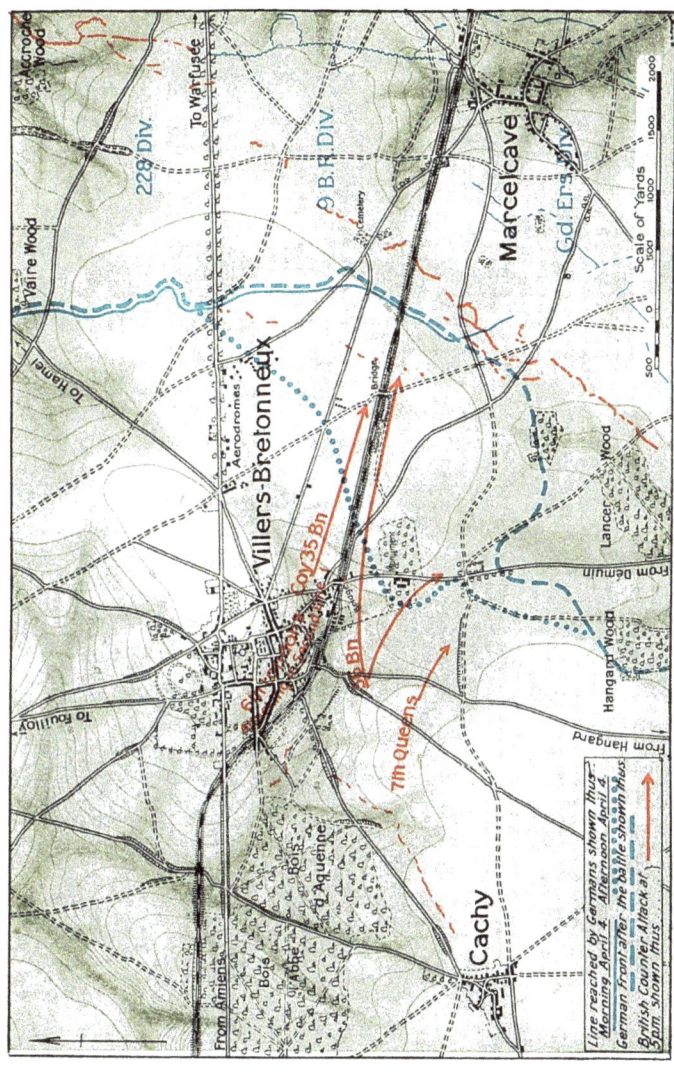

First Villers-Bretonneux, 4th April, 1918

The positions held by British and Germans before the battle are indicated by the red and blue trenches respectively.

Map No. 2.

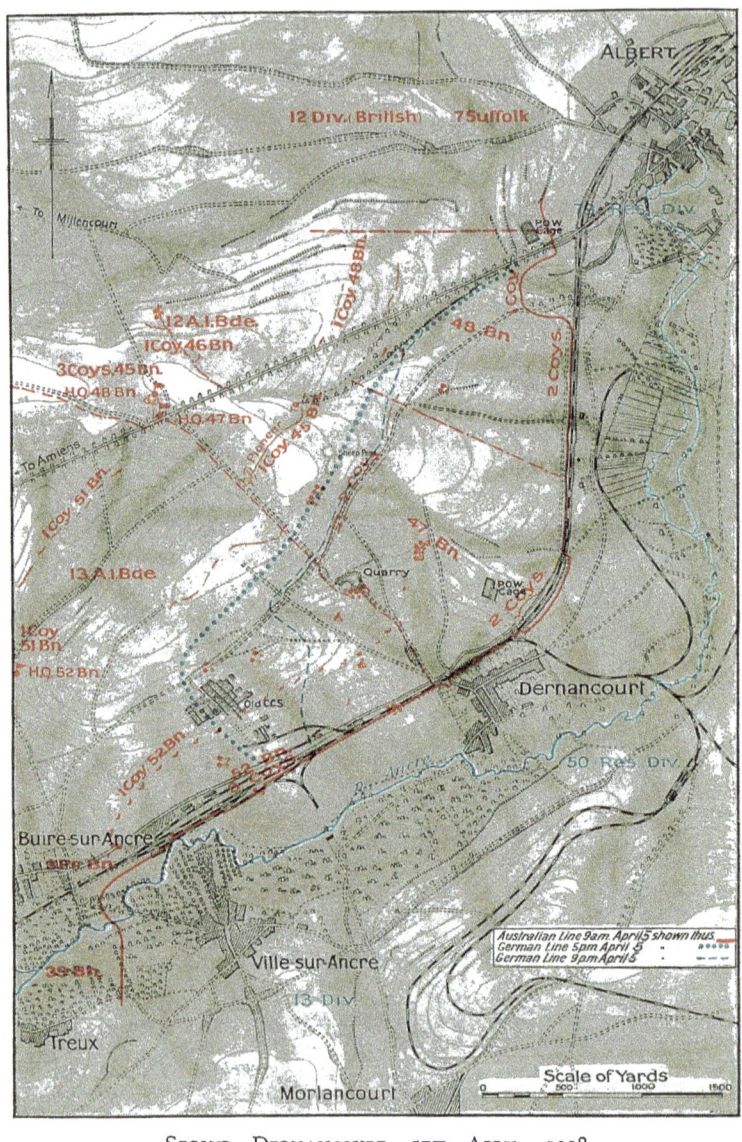

SECOND DERNANCOURT, 5TH APRIL, 1918
The dispositions are those existing at 9 a.m., when the German infantry delivered the main attack.

Map No. 3.

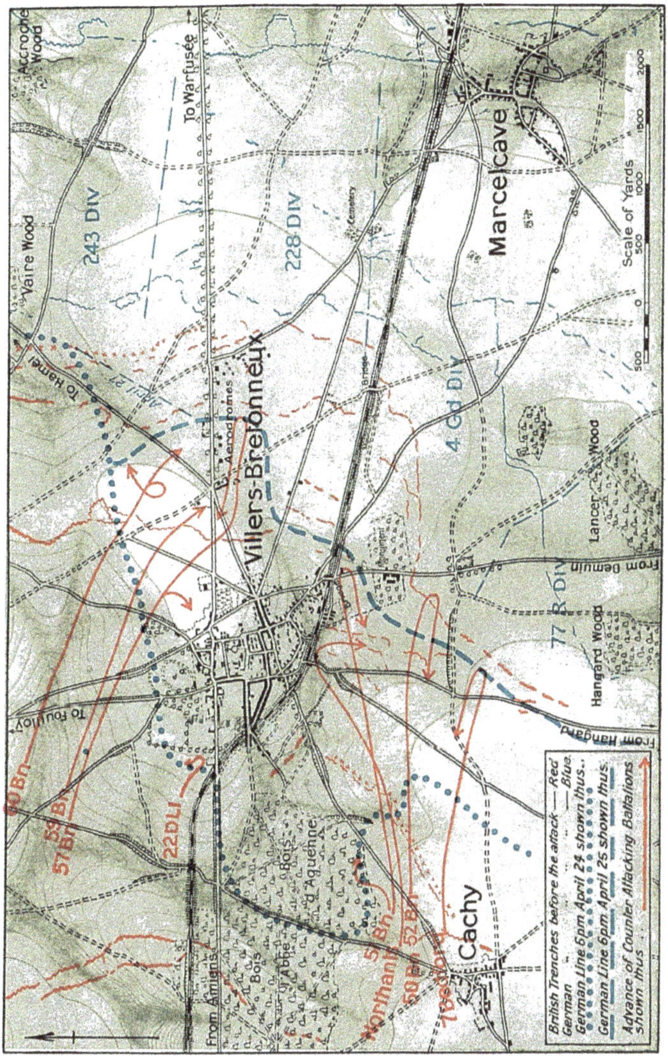

SECOND VILLERS-BRETONNEUX, 24TH-25TH APRIL, 1918

Showing the limits of the German advance and the direction of the several units in the counter-attack.

Map No. 4.

THE REGION OF THE BRITISH OPERATIONS IN MESOPOTAMIA AND
NORTH-WEST PERSIA
(Mountains are shown only where necessary for the reader's guidance.)

THE
AUSTRALIAN IMPERIAL FORCE IN FRANCE
DURING THE ALLIED OFFENSIVE, 1918

VOLUME VI

LIST OF MAPS

1 The attack by Australian Corps, 8th August, 1918
2 The front from Lihons to Albert after the Battle of Amiens

Map No. 1

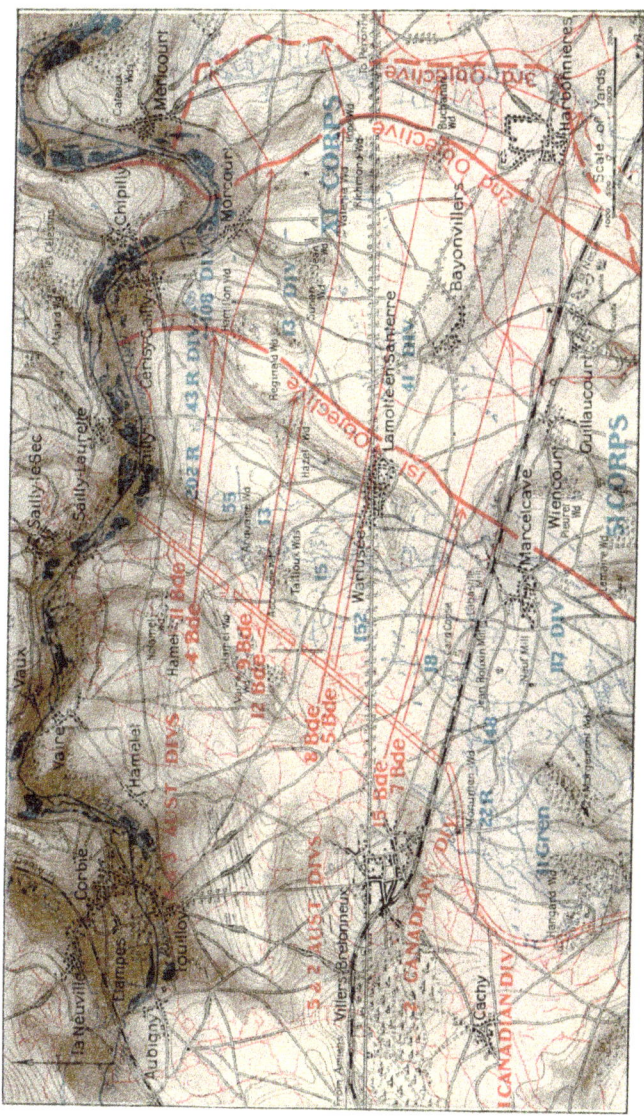

THE ATTACK BY AUSTRALIAN CORPS, 8TH AUGUST 1918

The map shows diagrammatically the Australian divisions that advanced in the several stages. British trenches, formations and objectives are printed in red, German in blue (German regiments are indicated by their numbers).

Light contours 5 metres, dark 20 metres.

Map No. 2

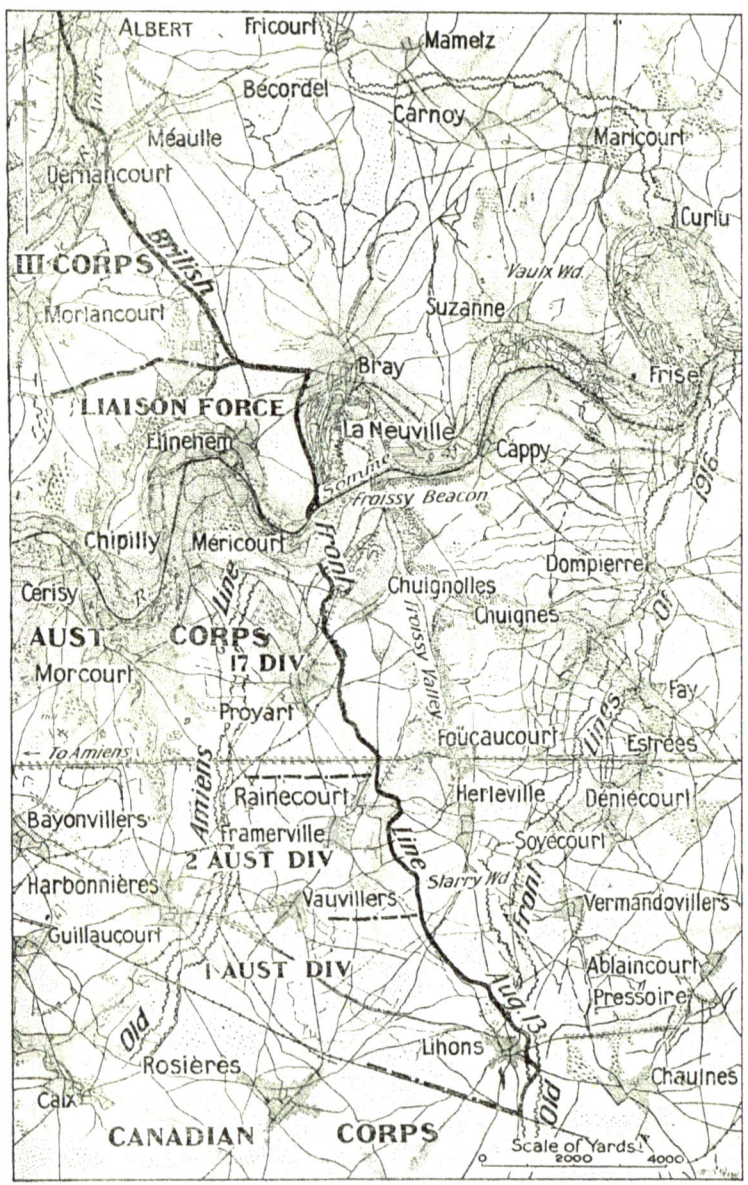

THE FRONT FROM LIHONS TO ALBERT AFTER THE BATTLE OF AMIENS.

THE
AUSTRALIAN IMPERIAL FORCE IN SINAI AND PALESTINE

1914-1918

VOLUME VII

LIST OF MAPS

1. Turkey in Asia, showing Allied pressure early in 1917
2. Sinai Peninsula, showing main routes across the desert
3. Communications about July, 1916
4. Romani—Position at dusk, 3rd August, 1916
5. Romani—Position at 4 p.m., 4th August, 1916
6. Romani—Position at 5 a.m., 5th August, 1916
7. Romani-Katia—Position at 5 p.m., 5th August, 1916
8. British attack at Bir el Abd
9. Magdhaba—Position at dusk, 23rd December, 1916
10. Battle of Rafa
11. Rafa—Attack by N.Z.M.R. Brigade and I.C.C. Brigade
12. First Battle of Gaza—Position at dusk, 26th March, 1917
13. Second Battle of Gaza—Position at 2 p.m., 19th April, 1917
14. British and Turkish lines of communication, prior to Allenby's attack on Gaza, October, 1917
15. Beersheba—Charge by 4th A.L.H. Brigade—Position at dusk, 31st October, 1917
16. Gaza—Allenby's attack—Position about 6 p.m., 31st October, 1917
17. Khuweilfe, 2nd-3rd November, 1917
18. Khuweilfe—Position at dusk, 7th November, 1917
19. "Breaking through," 10 p.m., 7th November, 1917
20. Advance up the Maritime Plain—Position at 7 a.m., 14th November, 1917
21. Turkish attack on Nahr el Auja line, 25th November, 1917
22. Position prior to fall of Jerusalem, evening of 7th December, 1917
23. Jerusalem water supply after the British occupation
24. Advance on Jericho—Position at noon, 20th February, 1918
25. Capture of Jericho—Position on 21st February, 1918, after Turks had evacuated the town
26. The opposing front lines (between the two Aujas), February, 1918
27. Crossing of Jordan, 22nd-23rd March, 1918
28. Amman Raid—First attack by Anzacs and I.C.C. Brigade— Position at dusk, 27th March, 1918
29. Amman Raid—Night attack—Position at dawn, 30th March, 1918
30. Amman Raid—Position on 30th March, 1918, immediately prior to withdrawal

MAPS

31 The fighting at Ghoraniye and Musallabeh, 11th-12th April, 1918
32 Es Salt Raid—Position at midnight, 30th April, 1918
33 Turkish attack on 4th A.L.H. Brigade—Position about 8 a.m., 1st May, 1918
34 Turkish attack on 4th A.L.H. Brigade—Grant's position at dusk, 1st May, 1918
35 Es Salt Raid—Position just prior to withdrawal, 2nd May, 1918
36 The counter-attack at Abu Tellul, 14th July, 1918
37 British and Turkish lines of communication, Summer of 1918
38 Commencement of Battle of Sharon, 19th September, 1918
39 Battles of Sharon and Samaria. Advance of British cavalry—Position at 6 p.m., 20th September, 1918
40 Operations of 5th A.L.H. Brigade, 19th-20th September, 1918
41 Operations of 5th A.L.H. Brigade, 21st September, 1918
42 Chaytor's advance on Es Salt and Amman, 22nd September, 1918
43 Capture of Amman by Chaytor's Force, 25th September, 1918
44 The action at Semakh, 25th September, 1918
45 The action at Tiberias, 25th September, 1918
46 Crossing of the Jordan at Jisr Benat Yakub, 28th September, 1918
47 Advance on Damascus, 28th September, 1918
48 Damascus and environs, showing route taken by 3rd Australian Light Horse Brigade through the city
49 British and Turkish lines of communication after the capture of Aleppo

MAP

TURKEY IN ASIA, SHOWING

No. 1.

ALLIED PRESSURE EARLY IN 1917.

Map No. 2

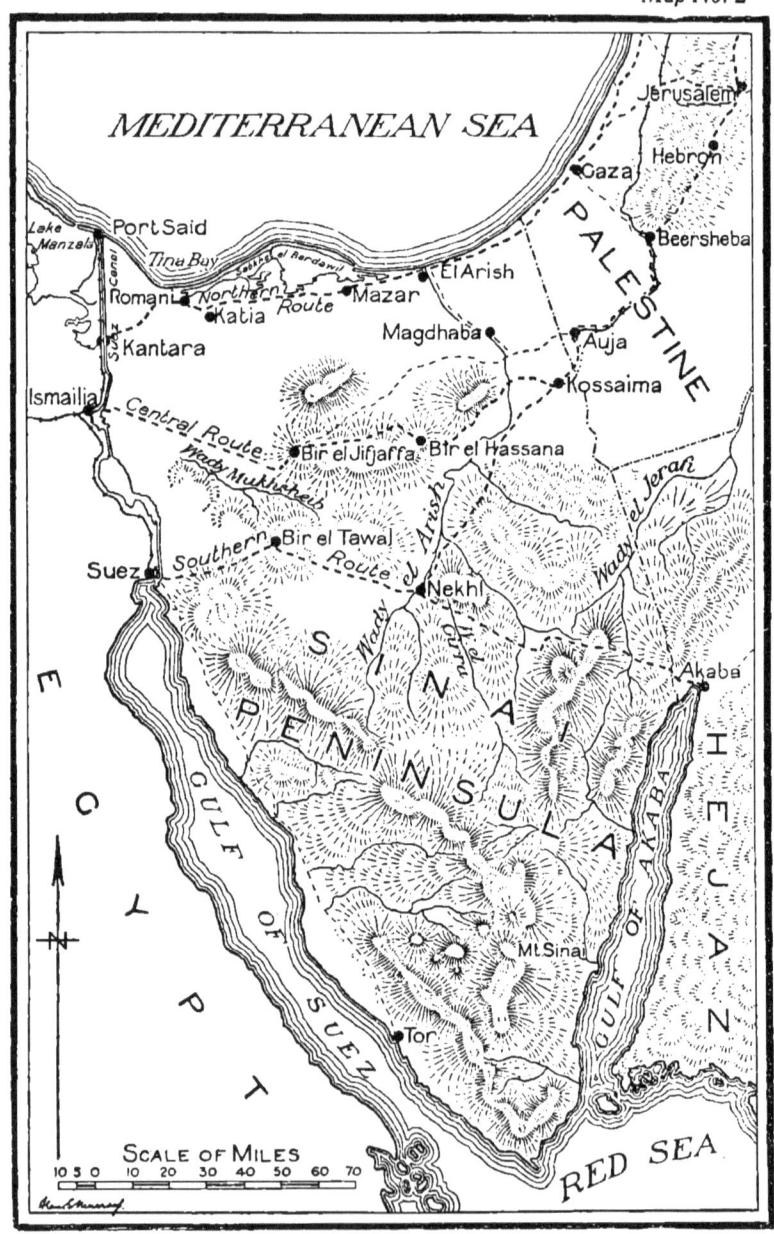

SINAI PENINSULA, SHOWING MAIN ROUTES ACROSS THE DESERT.

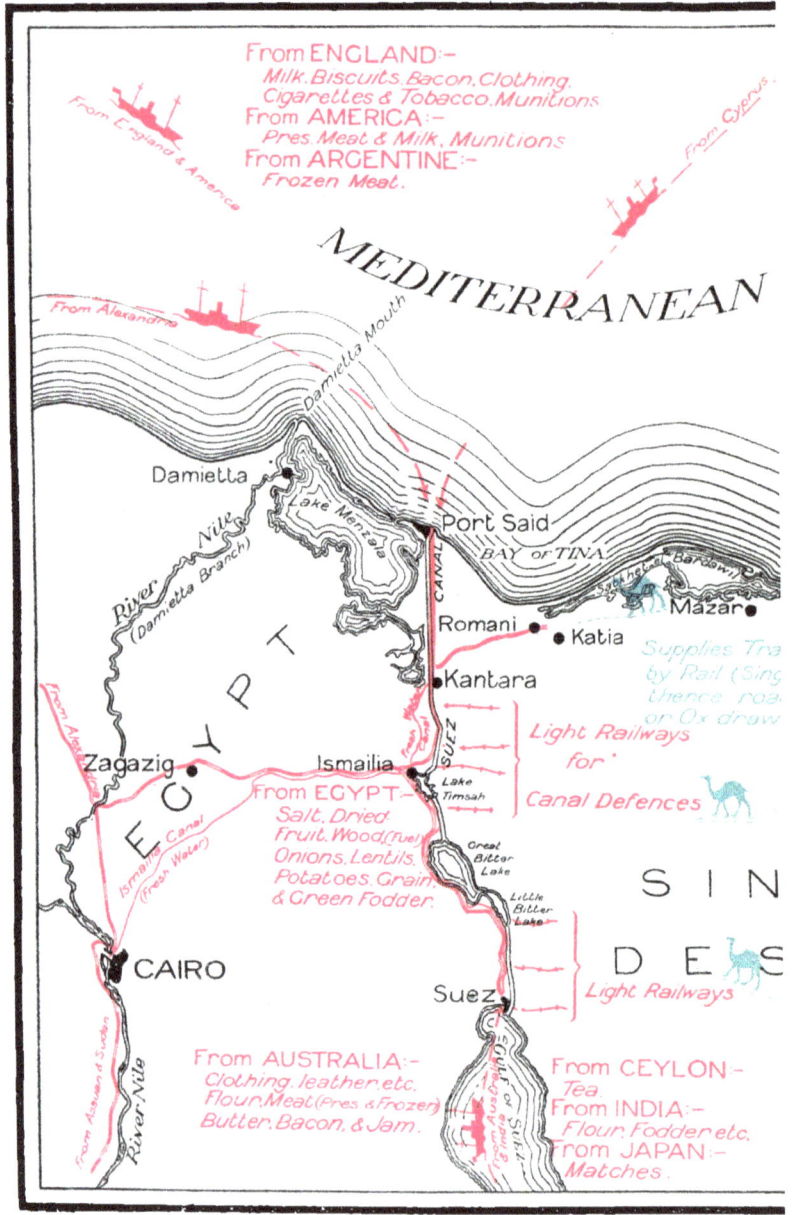

No. 3.

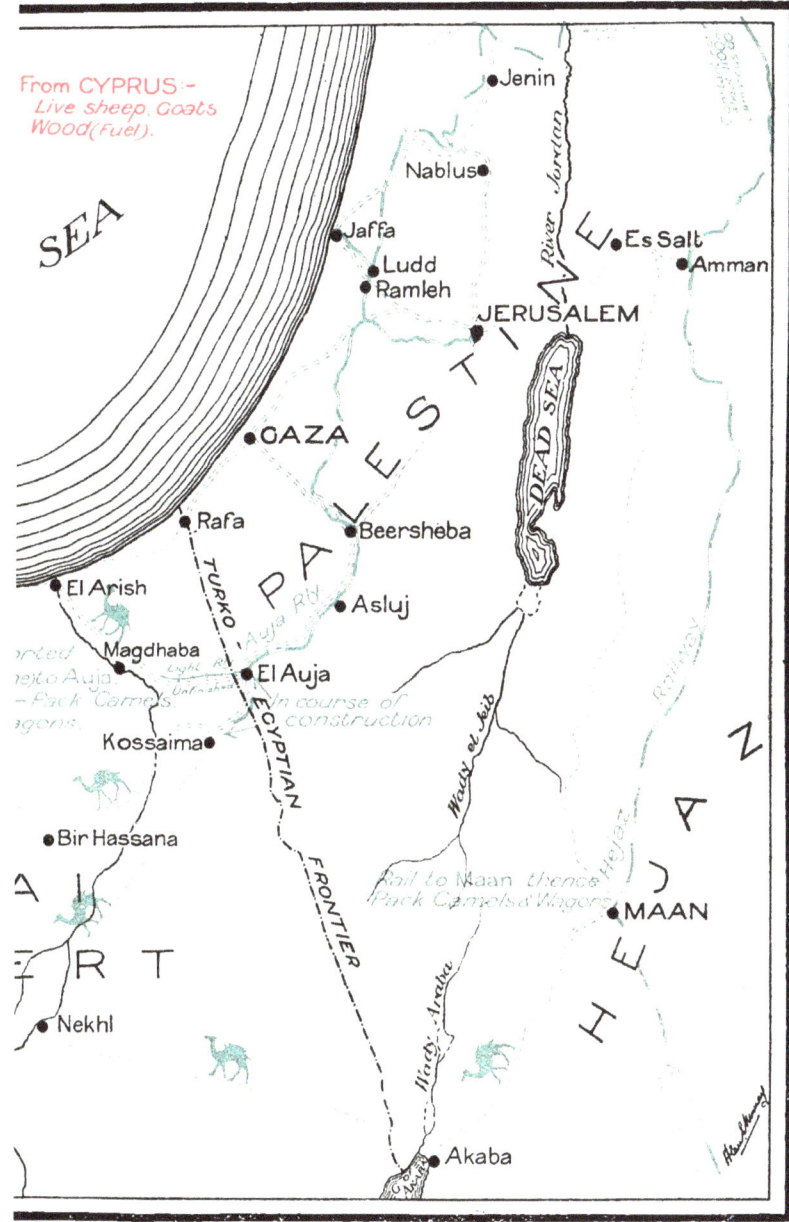

ABOUT JULY, 1916.

Map No. 4

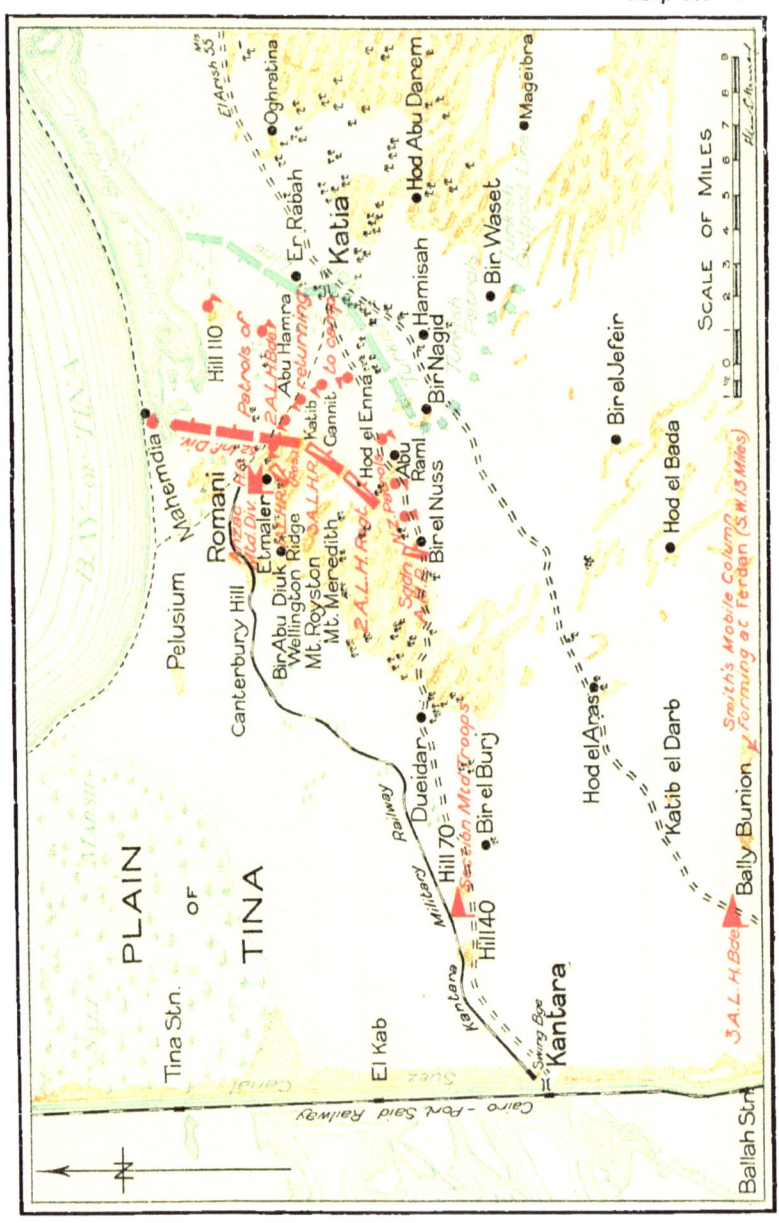

Romani—Position at dusk, 3rd August, 1916.

Map No. 5

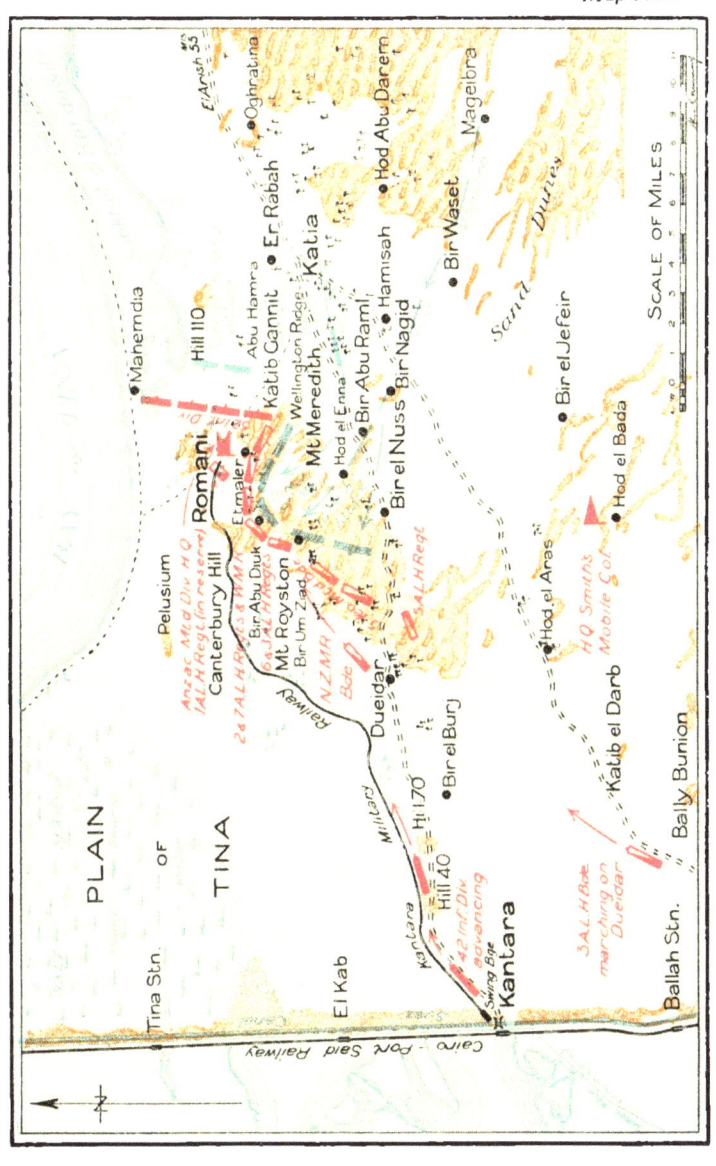

Romani—Position at 4 p.m., 4th August, 1916. (Certain advanced units of the 42nd Division were also near Pelusium and Romani.)

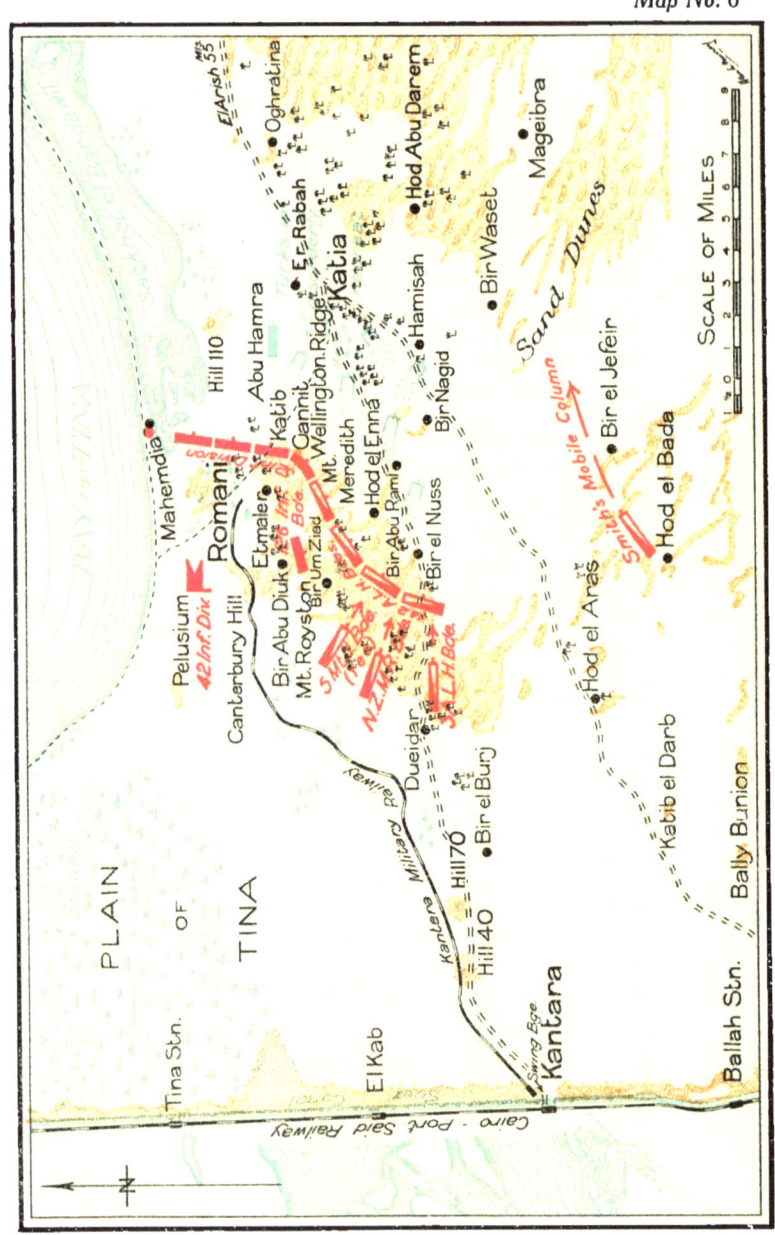

Romani—Position at 5 a.m., 5th August, 1916.

Map No. 7

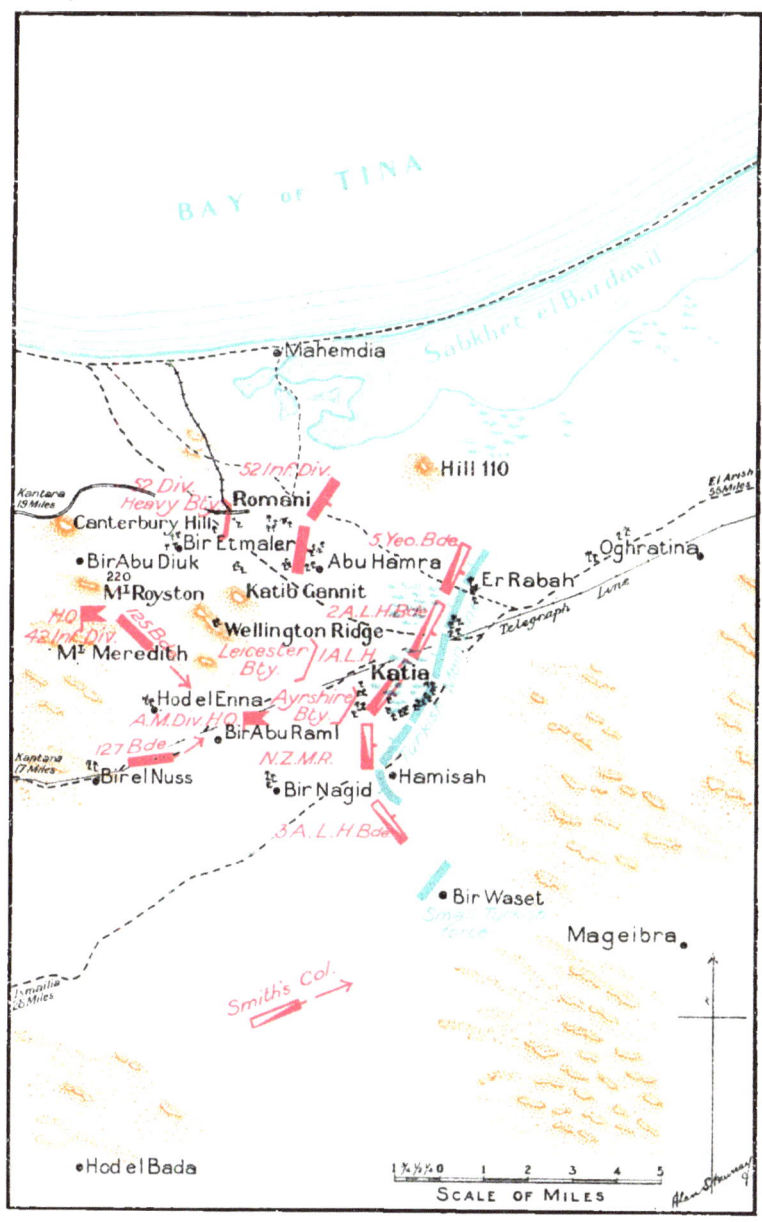

ROMANI-KATIA—POSITION AT 5 P.M., 5TH AUGUST, 1916.

Map No. 8

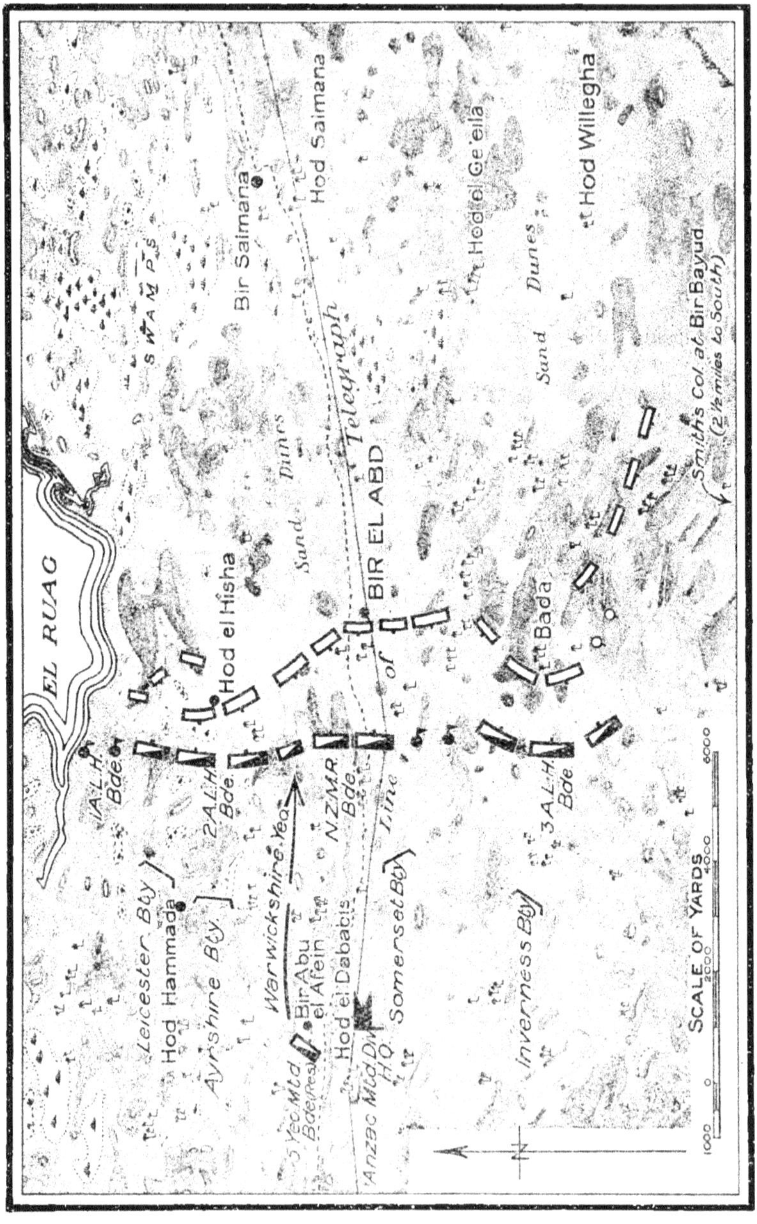

British attack at Bir el Abd.

Map No. 9

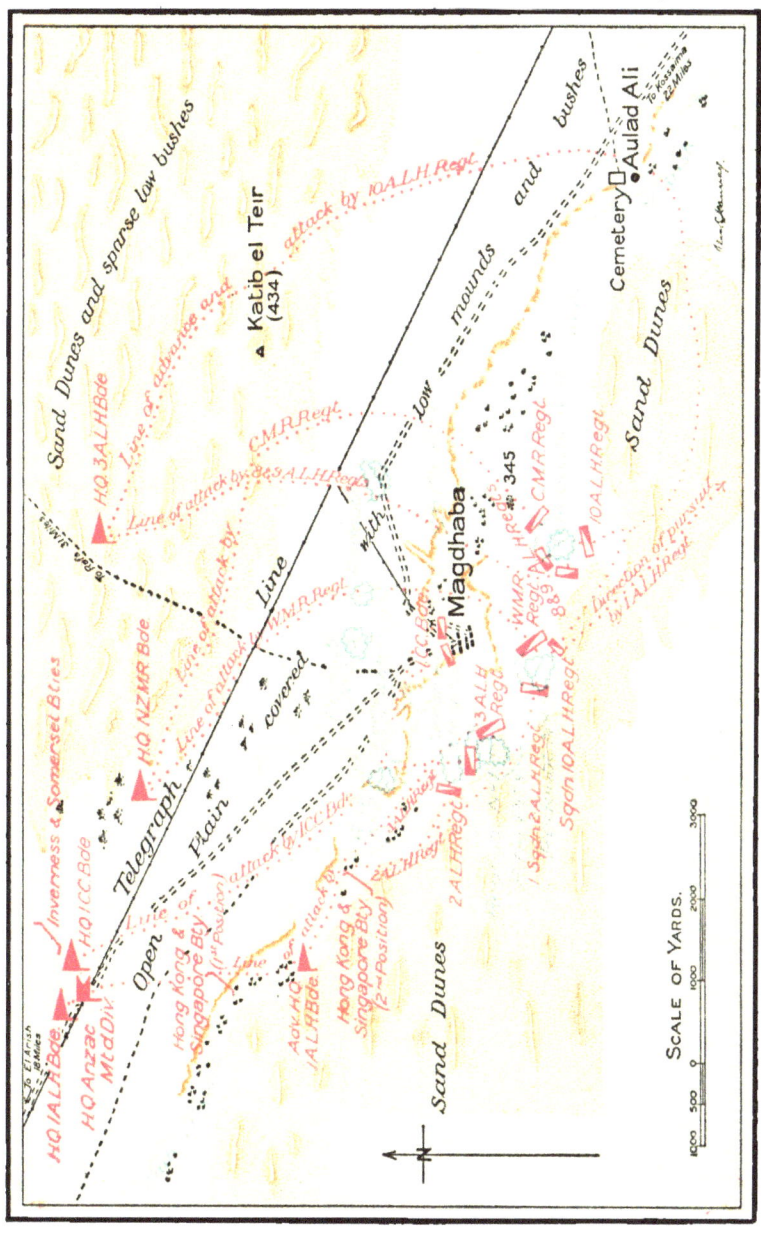

Magdhaba—Position at dusk on 23rd December, 1916.

Map No. 10

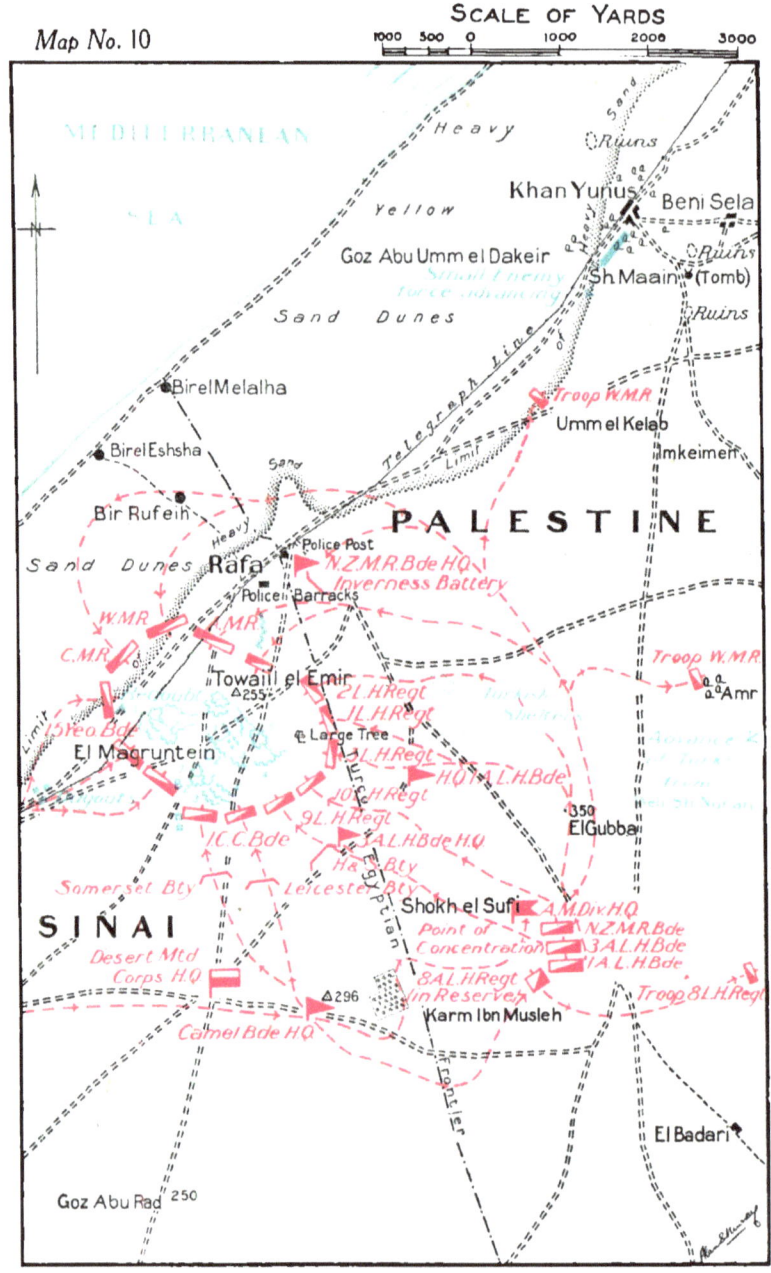

BATTLE OF RAFA.

Map No. 11

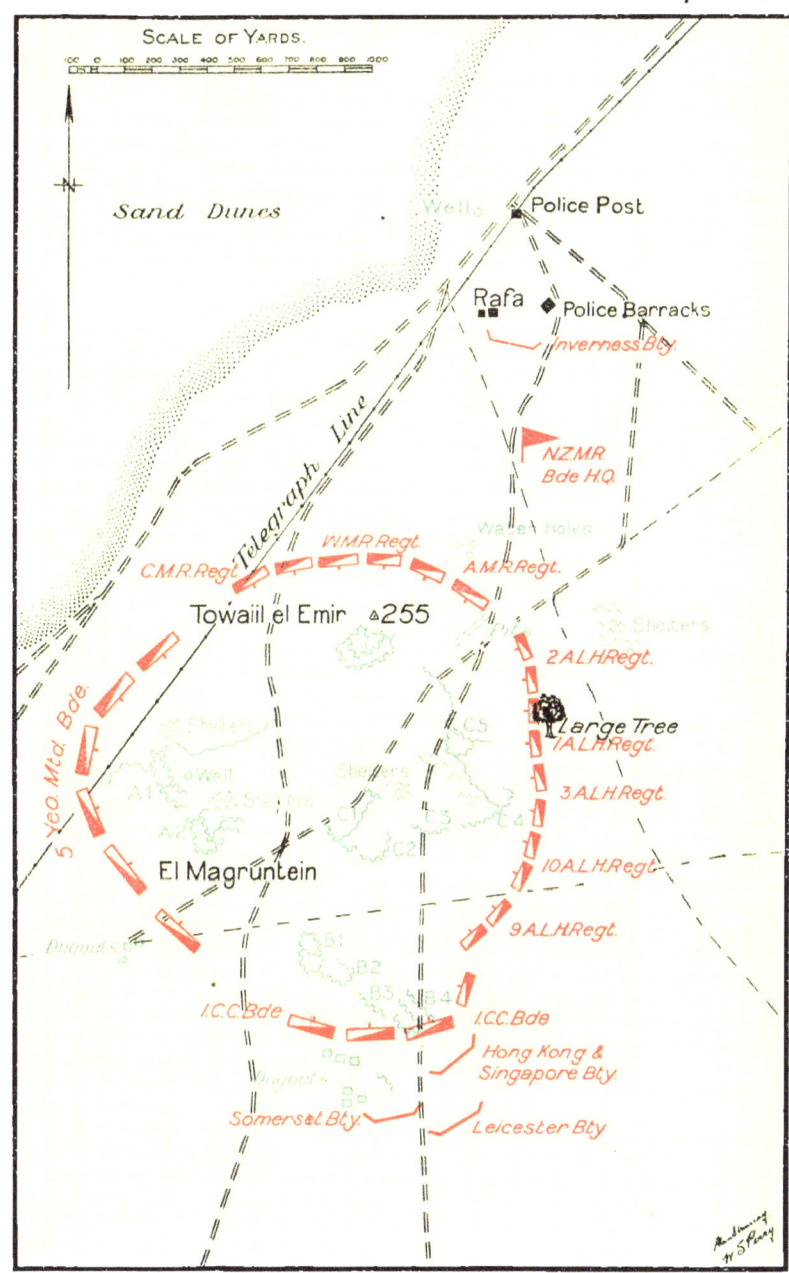

Rafa—Attack by N.Z.M.R. Brigade and I.C.C. Brigade.

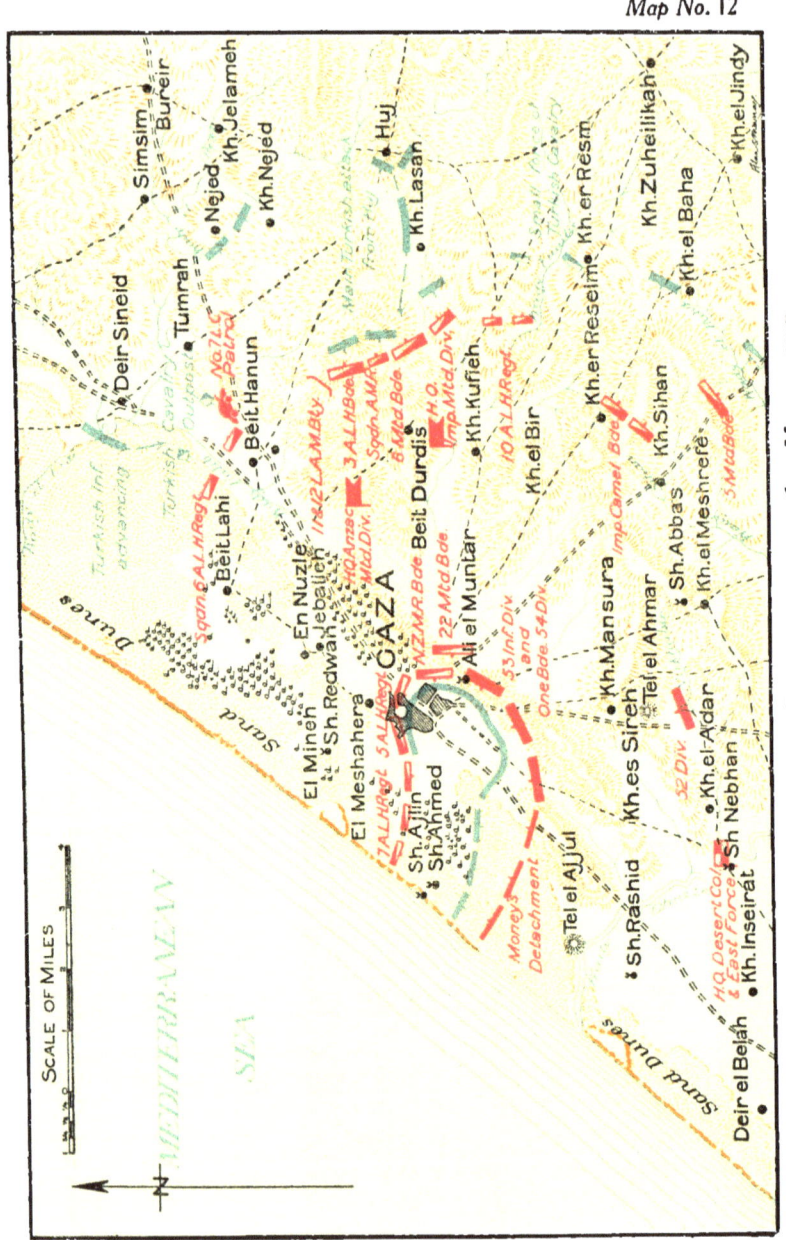

Map No. 12

First battle of Gaza—Position at dusk, 26th March, 1917.

MAP

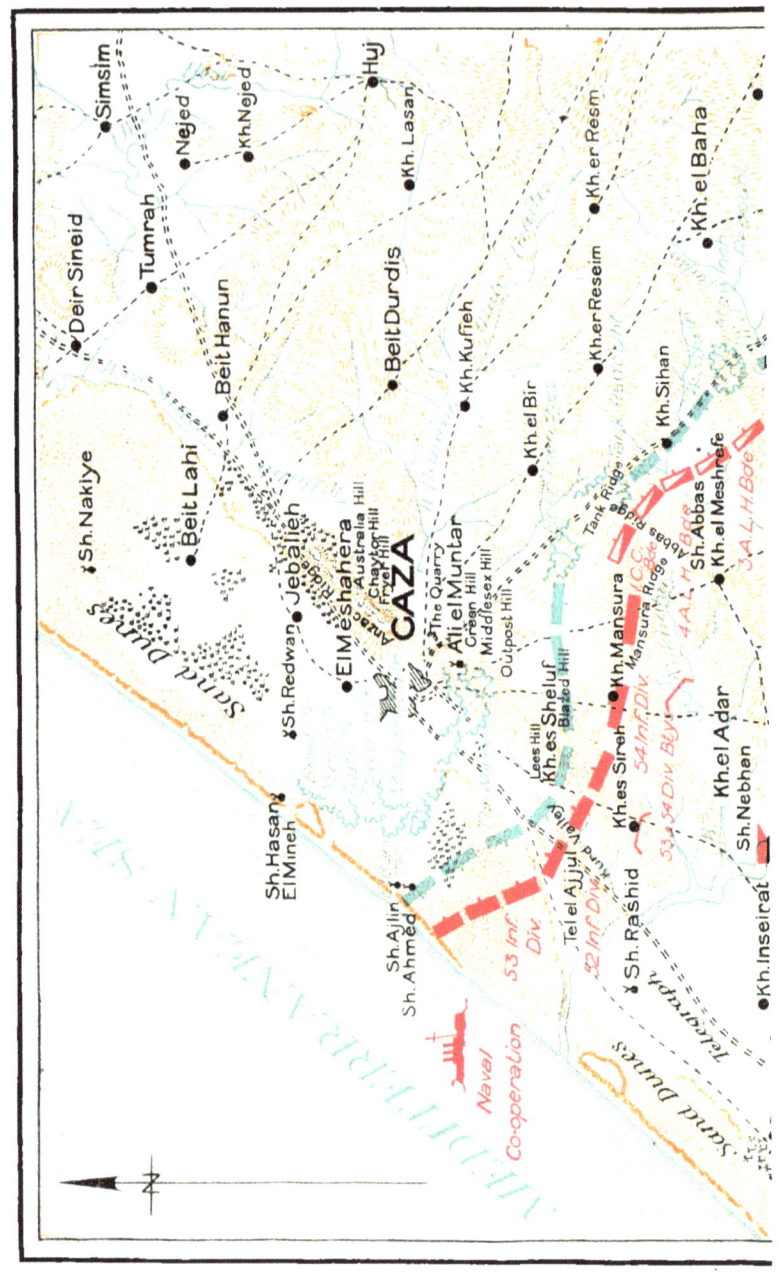

No. 13.

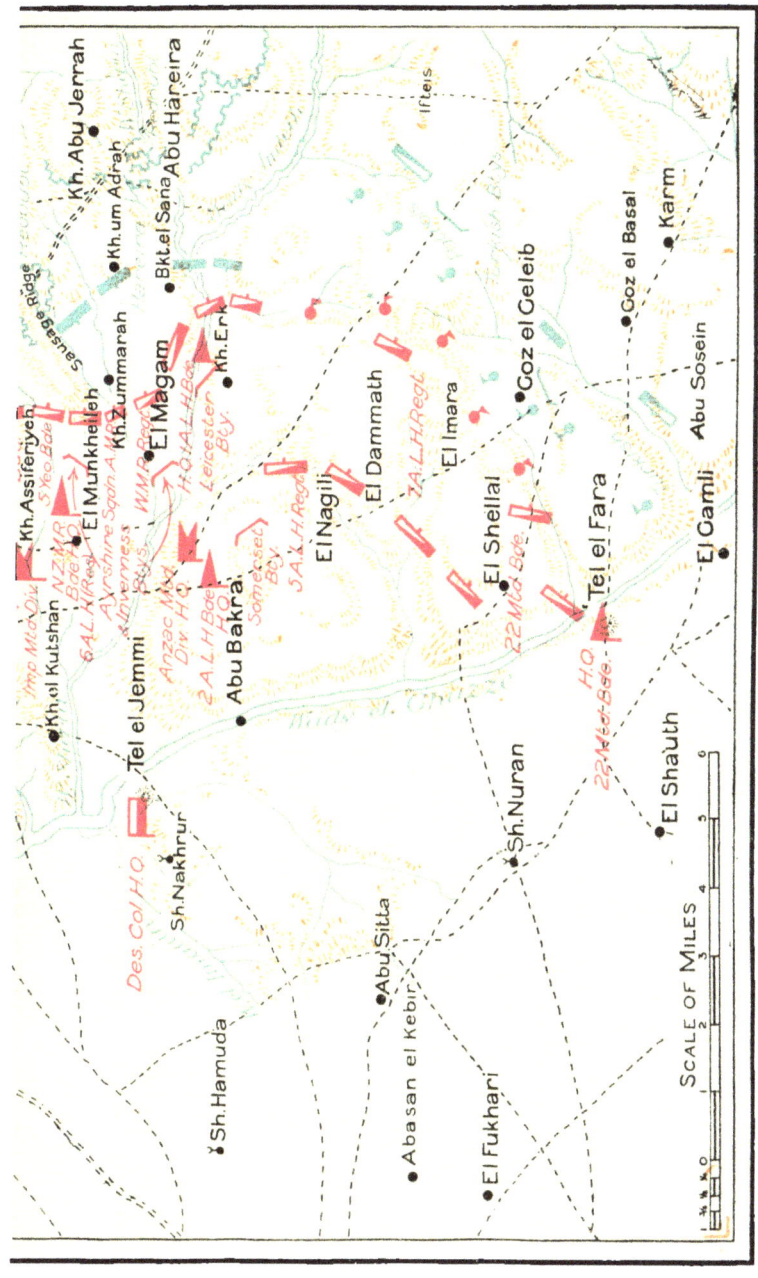

MAP

No. 14.

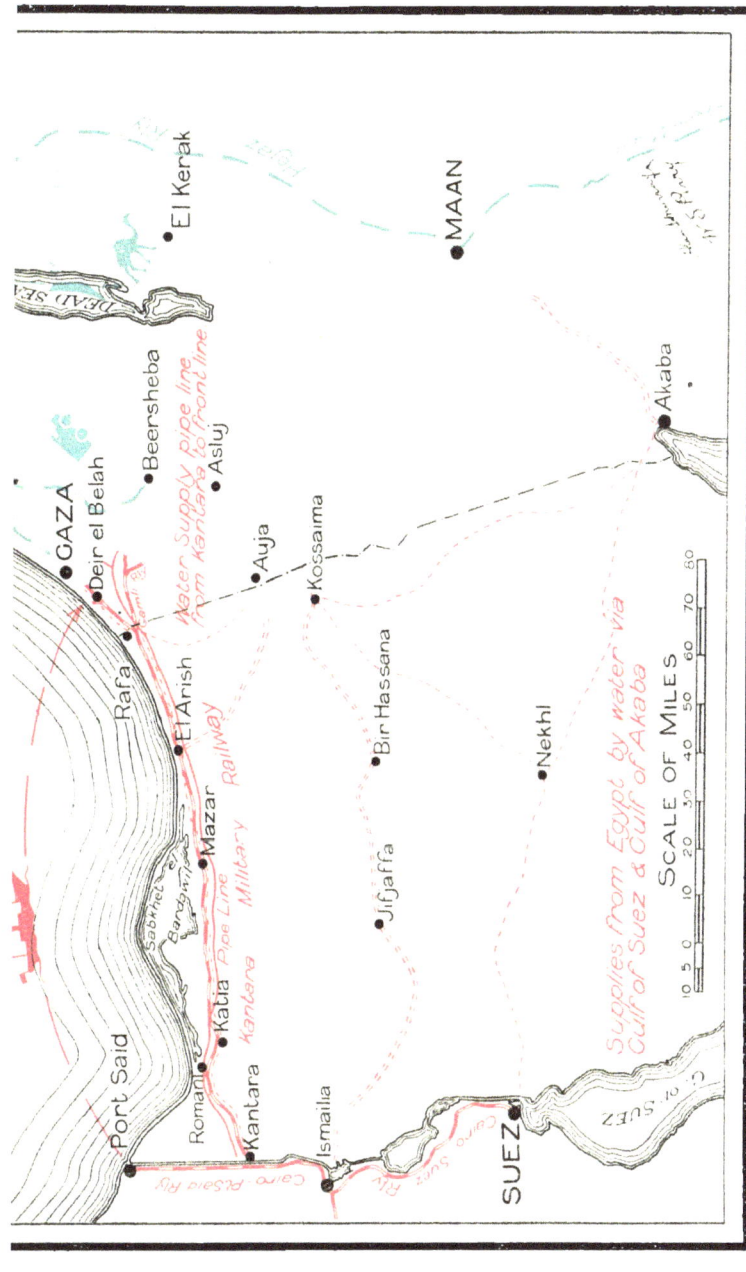

British and Turkish lines of communication prior to Allenby's attack on Gaza, October, 1917.

Map No. 15

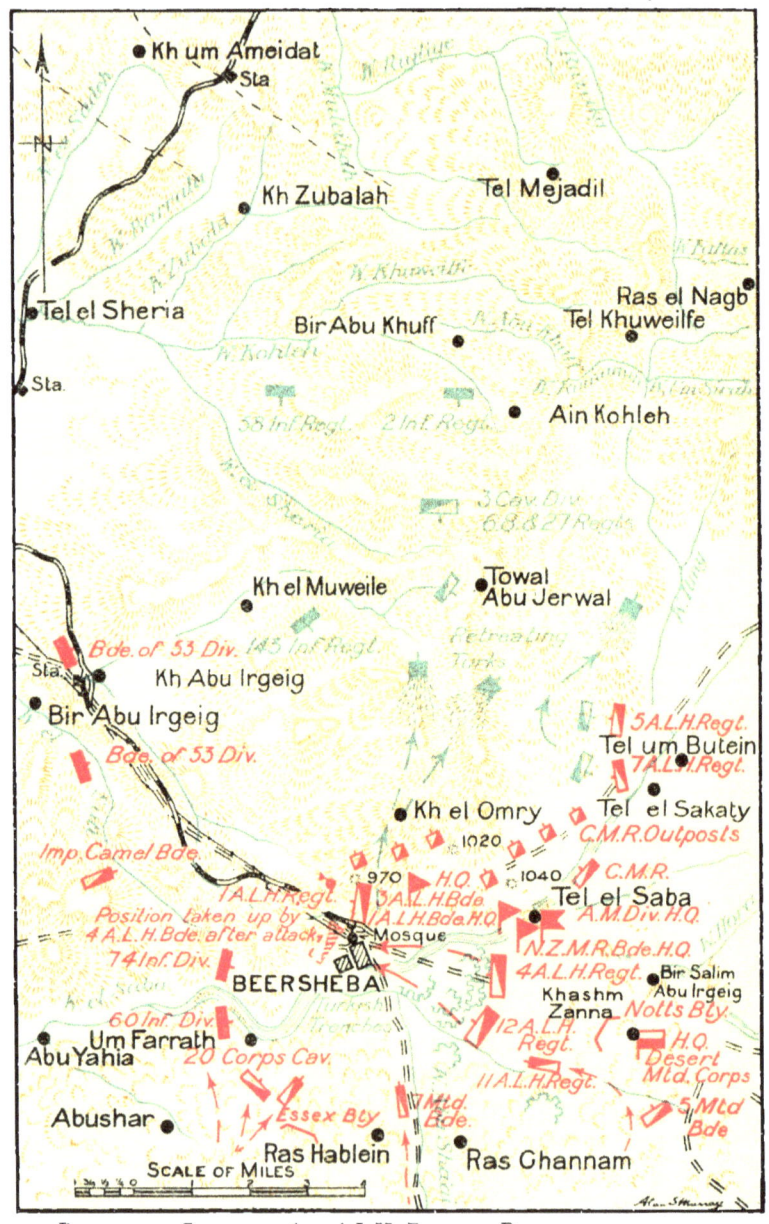

BEERSHEBA—CHARGE BY 4TH A.L.H. BRIGADE—POSITION AT DUSK, 31ST OCTOBER, 1917.

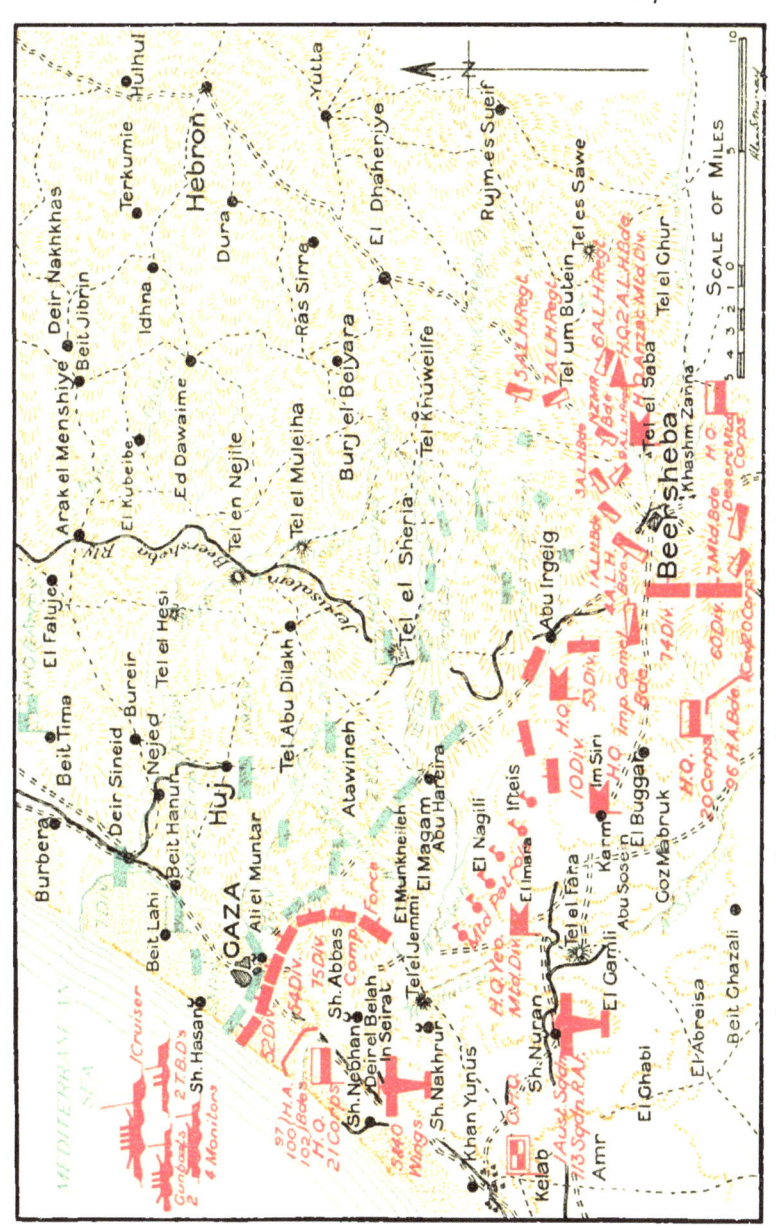

Gaza—Allenby's attack—Position at about 6 p.m., 31st October, 1917.

Map No. 17

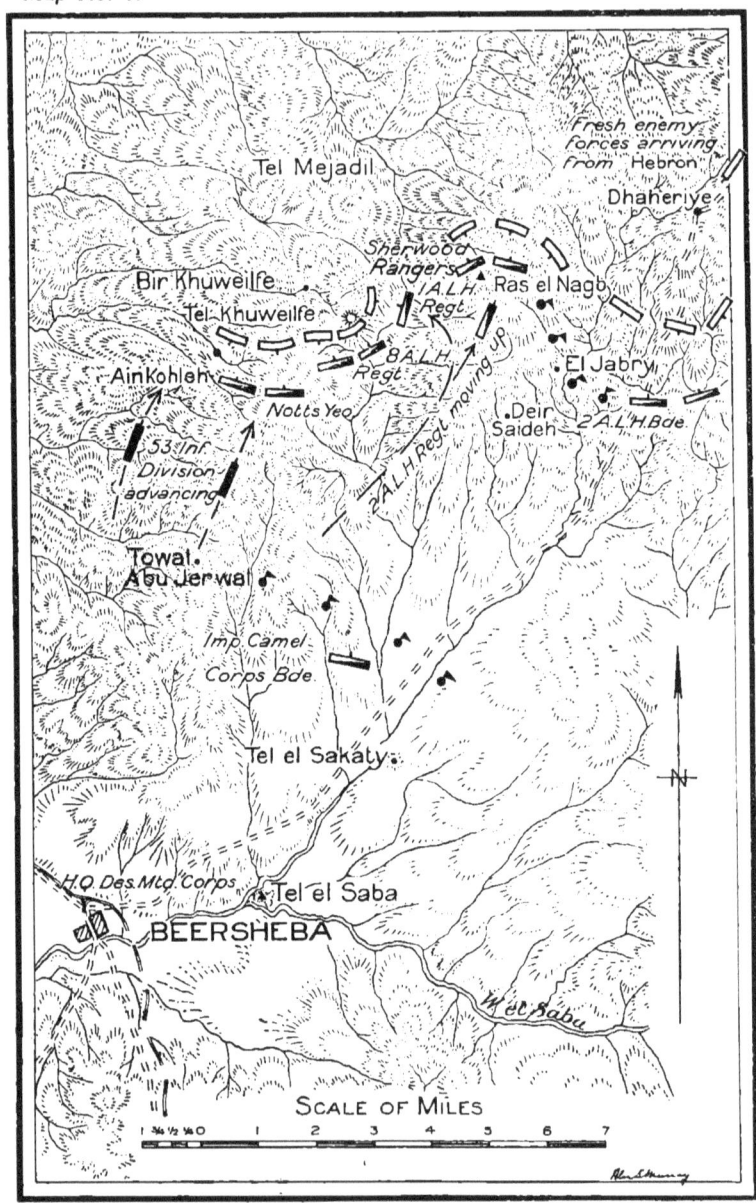

KHUWEILFE, 2ND-3RD NOVEMBER, 1917.

Map No. 18

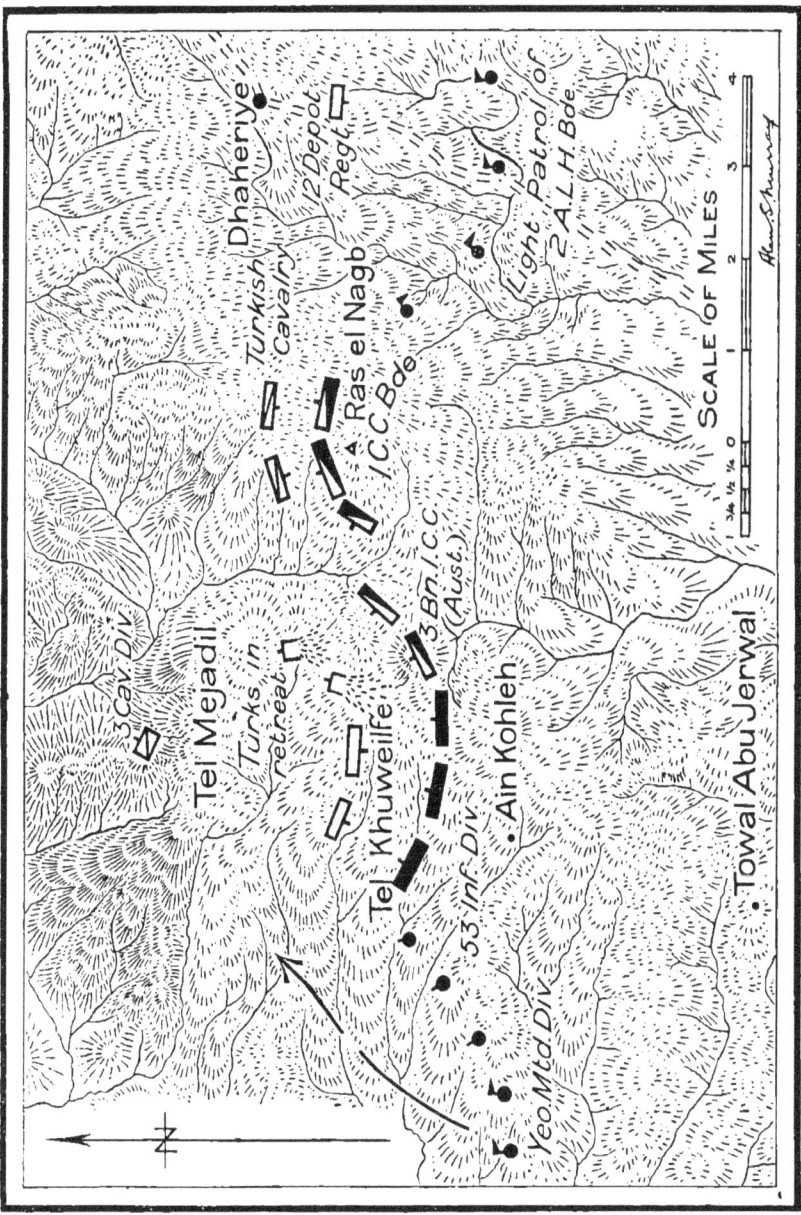

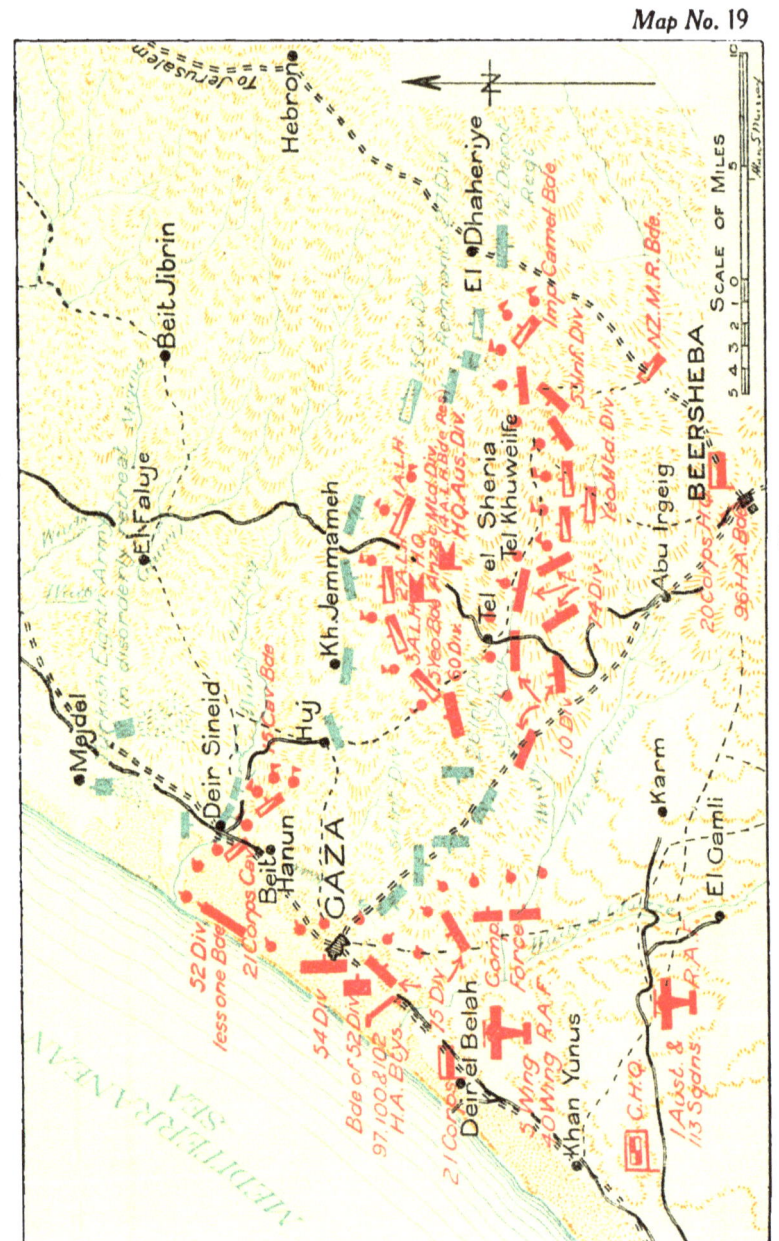

"Breaking through," 10 p.m., 7th November, 1917.

Map No. 20

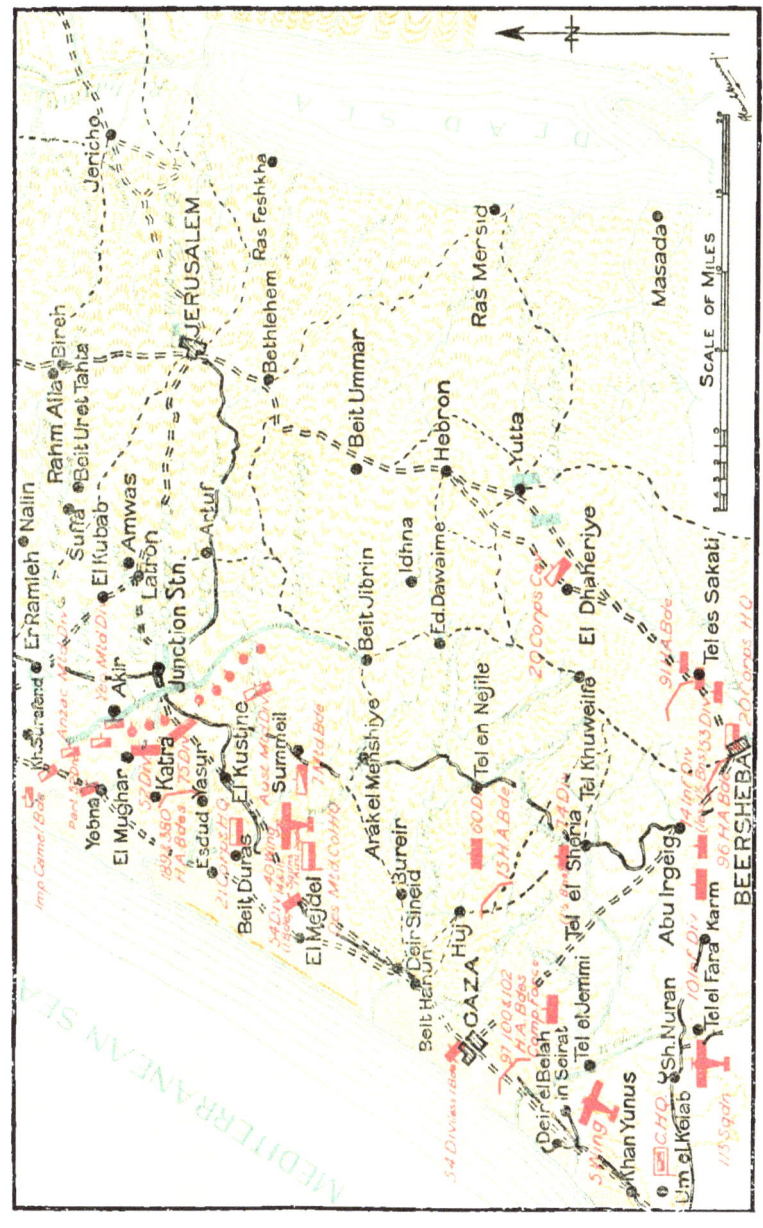

Advance up the Maritime Plain—Position at 7 a.m., 14th November, 1917.

Map No. 21

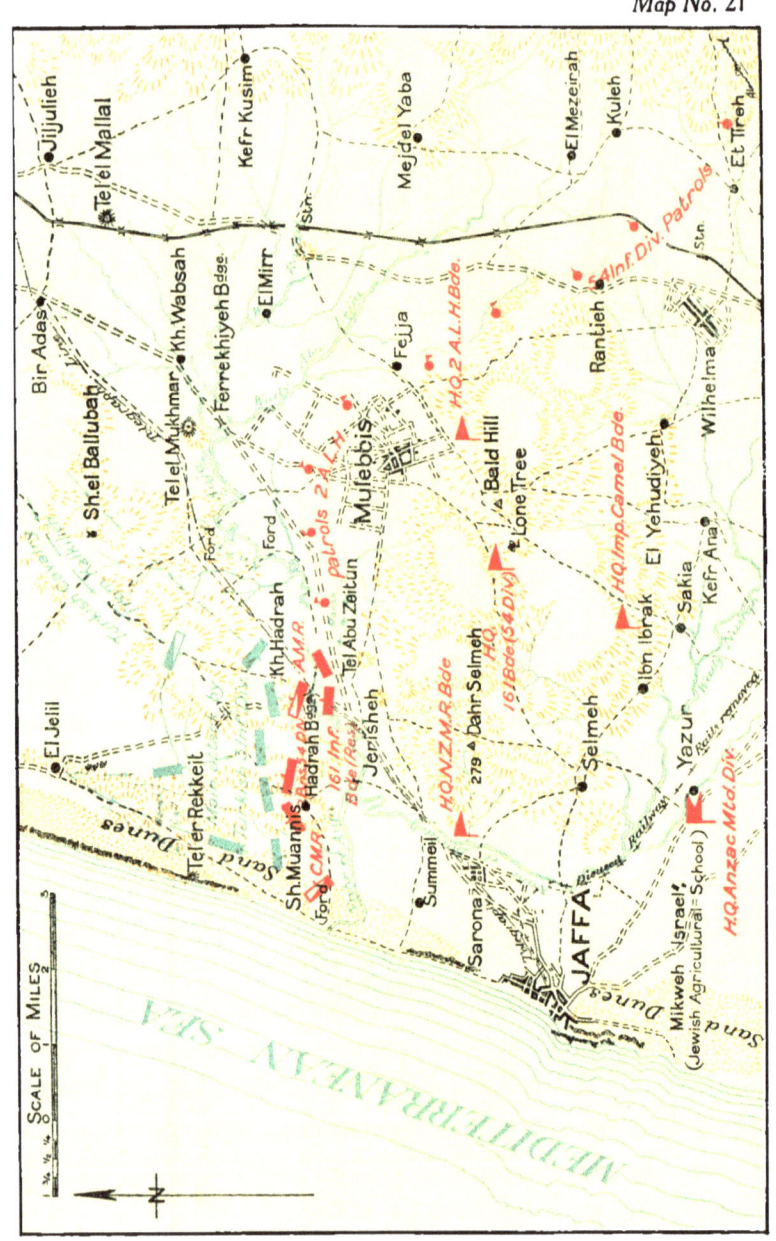

MAP

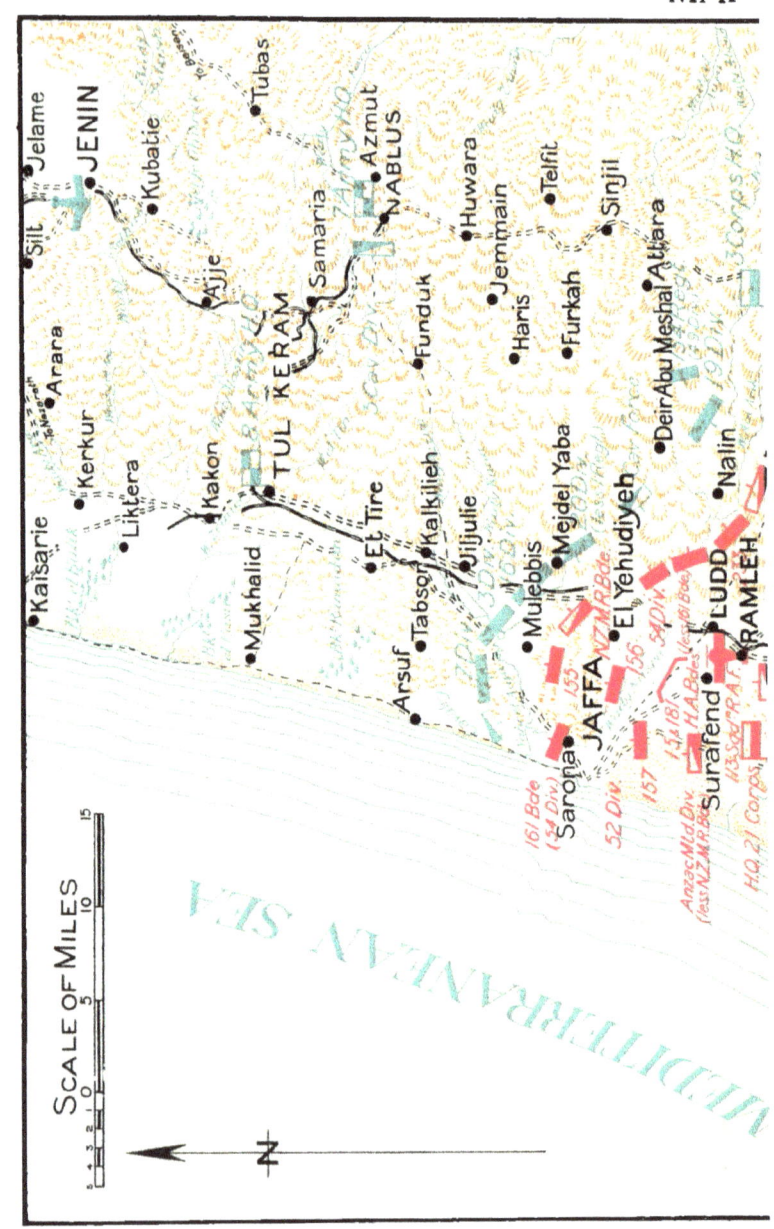

No. 22.

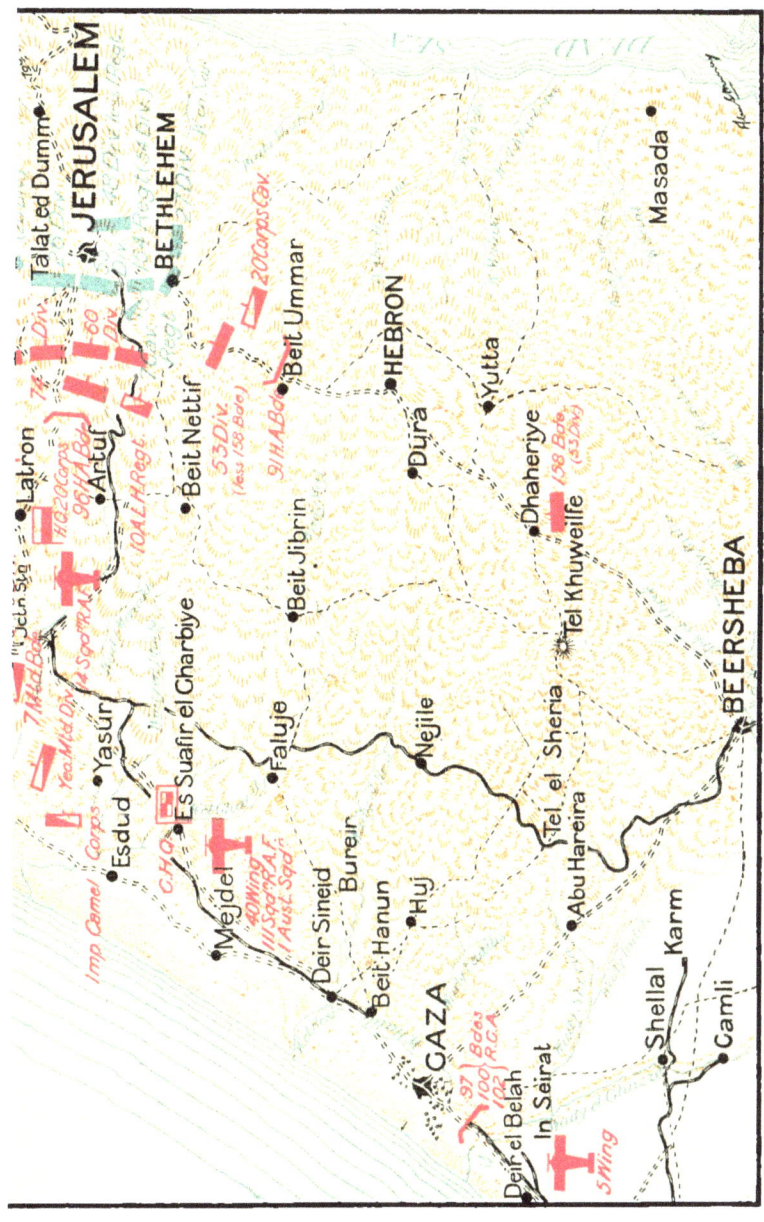

Position prior to fall of Jerusalem. Evening of 7th December, 1917.

Map No. 23

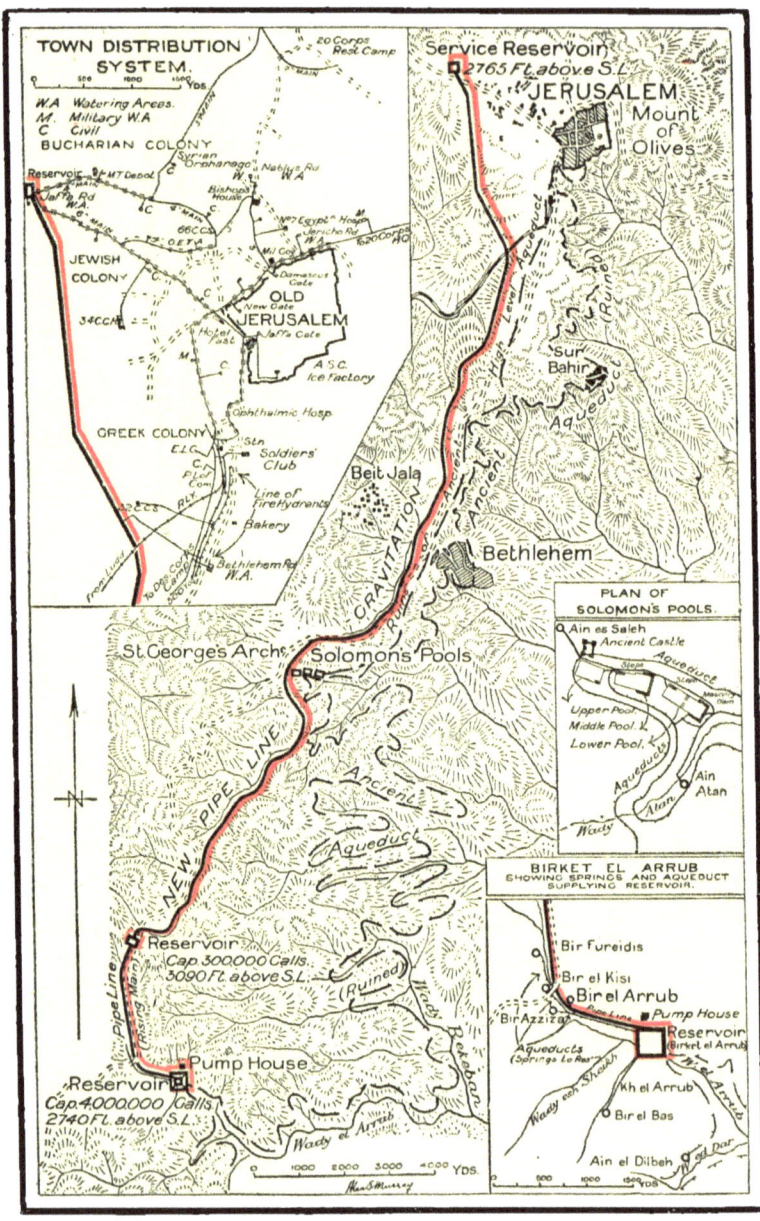

Jerusalem water supply after the British occupation. (See p. 648.)

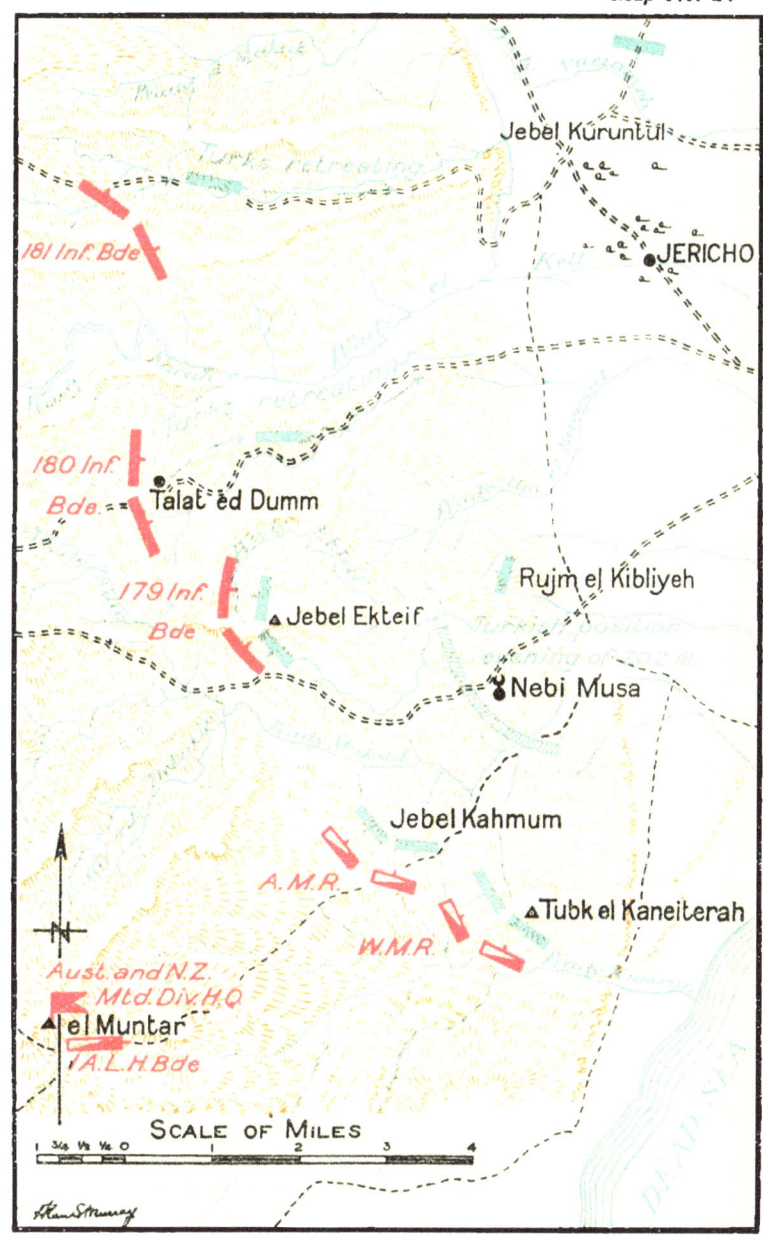

Advance on Jericho—Position at noon, 20th February, 1918.

Map No. 25

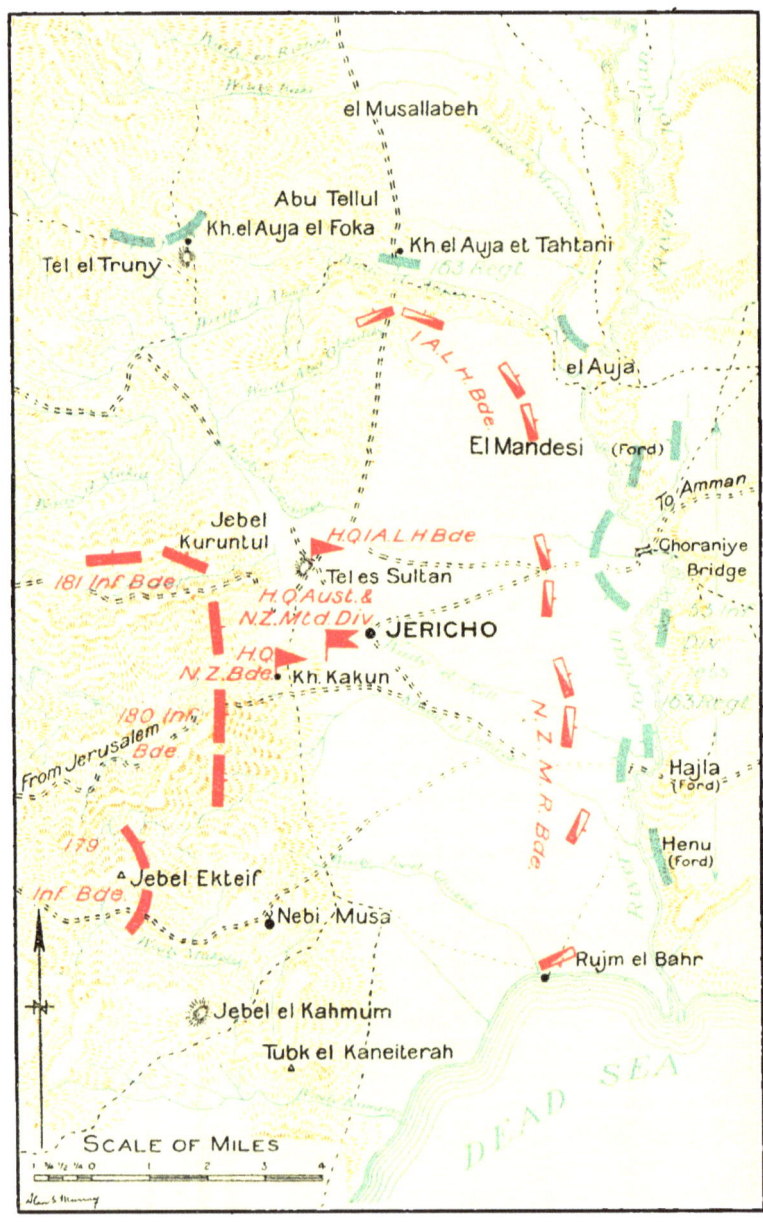

CAPTURE OF JERICHO—POSITION ON 21ST FEBRUARY, 1918, AFTER TURKS HAD EVACUATED THE TOWN.

Map No. 26

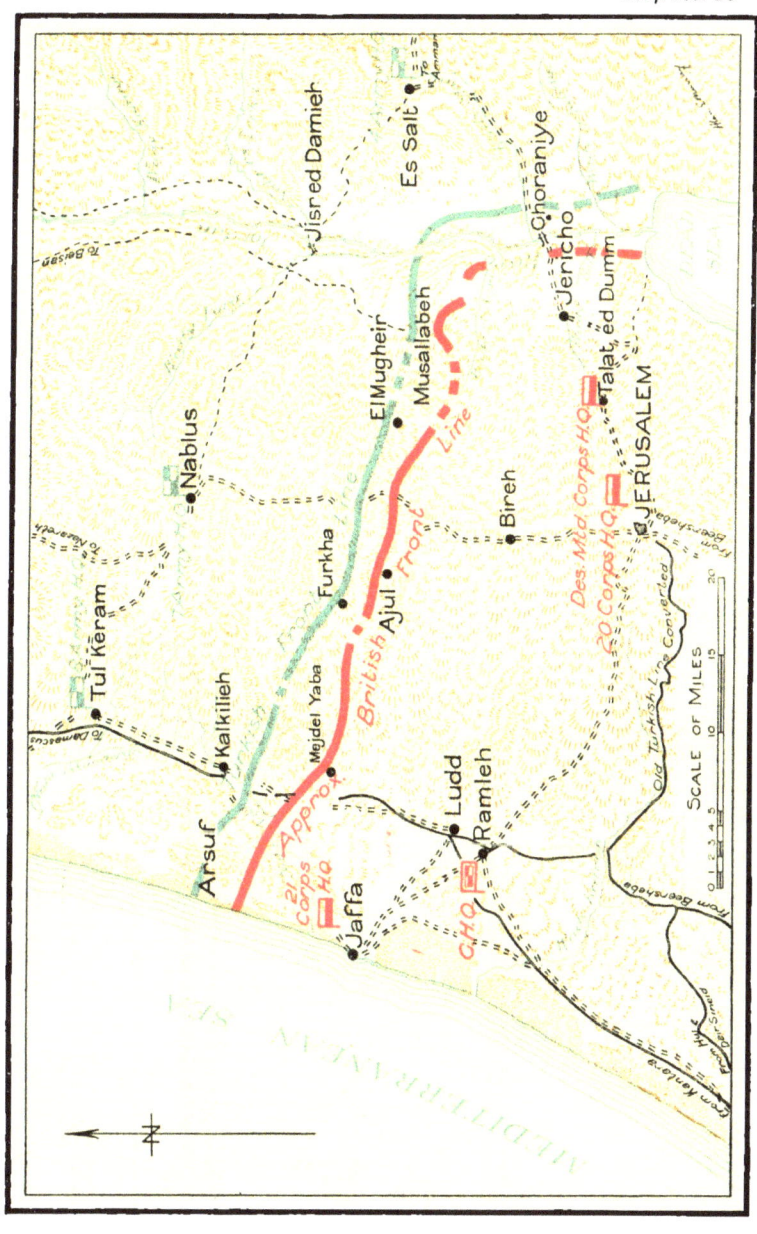

The opposing front lines (between the two Aujas), February, 1918.

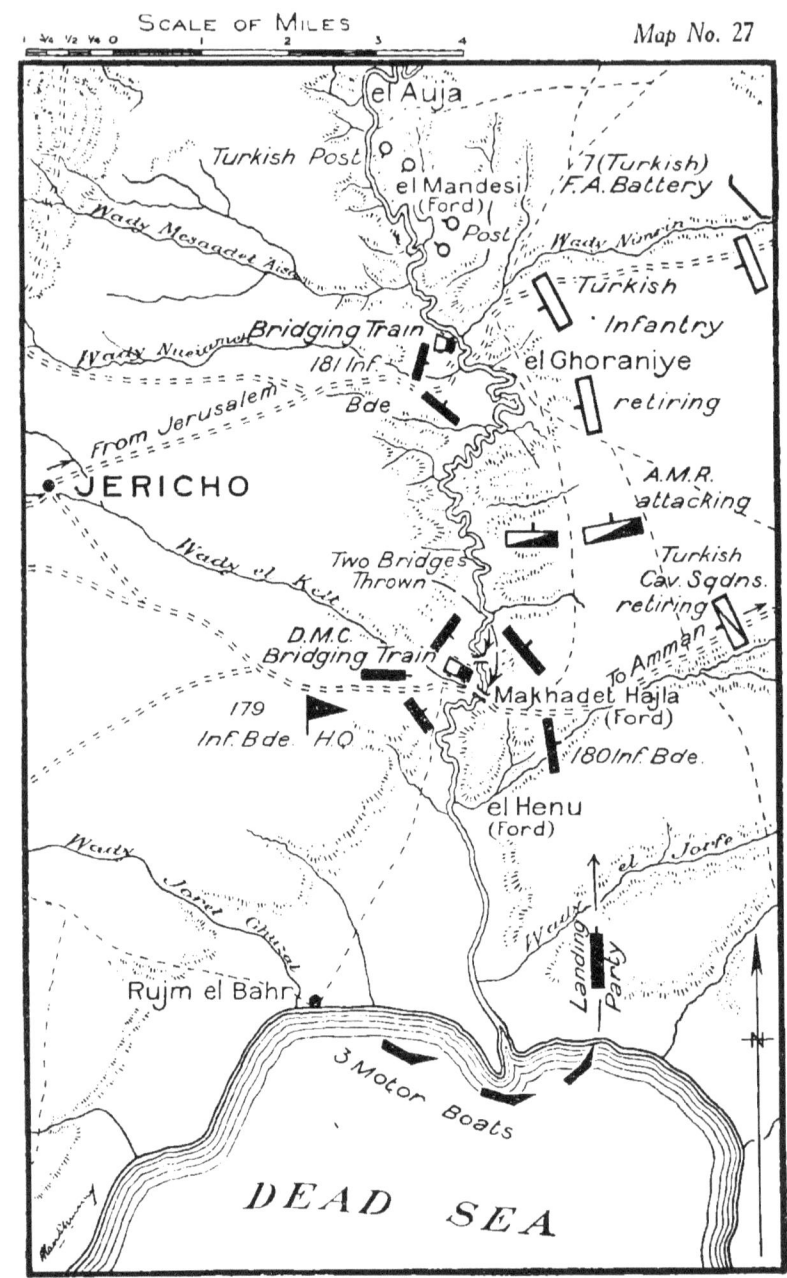

Crossing of Jordan, 22nd-23rd March, 1918.

Map No. 28

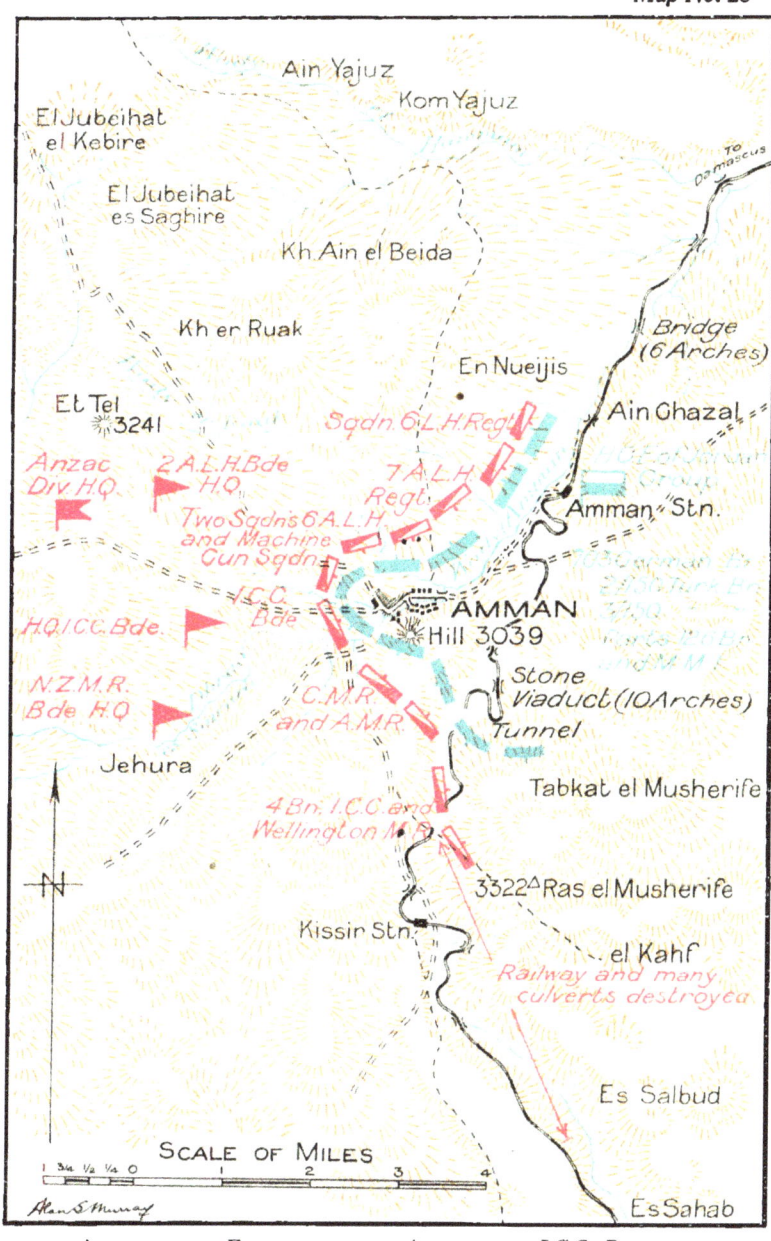

AMMAN RAID—FIRST ATTACK BY ANZACS AND I.C.C. BRIGADE—
POSITION AT DUSK, 27TH MARCH, 1918.

Map No. 29

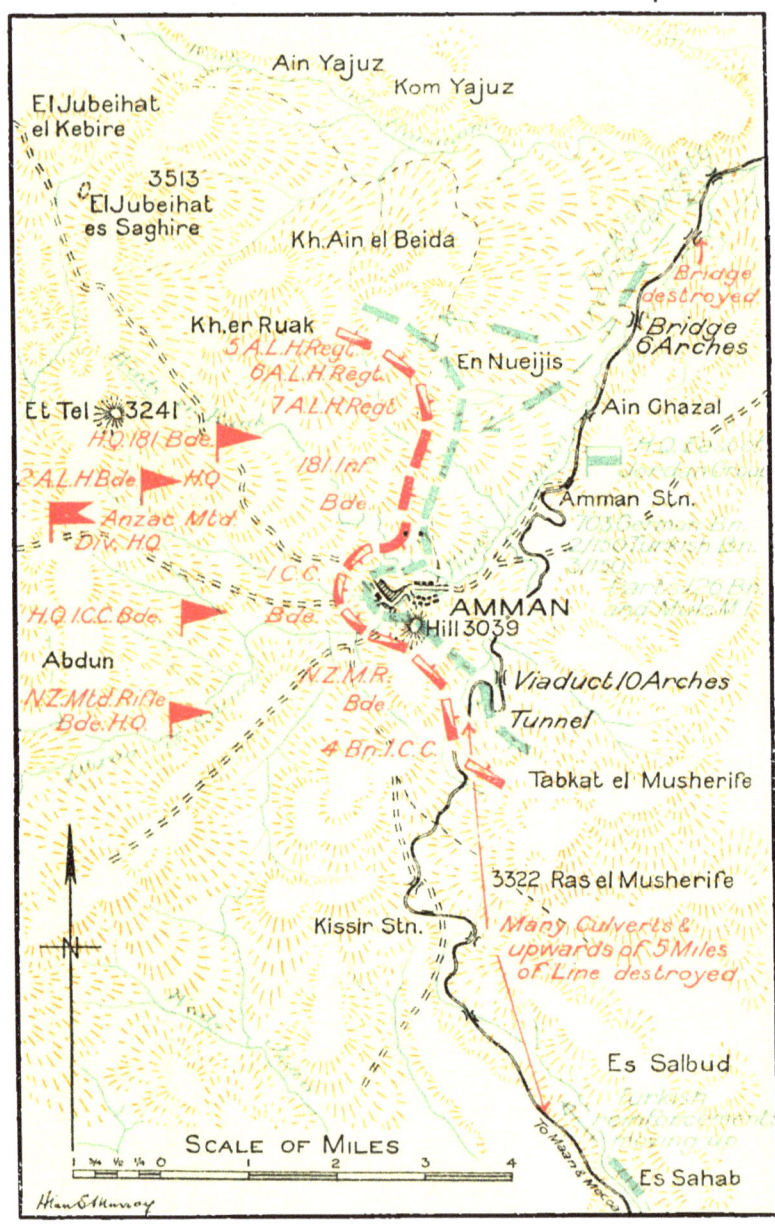

Amman raid—Night attack—Position at dawn, 30th March, 1918.

AMMAN RAID—POSITION ON 30TH MARCH, 1918, IMMEDIATELY PRIOR TO WITHDRAWAL.

Map No. 31

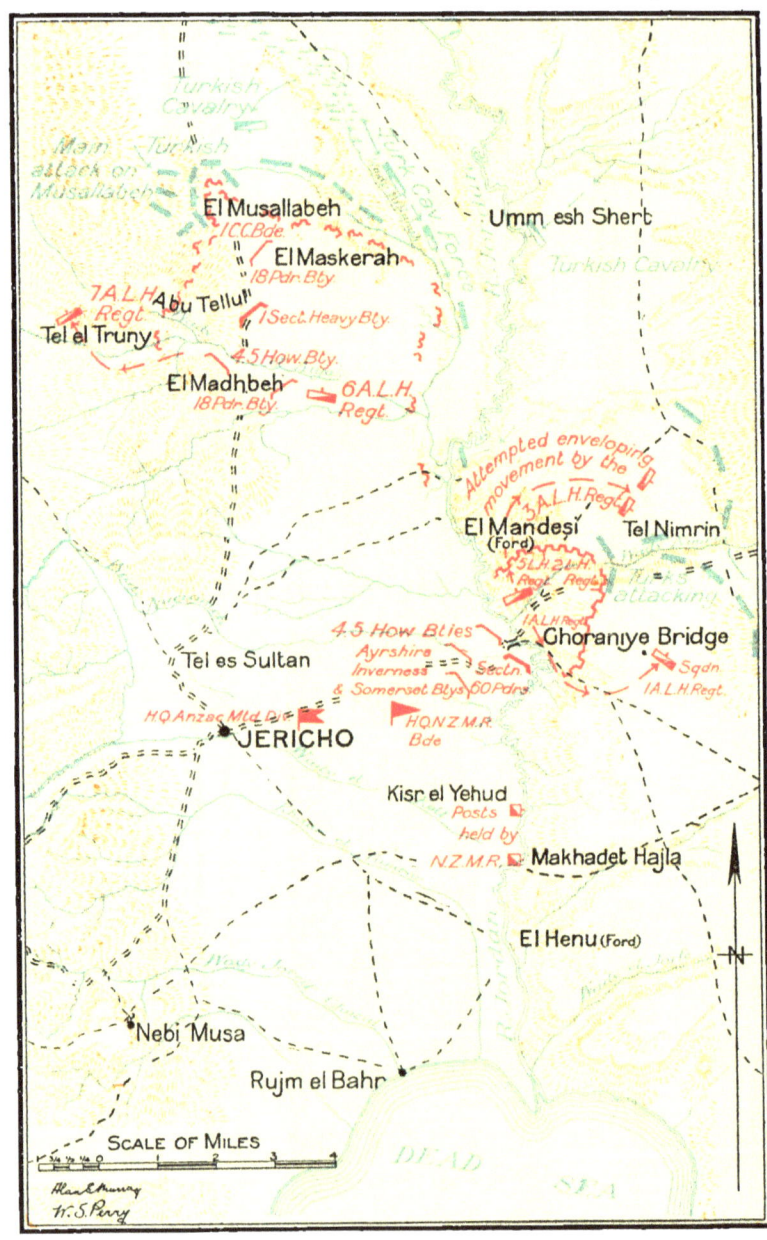

THE FIGHTING AT GHORANIYE AND MUSALLABEH, 11TH–12TH APRIL, 1918.

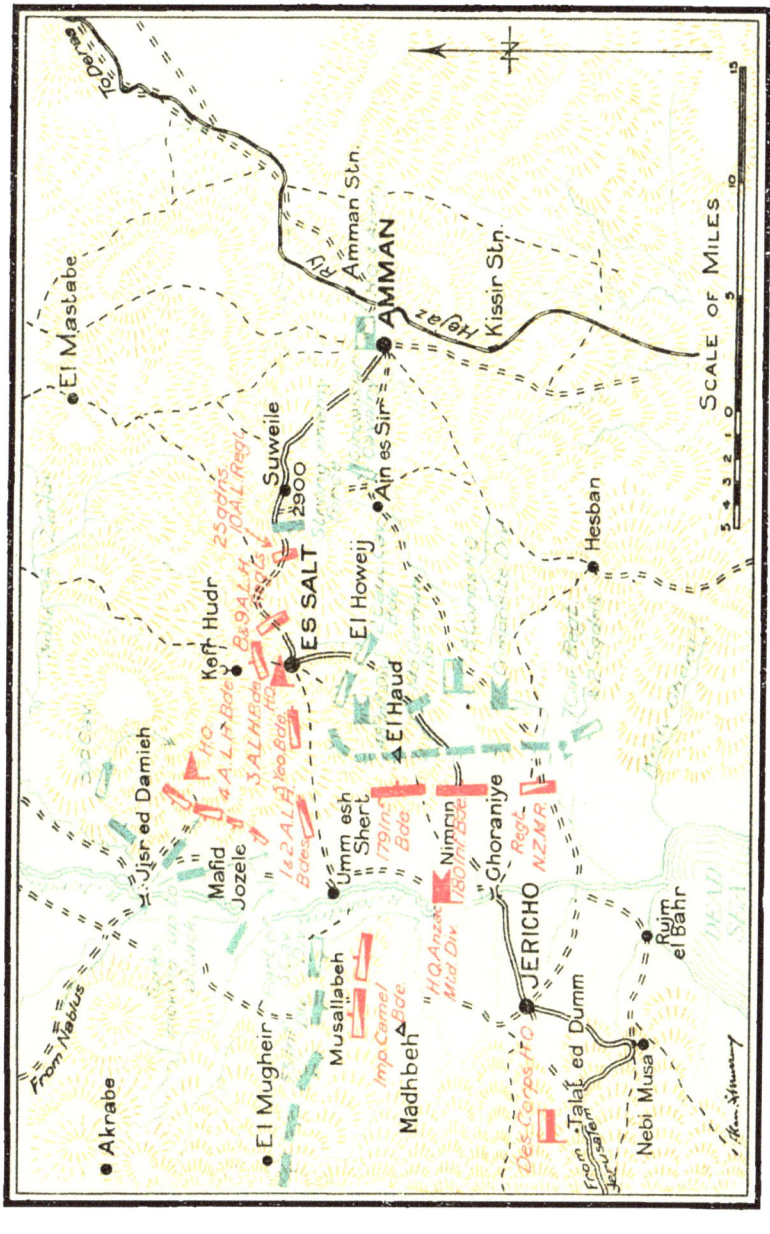

Map No. 32

Es Salt Raid—Position at Midnight, 30th April, 1918.

Map No. 33

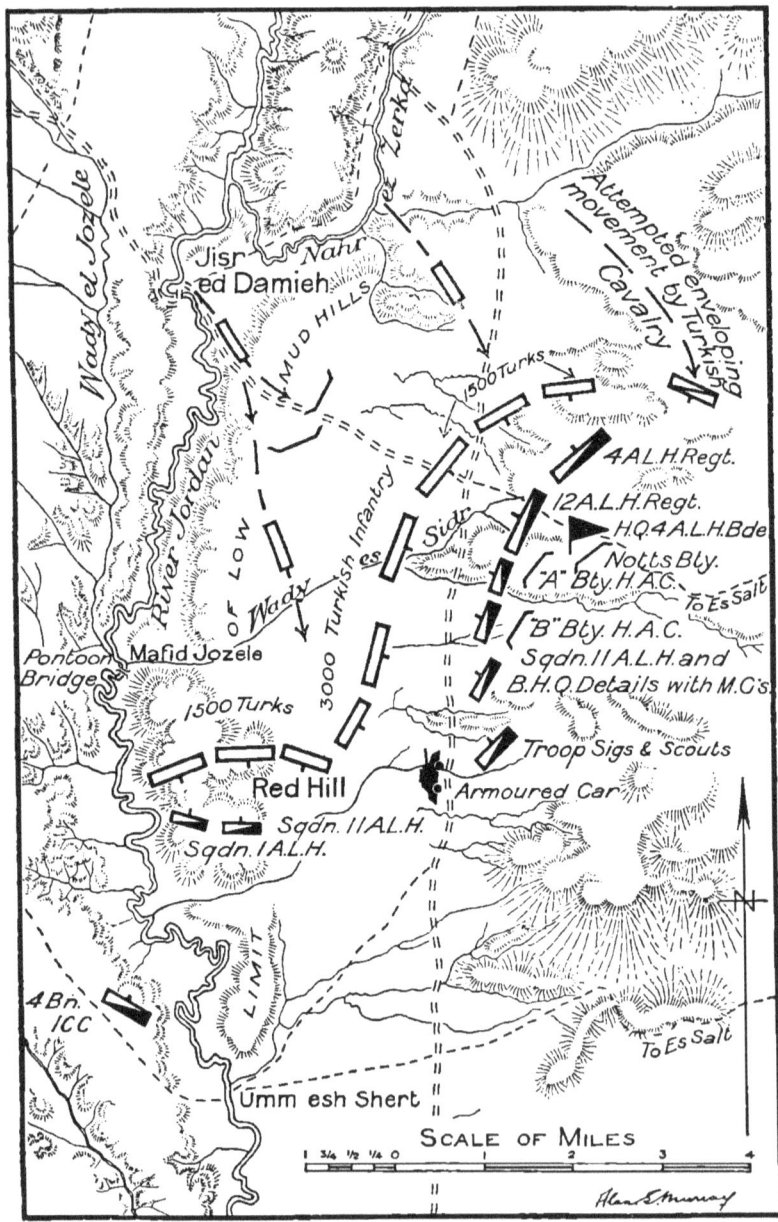

TURKISH ATTACK ON 4TH A.L.H. BRIGADE—POSITION ABOUT 8 A.M., 1ST MAY, 1918.

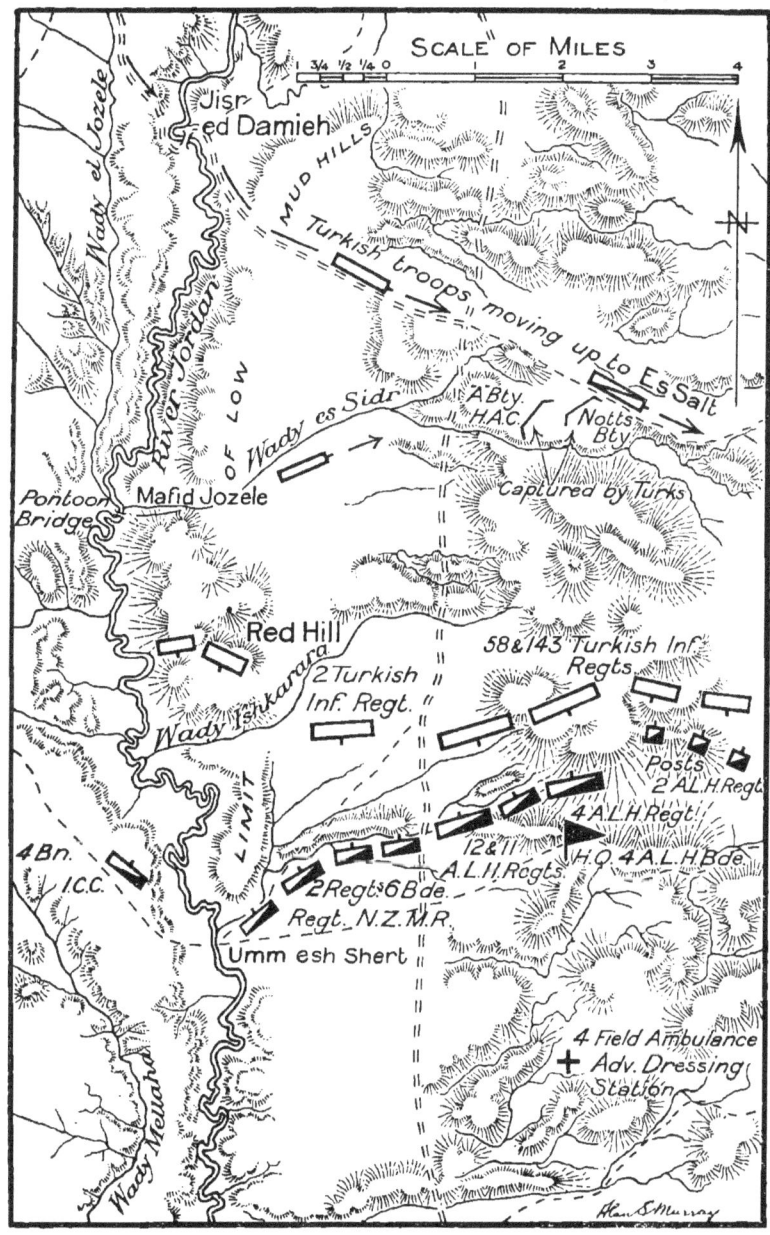

Turkish attack on 4th A.L.H. Brigade—Grant's position at dusk on 1st May, 1918.

MAP

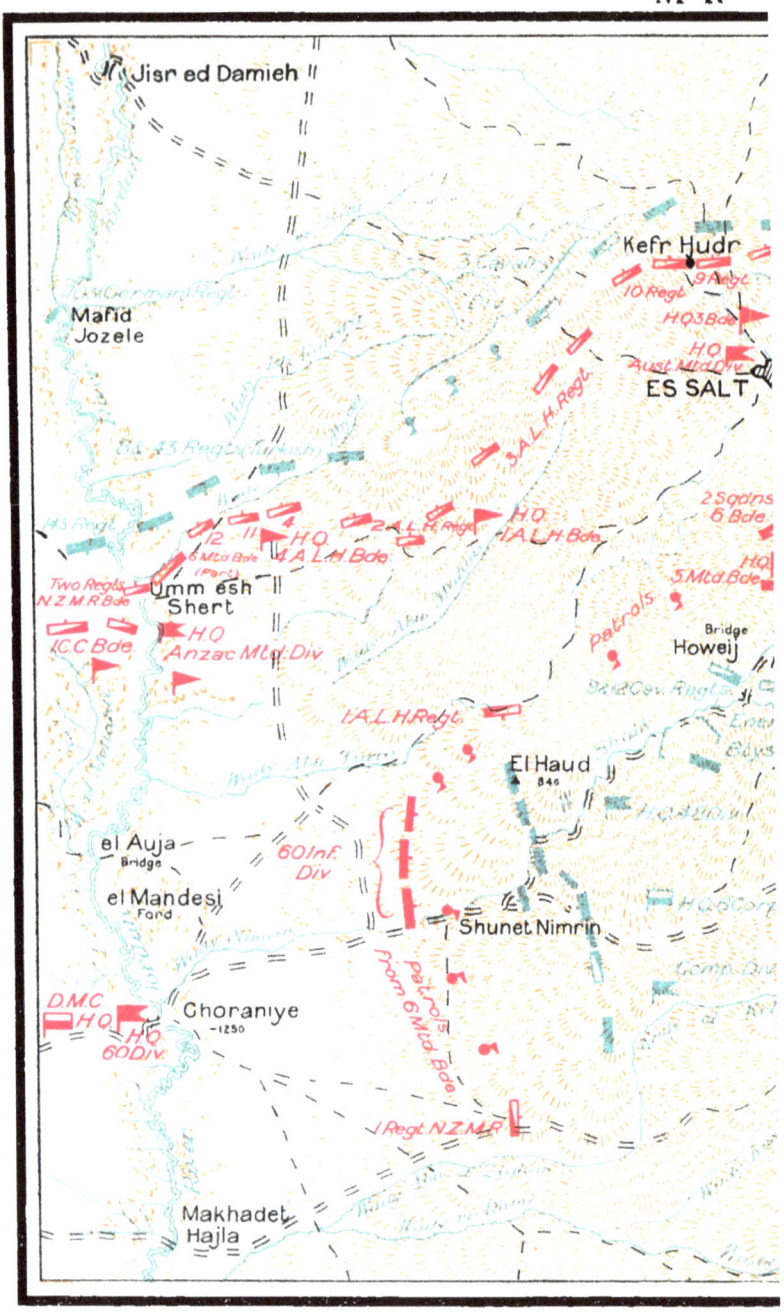

Es Salt raid—Position just

No. 35.

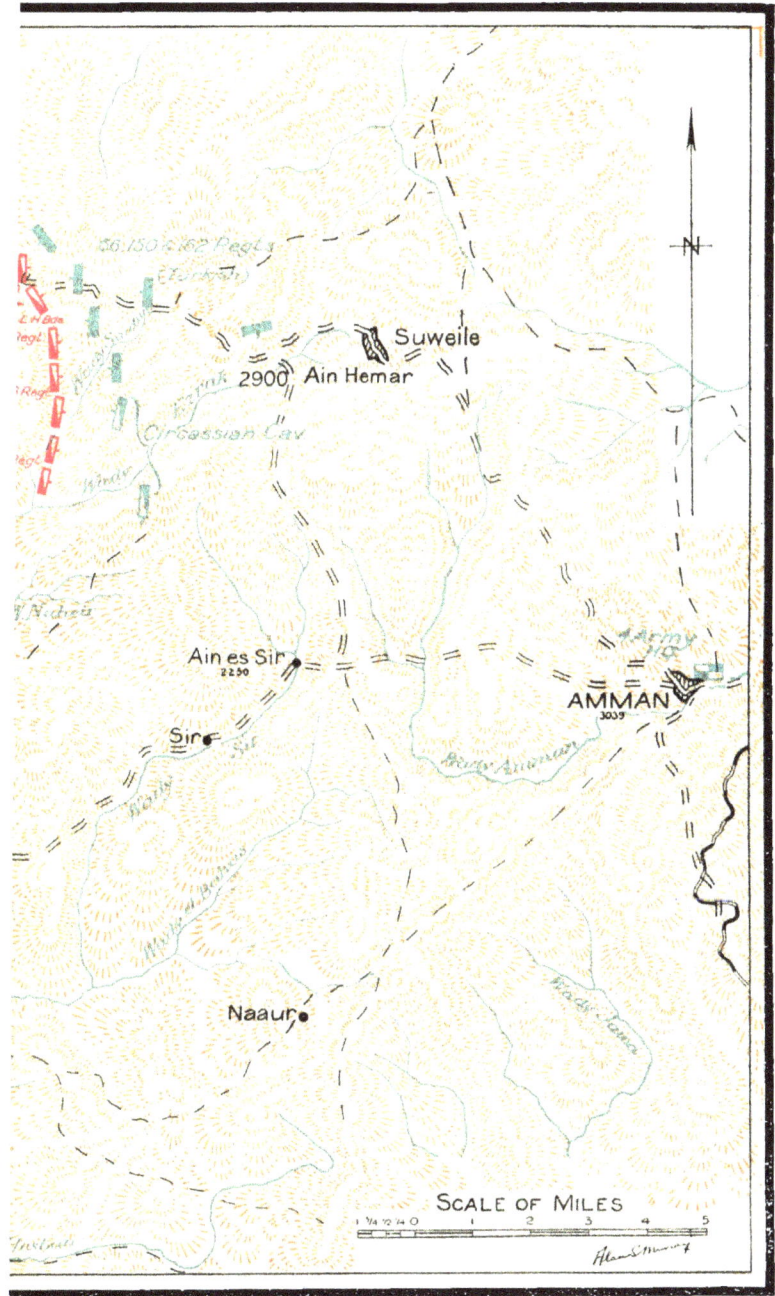

TO WITHDRAWAL, 2ND MAY, 1918.

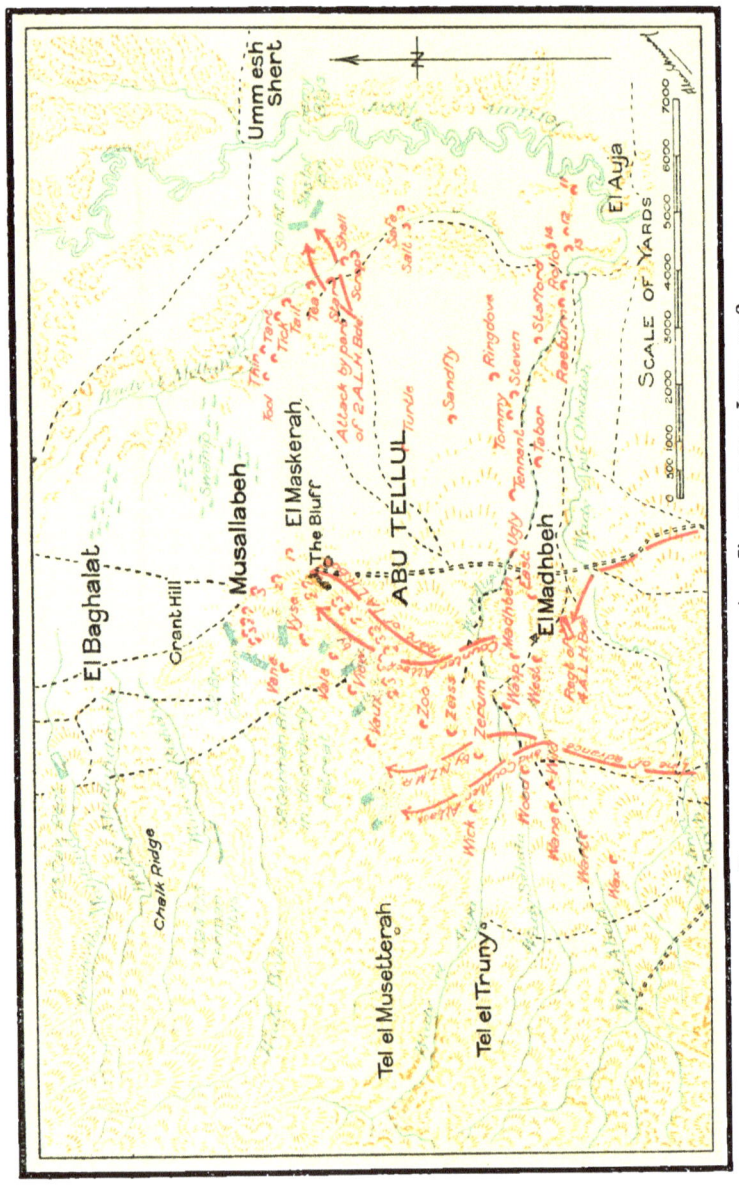

Map No. 36

The counter-attack at Abu Tellul, 14th July, 1918.

MAP

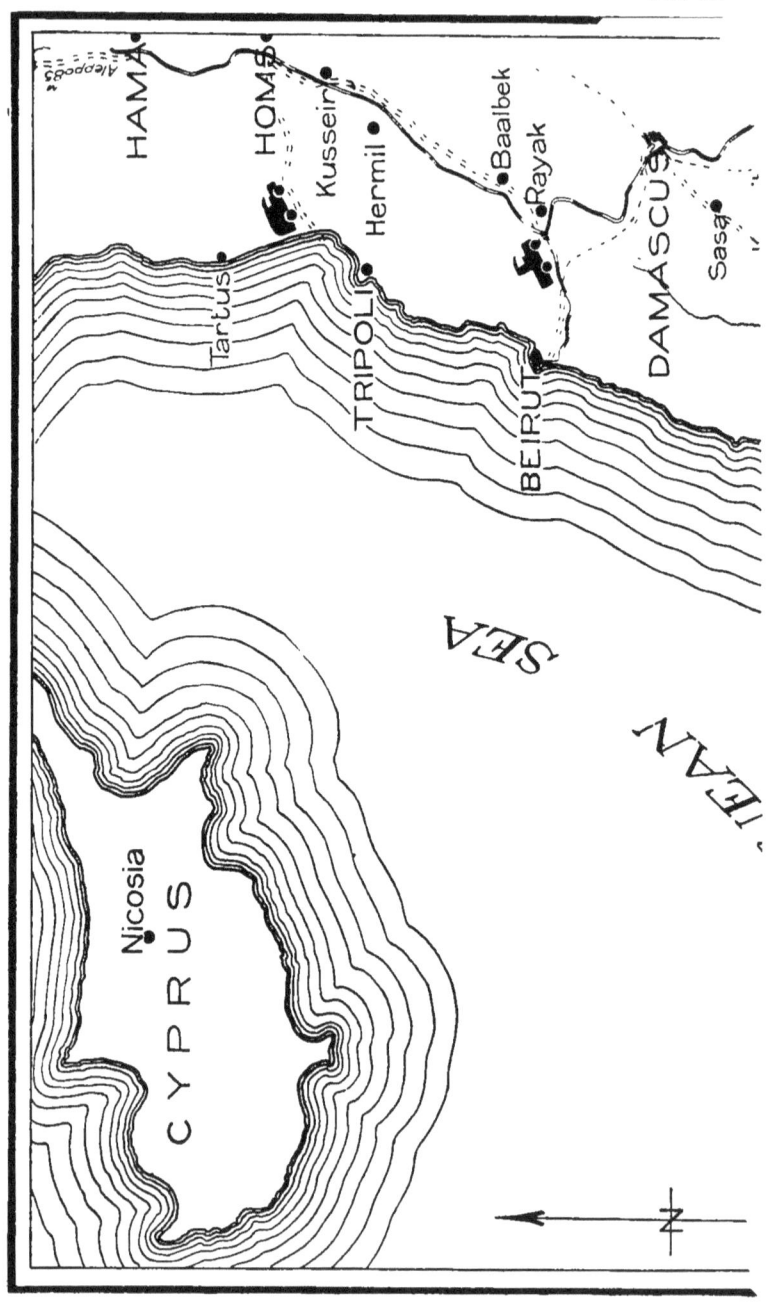

No. 37

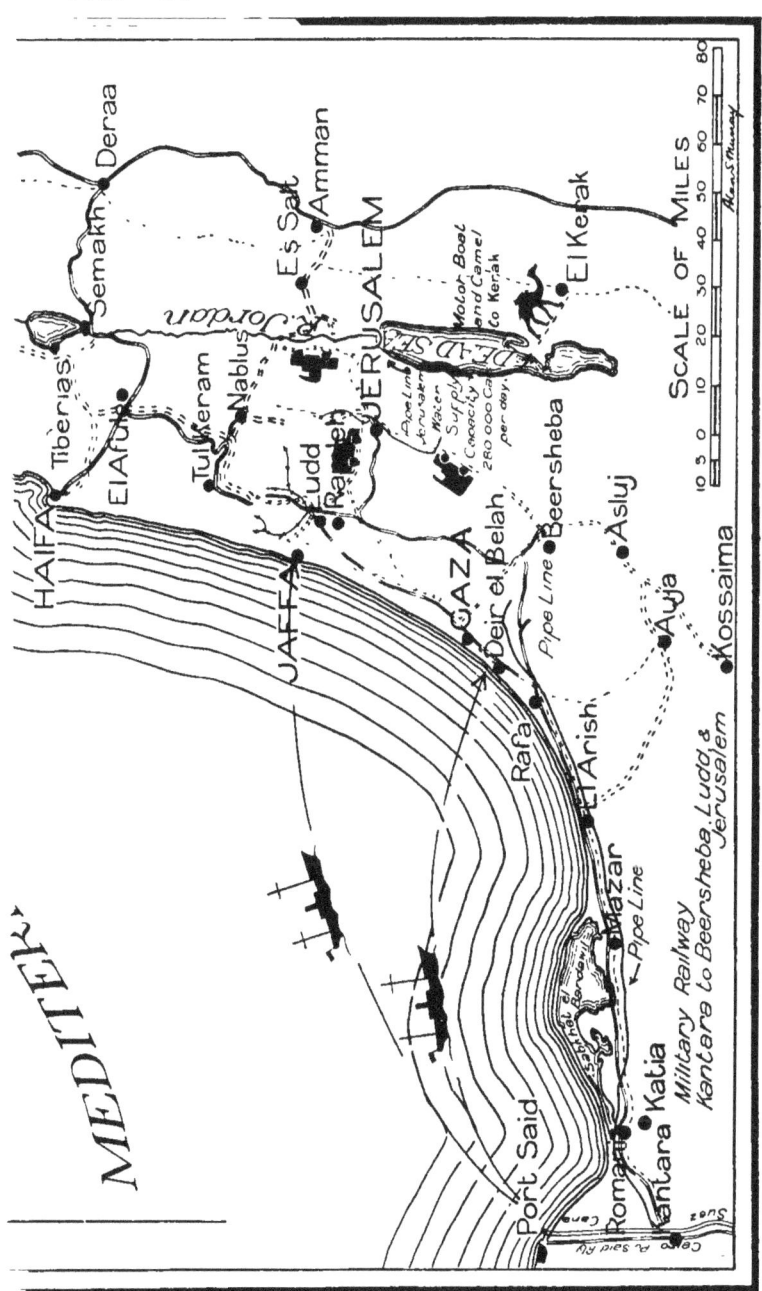

British and Turkish lines of communication, summer of 1918.

MAP

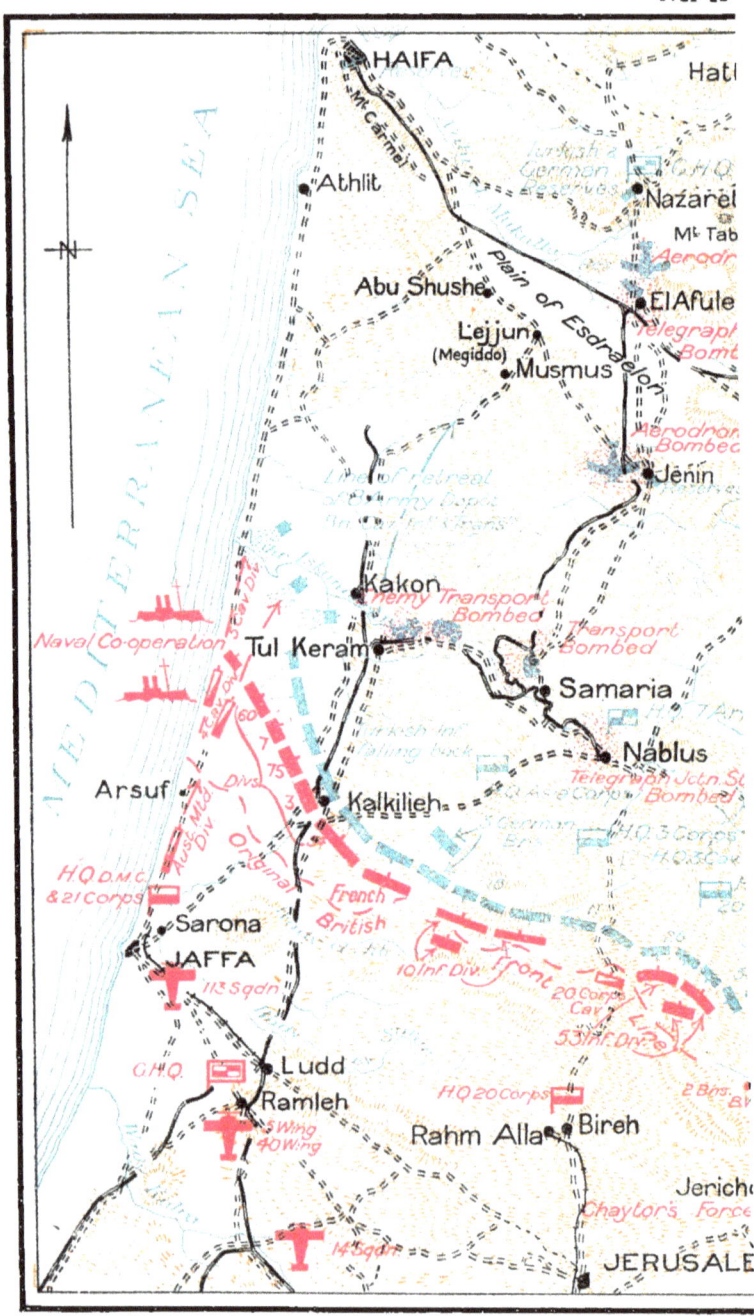

COMMENCEMENT OF BATTLE

No. 38.

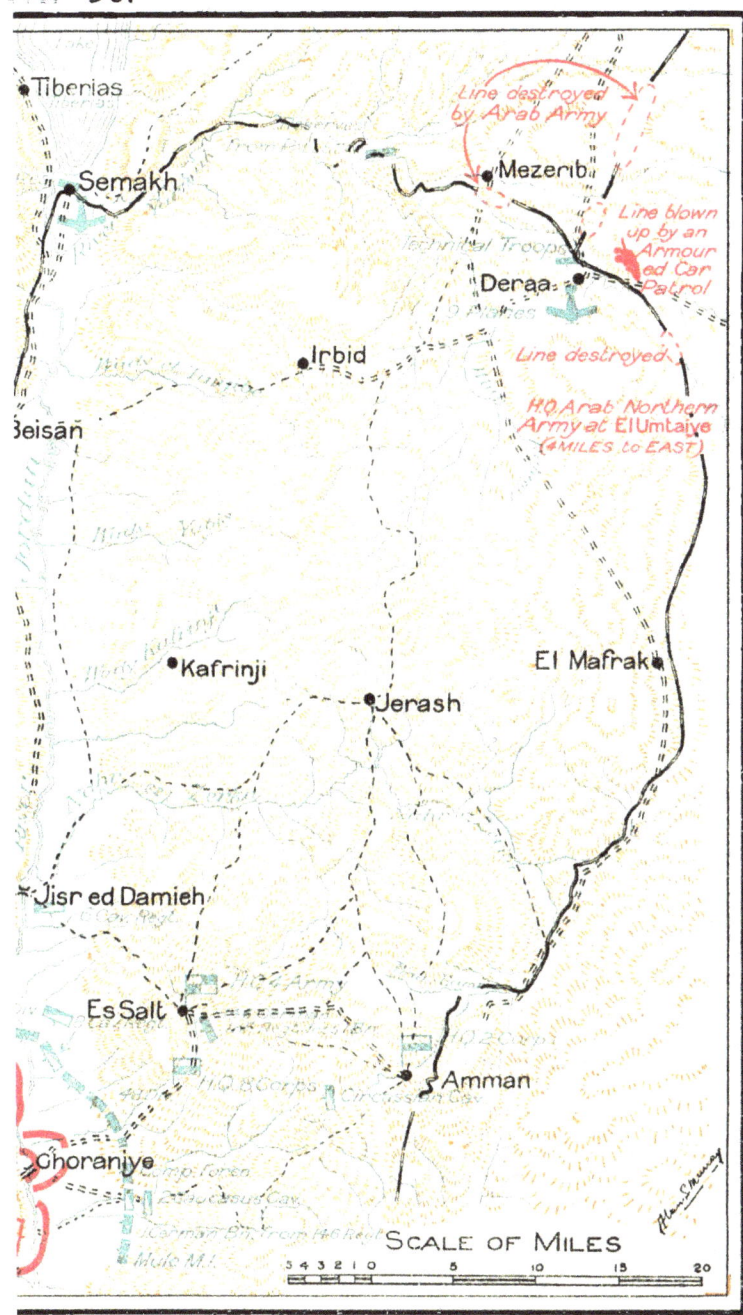

Map No. 39

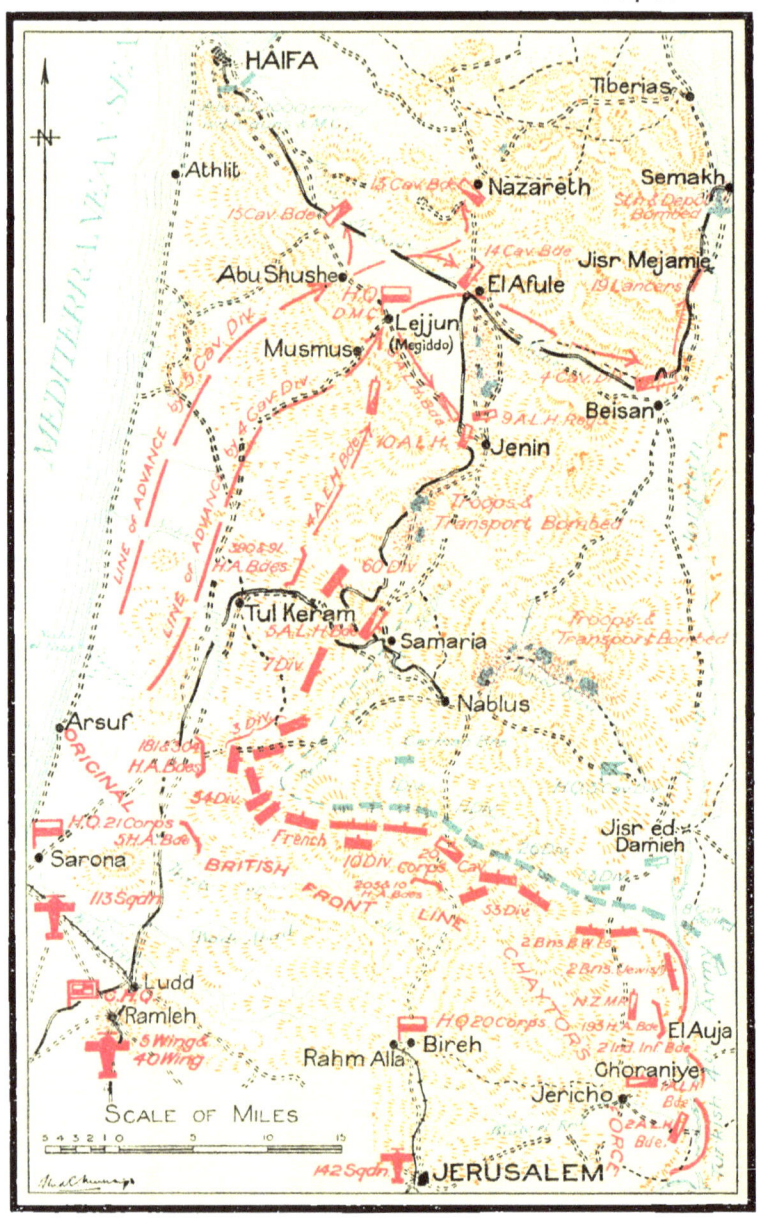

BATTLES OF SHARON AND SAMARIA. ADVANCE OF BRITISH CAVALRY—
POSITION AT 6 P.M. ON 20TH SEPTEMBER, 1918.

Map No. 40

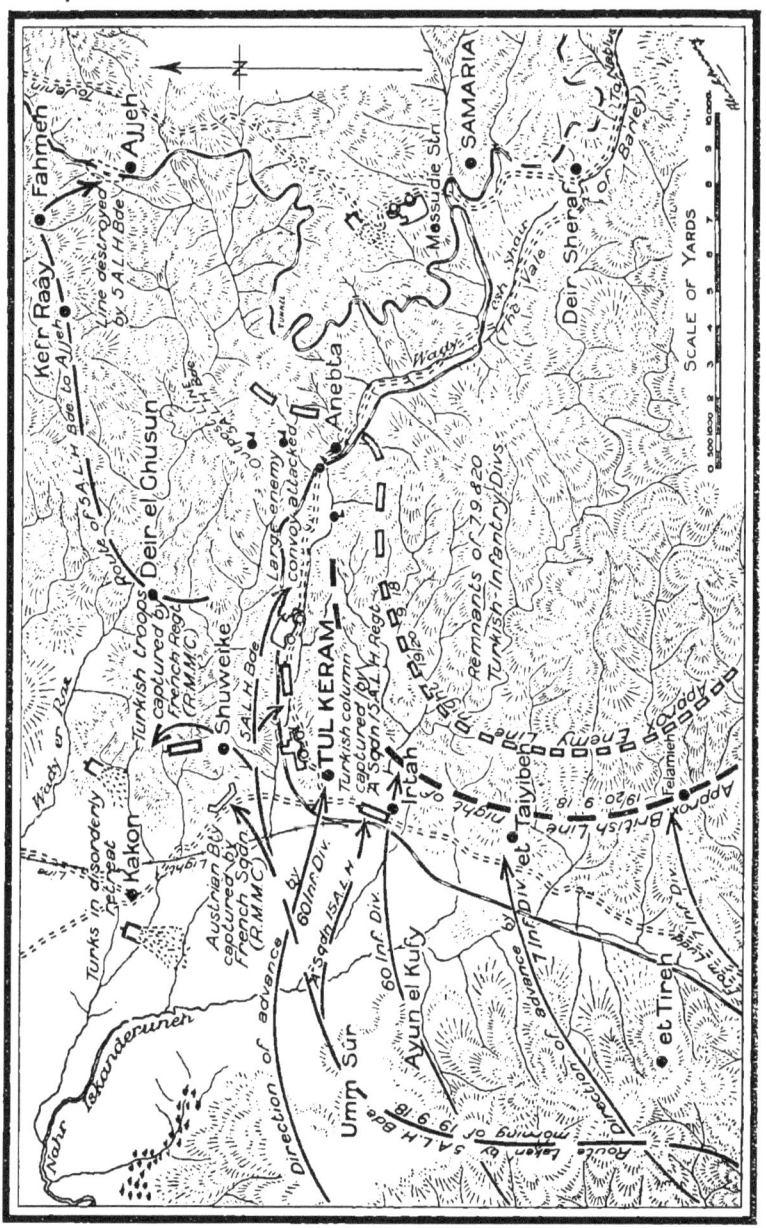

Operations of 5th A.L.H. Brigade 19th-20th September 1918

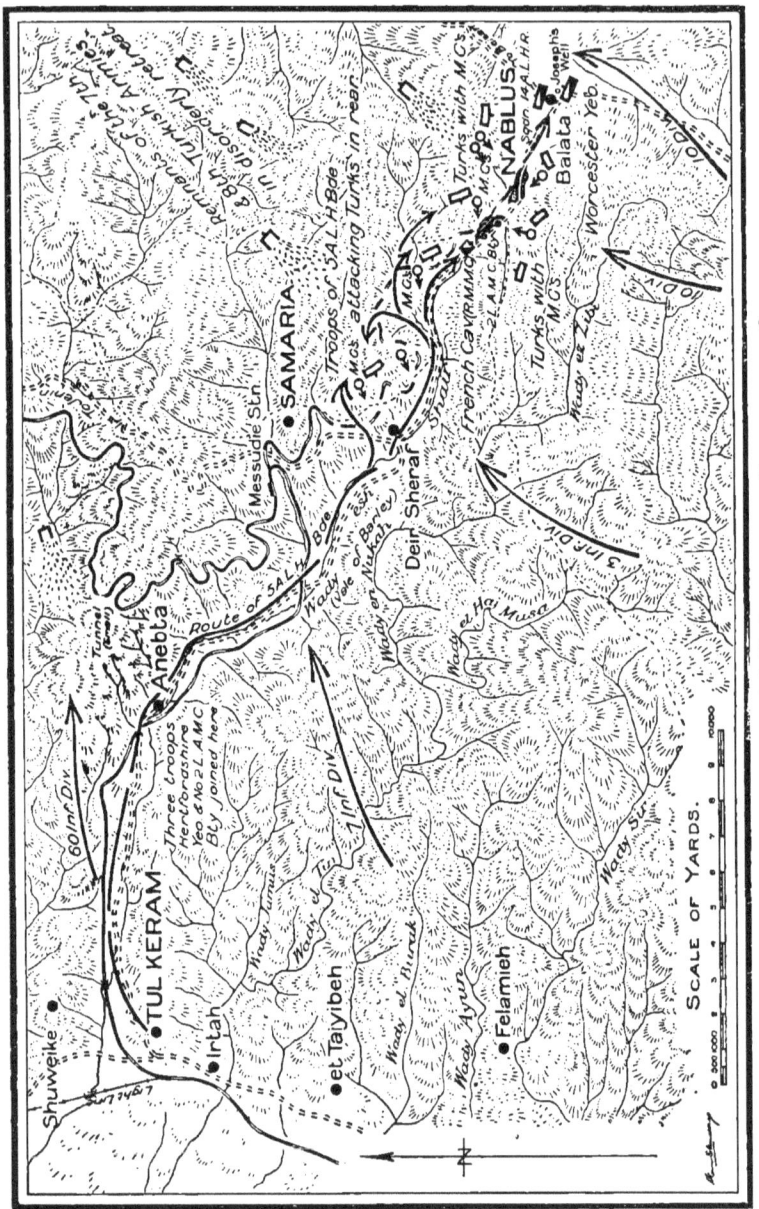

Map No. 41

Operations of 5th A.L.H. Brigade, 21st September, 1918.

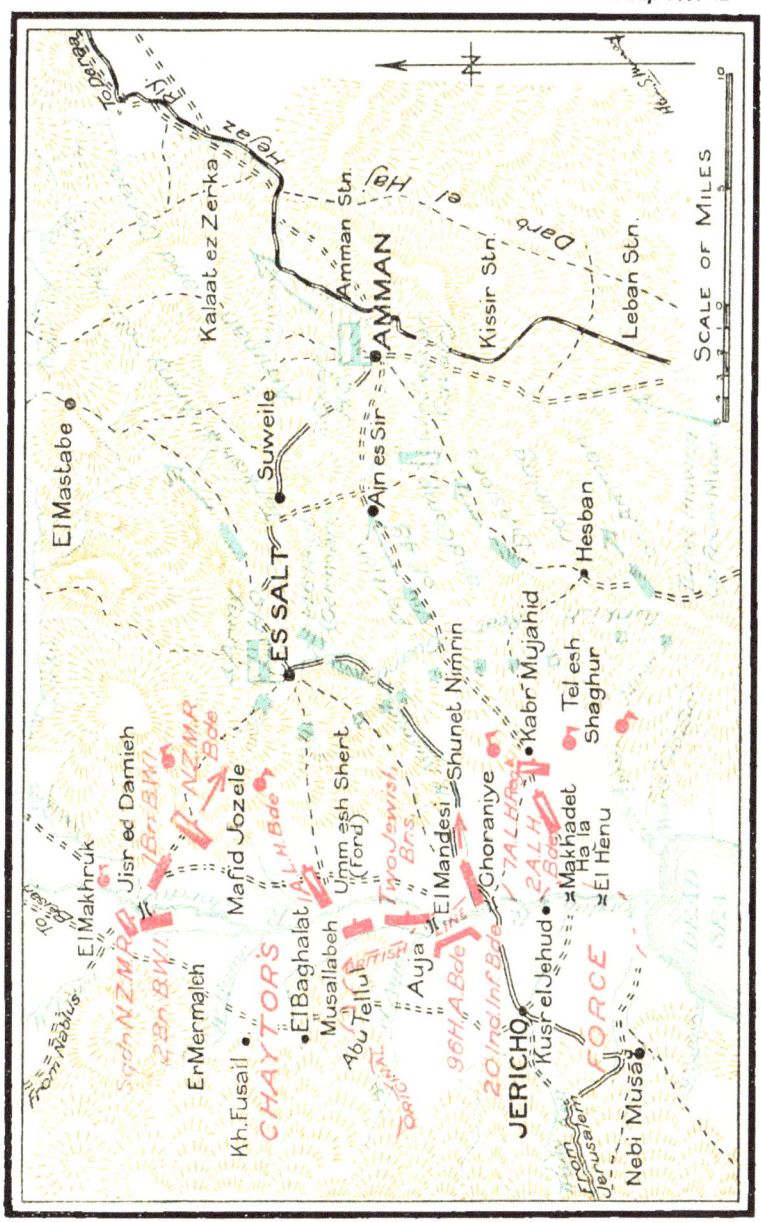

Map No. 42

Chaytor's advance on Es Salt and Amman, 22nd September, 1918.

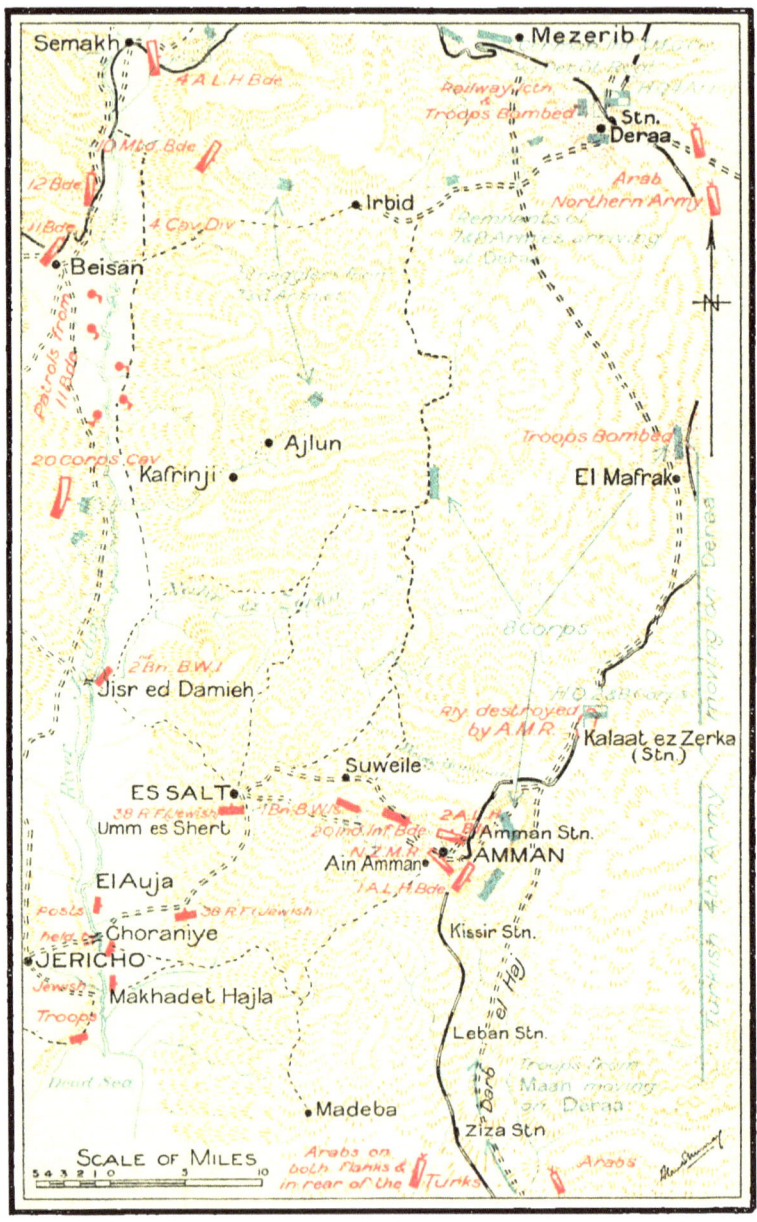

Map No. 43

CAPTURE OF AMMAN BY CHAYTOR'S FORCE, 25TH SEPTEMBER, 1918.

Map No. 44

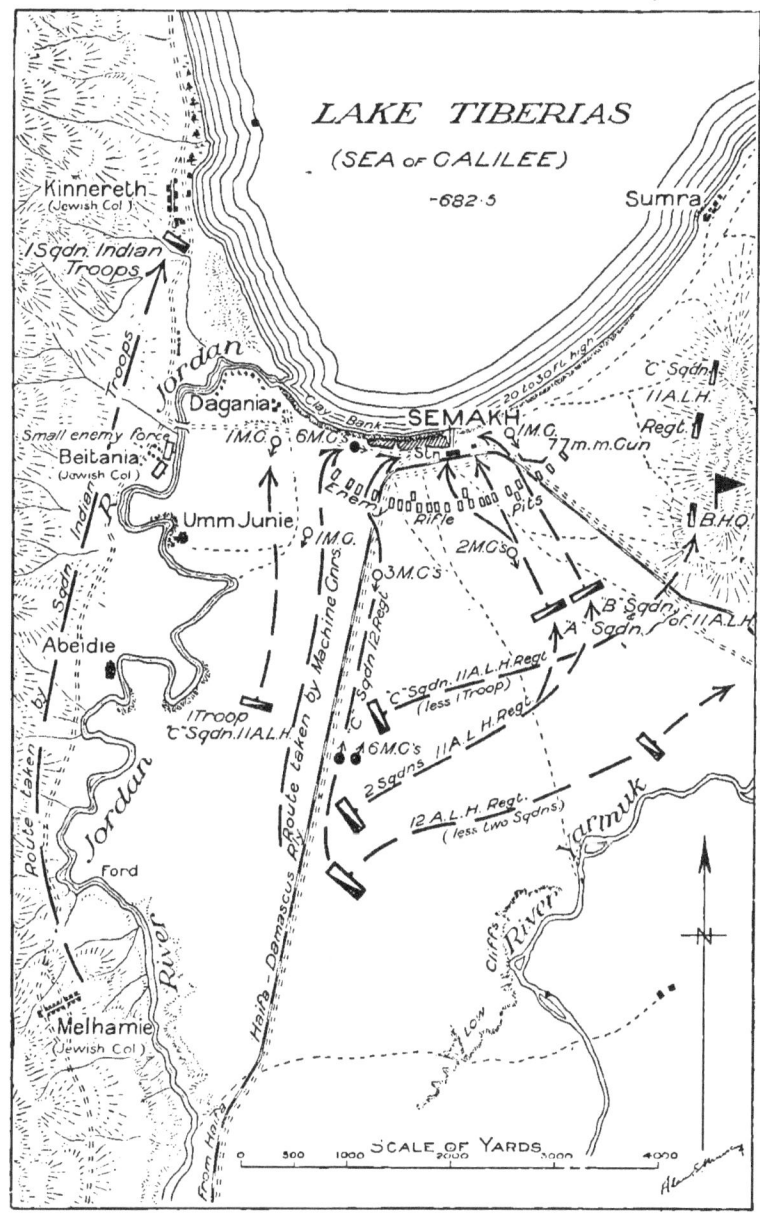

THE ACTION AT SEMAKH, 25TH SEPTEMBER, 1918.

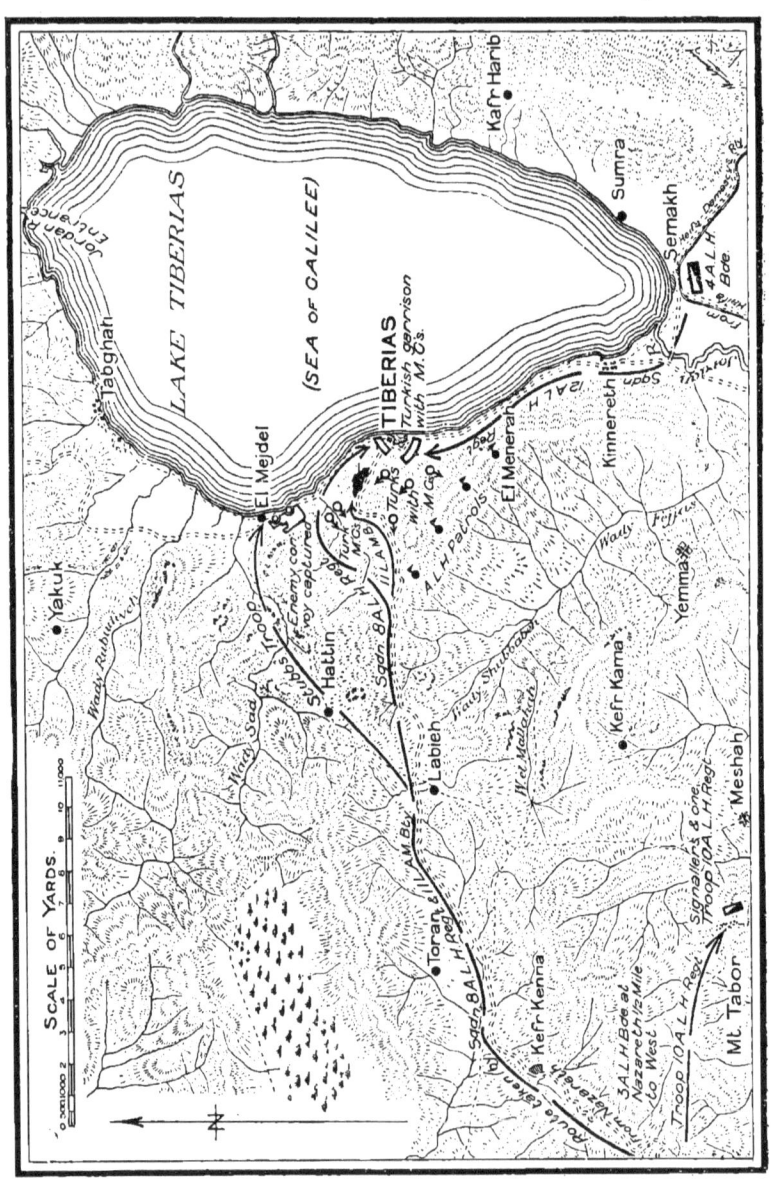

Map No. 45

The action at Tiberias, 25th September, 1918.

Map No 46

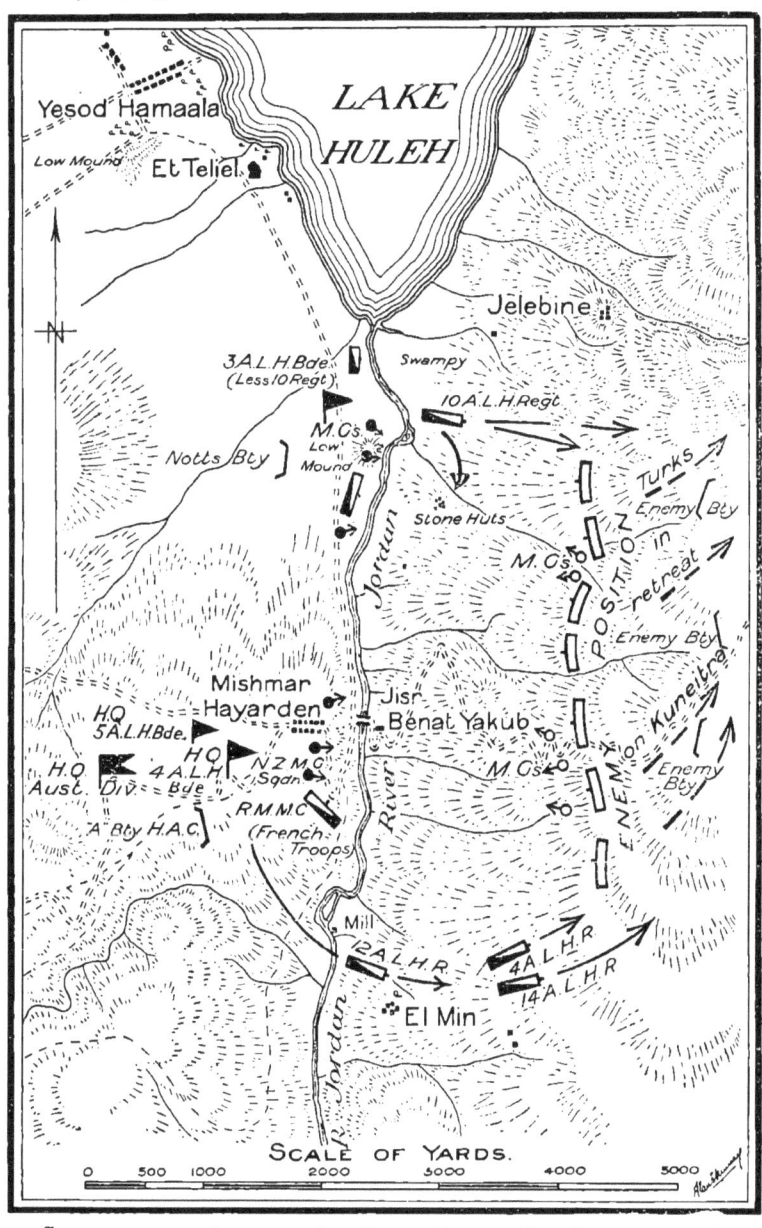

CROSSING OF THE JORDAN AT JISR BENAT YAKUB, 28TH SEPTEMBER, 1918.

MAP

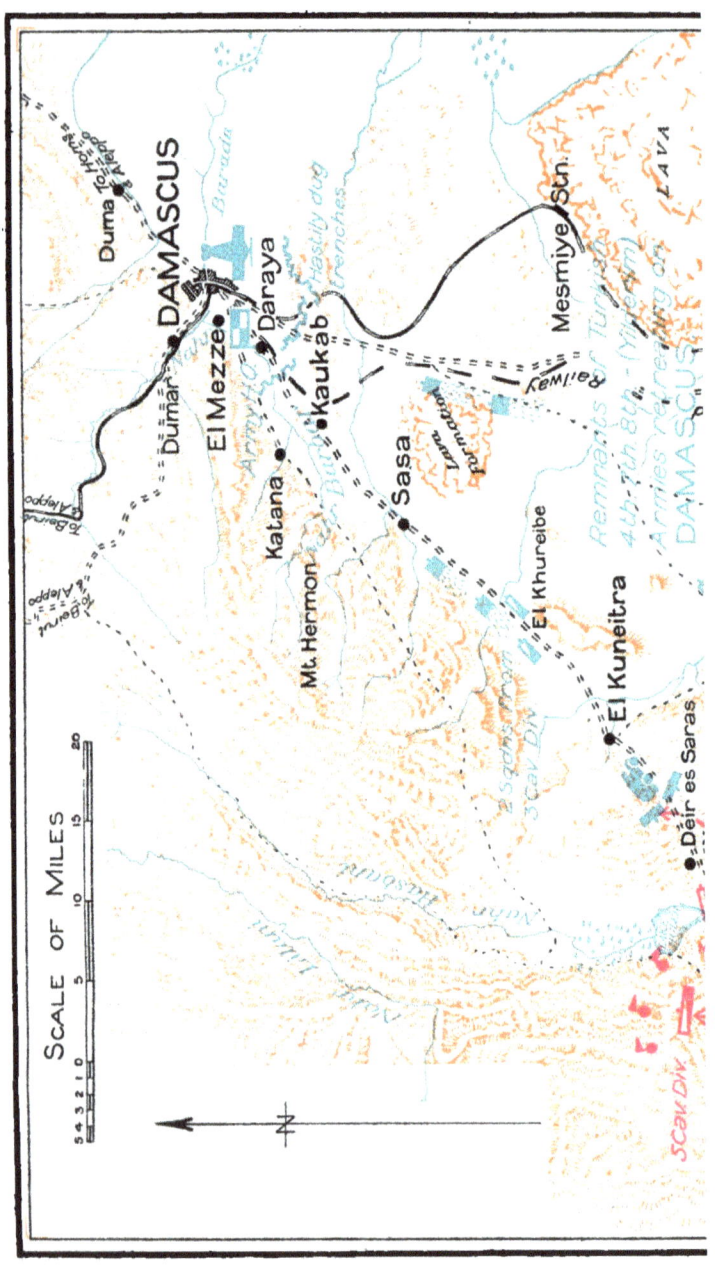

No. 47.

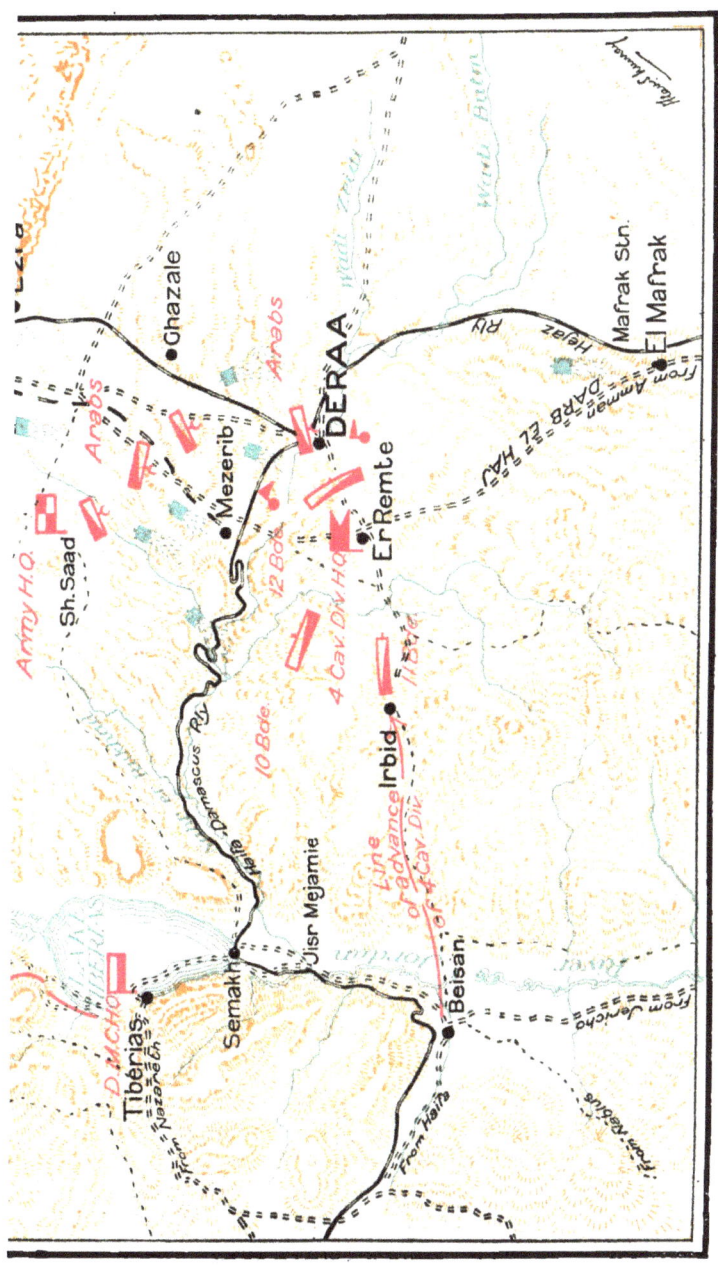

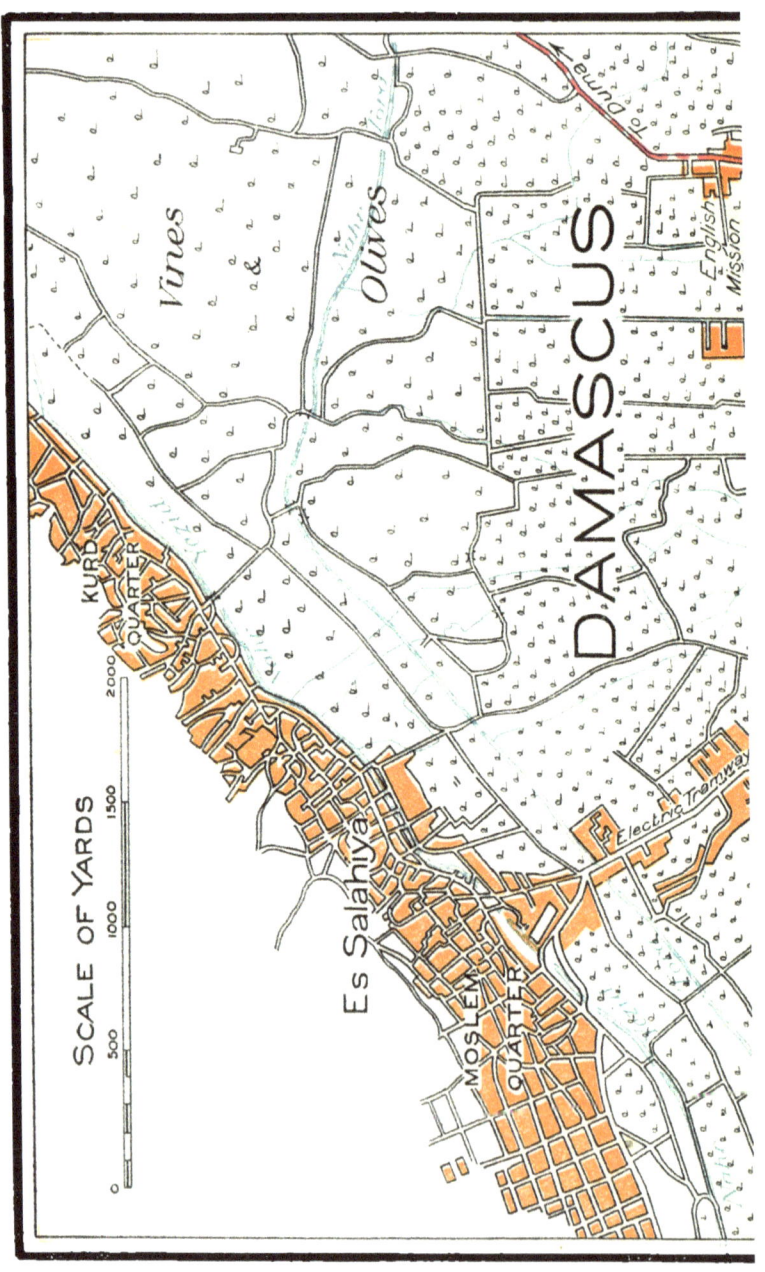

No. 48.

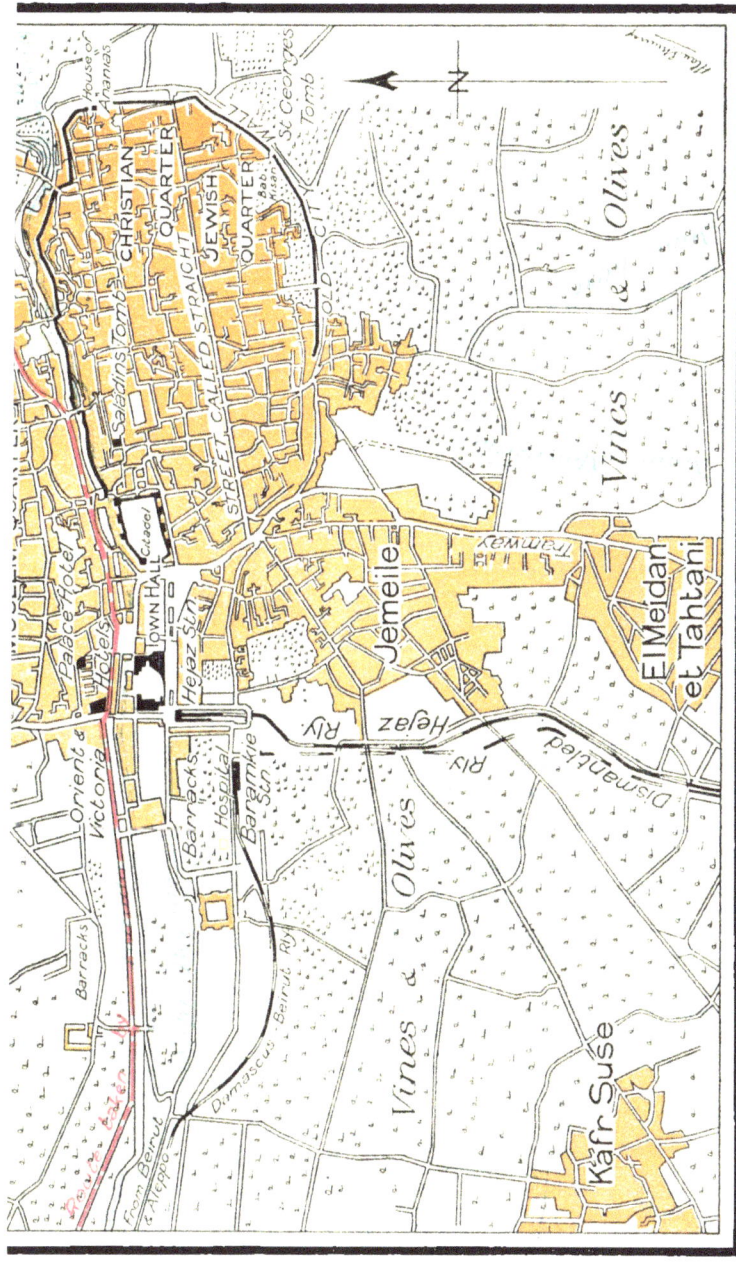

Damascus and environs, showing route taken by 3rd Australian Light Horse Brigade through the city.

MAP

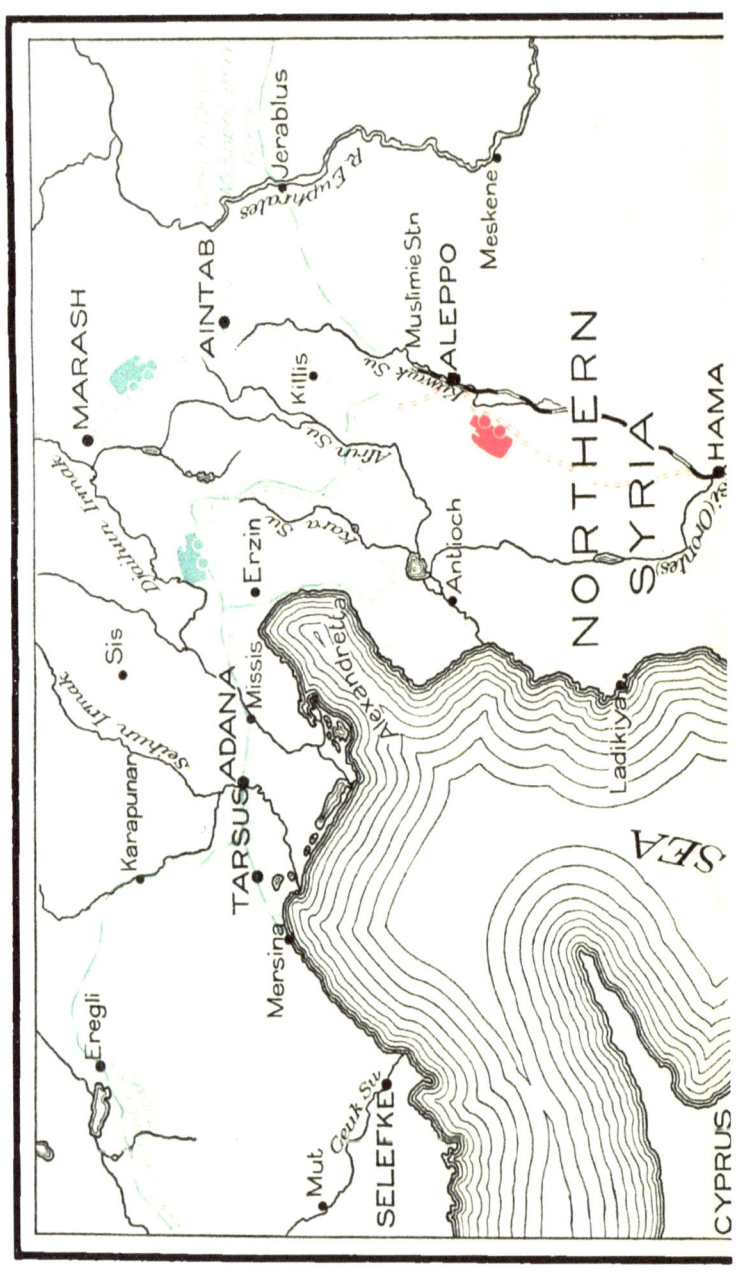

No. 49.

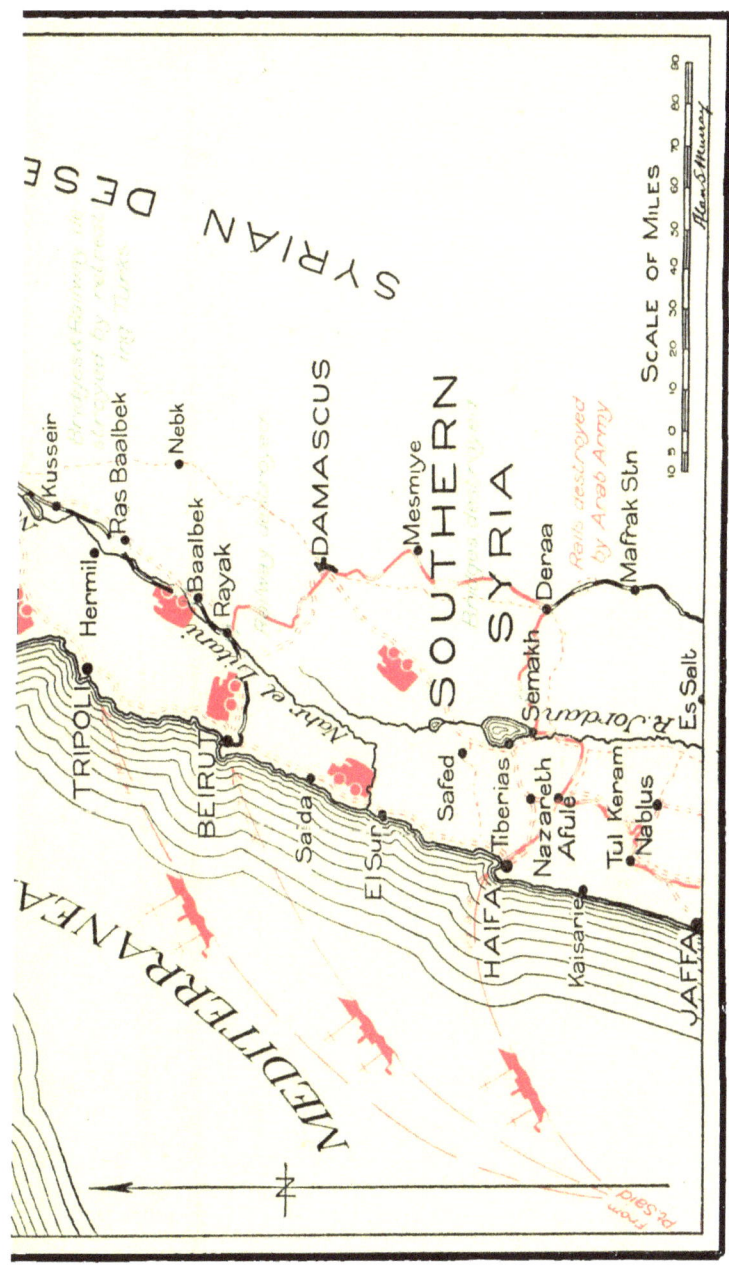

British and Turkish lines of communication after the capture of Aleppo.

THE
STORY OF ANZAC

FROM THE OUTBREAK OF WAR TO THE END
OF THE FIRST PHASE OF THE GALLIPOLI
CAMPAIGN, MAY 4, 1915

VOLUME VIII

LIST OF MAPS

1. Mesopotamia (South-eastern portion), showing area in which operations of Australian Half-Flight opened
2. Mesopotamia (North-western portion), showing area of later operations of Australian Half-Flight
3. Egypt
4. Sinai Desert, the scene of the campaign of 1916
5. Southern Palestine, showing the position before the Third Battle of Gaza
6. The country east of the Dead Sea, showing the Hejaz railway
7. Central Palestine, the scene of the Battle of Nablus
8. The Wady Fara, in which heavy bombing operations occurred on 21st September, 1918
9. Syria, showing the area of the last stages of the campaign against the Turks
10. North-eastern France, showing the areas illustrated by maps in this volume
11. Cambrai region, showing area of operations of No. 2 Squadron in November and December, 1917, and of No. 2 and No. 4 Squadrons in March, 1918
12. Section of a typical artillery map, showing method of ranging by reference to "clock-face"
13. Douai region, the "hunting" area of all British scout squadrons
14. The Lys region, showing area of operations of No. 3 Squadron, December, 1917-April, 1918, and of No. 2 and No. 4 Squadrons, May-September, 1918
15. Villers-Bretonneux region, showing area of operations of No. 3 Squadron, April-August, 1918
16. St. Quentin region, showing area of operations of No. 3 Squadron, September and October, 1918
17. Lille region, showing area of operations of No. 2 and No. 4 Squadrons, May-October, 1918
18. Tournai region, showing area of operations of No. 2 and No. 4 Squadrons, October and November, 1918
19. Ath region, showing area of operations of No. 2 and No. 4 Squadrons, October and November, 1918

Map No. 1

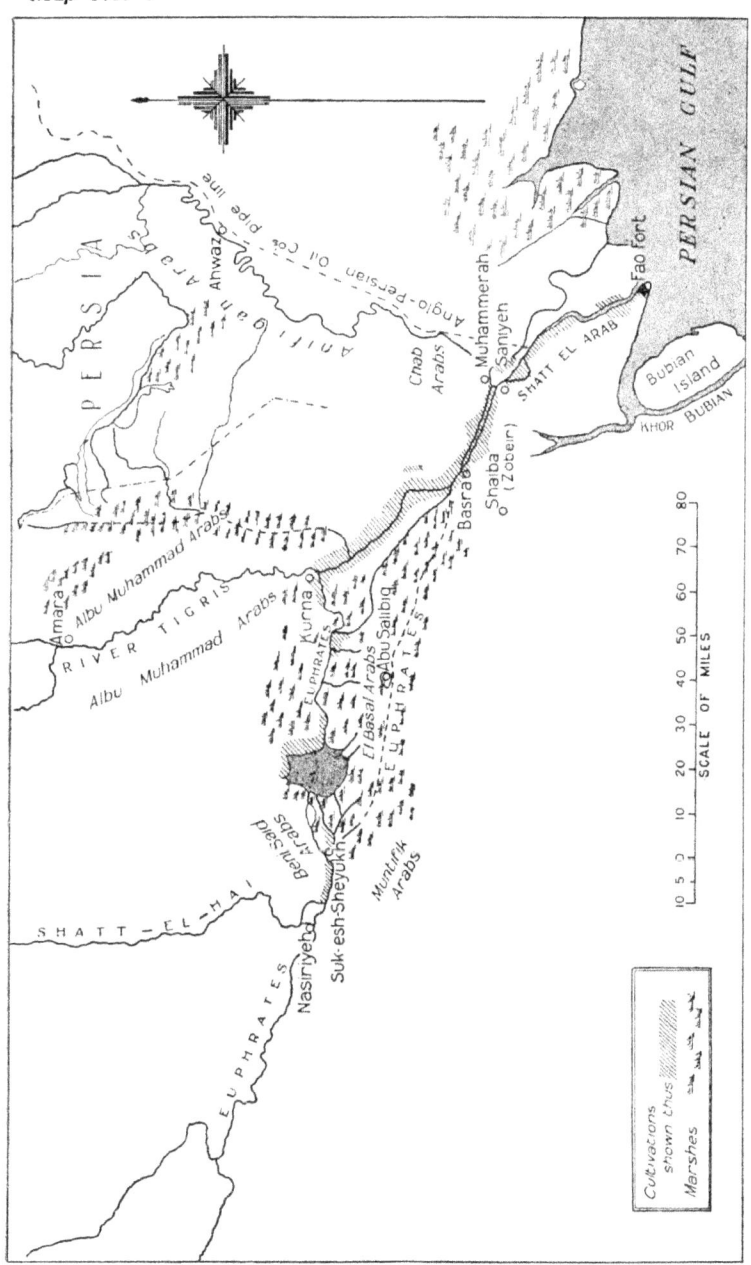

MESOPOTAMIA (SOUTH-EASTERN PORTION), SHOWING AREA IN WHICH OPERATIONS OF AUSTRALIAN HALF-FLIGHT OPENED

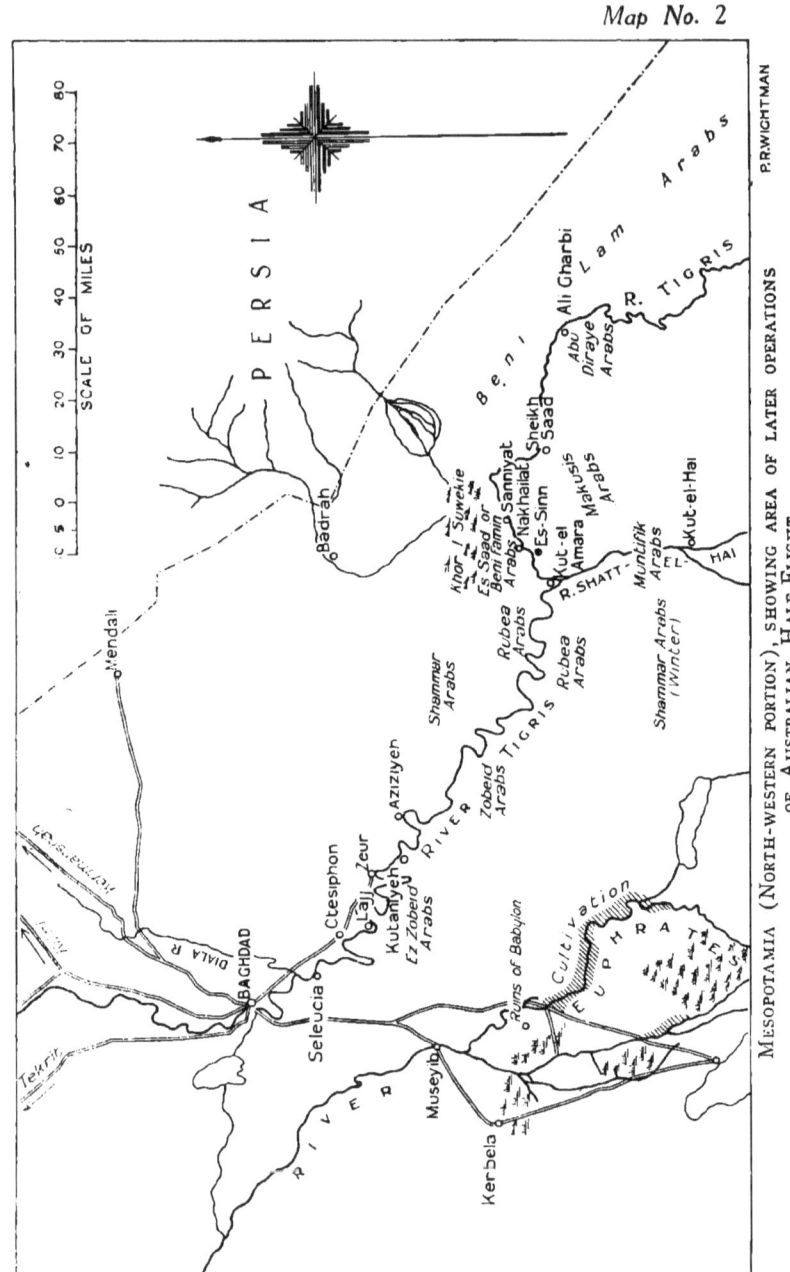

Map No. 2

Mesopotamia (North-western portion), showing area of later operations of Australian Half-Flight

Map No. 3

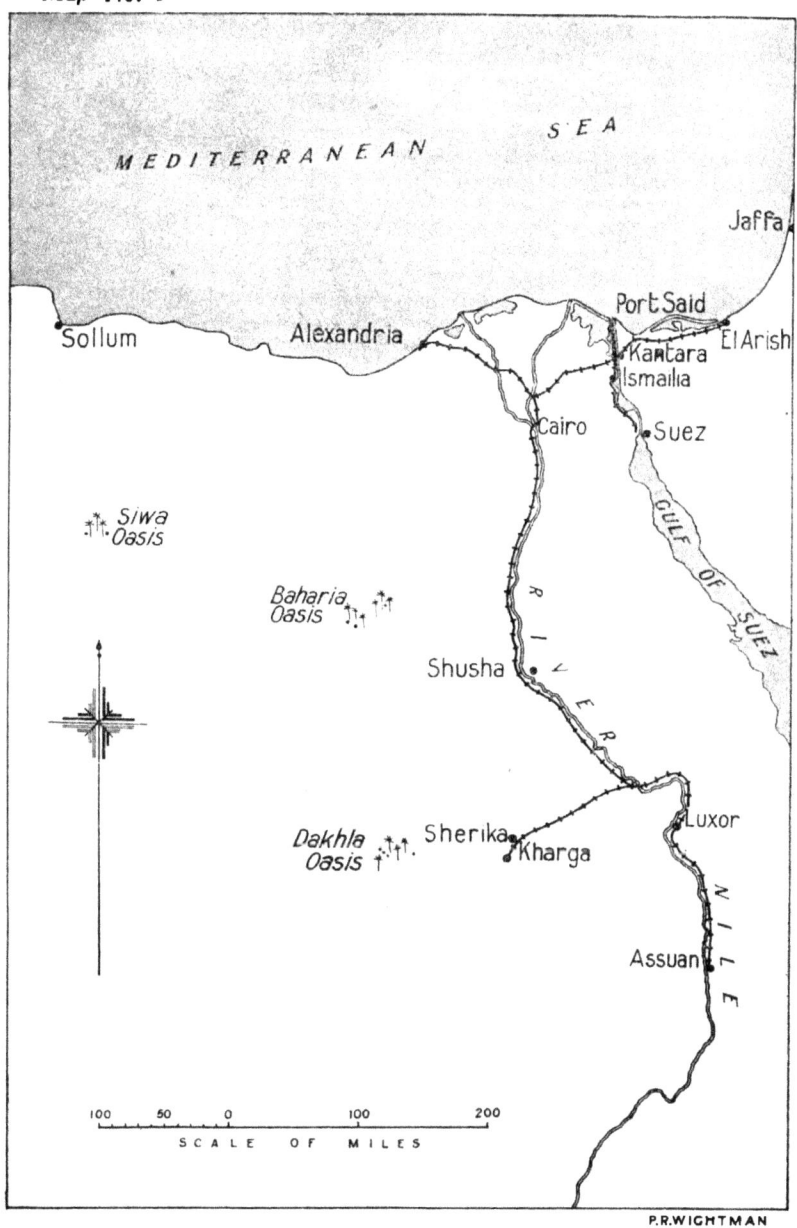

EGYPT

MAP

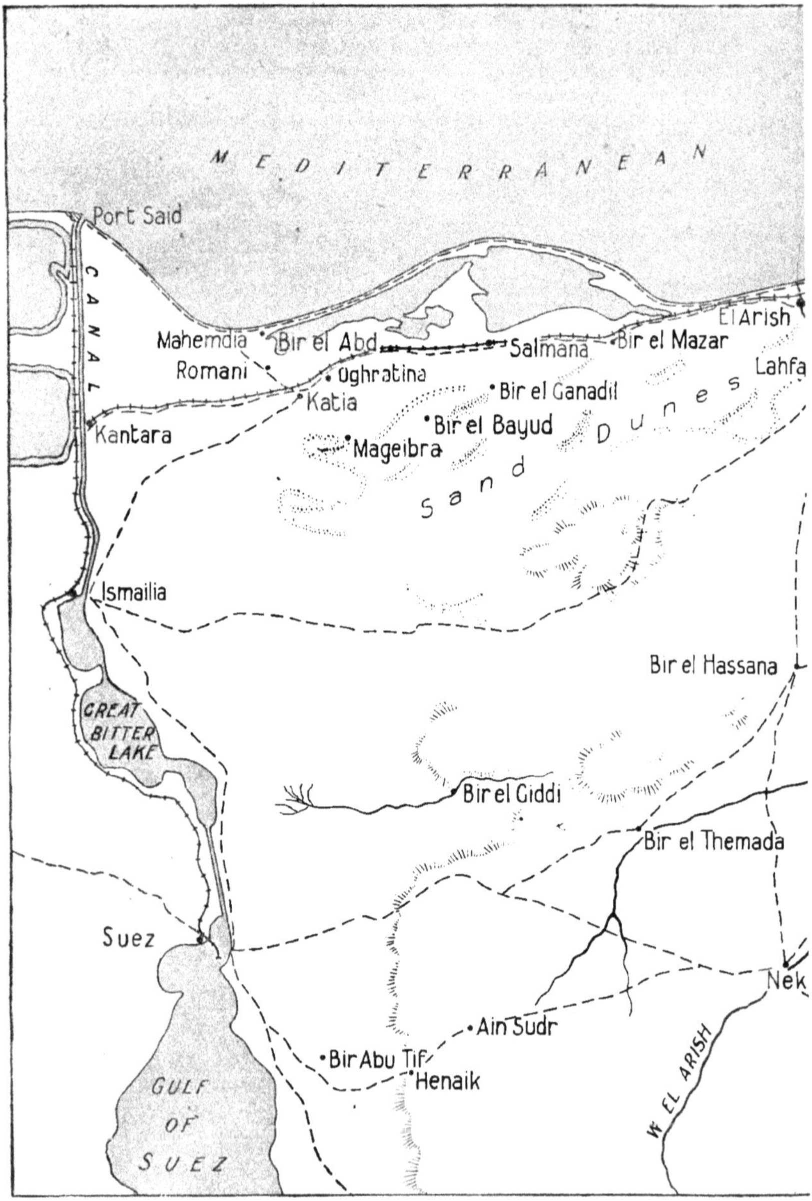

SINAI DESERT, THE SCE[NE

No. 4

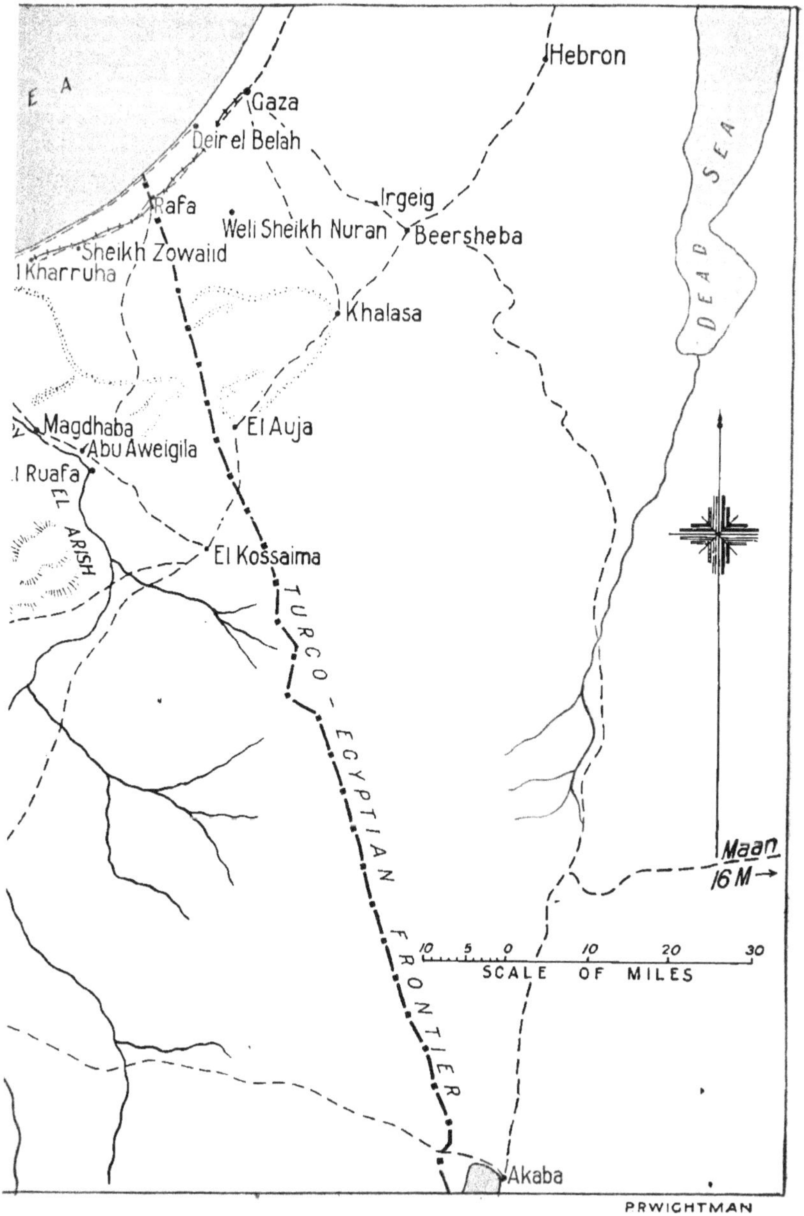

THE CAMPAIGN OF 1916

Map No. 5

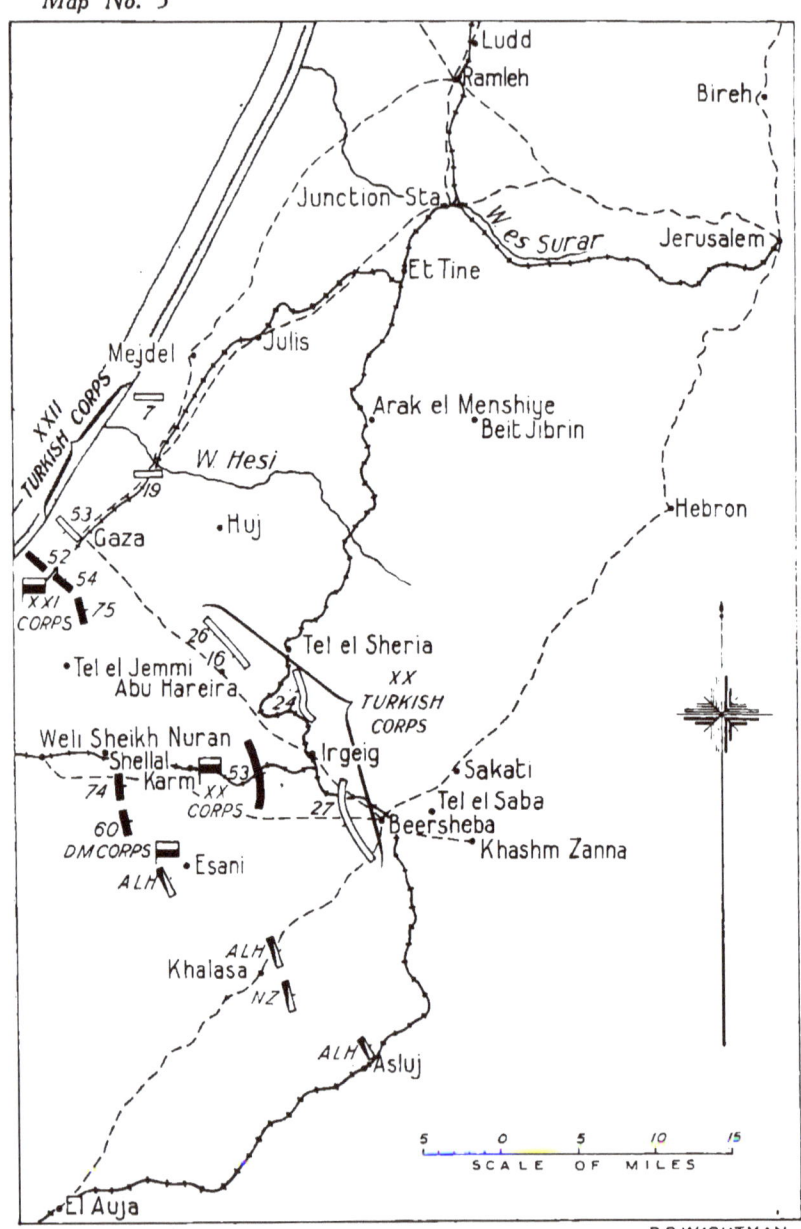

SOUTHERN PALESTINE, SHOWING THE POSITION BEFORE THE THIRD BATTLE OF GAZA

Map No. 6

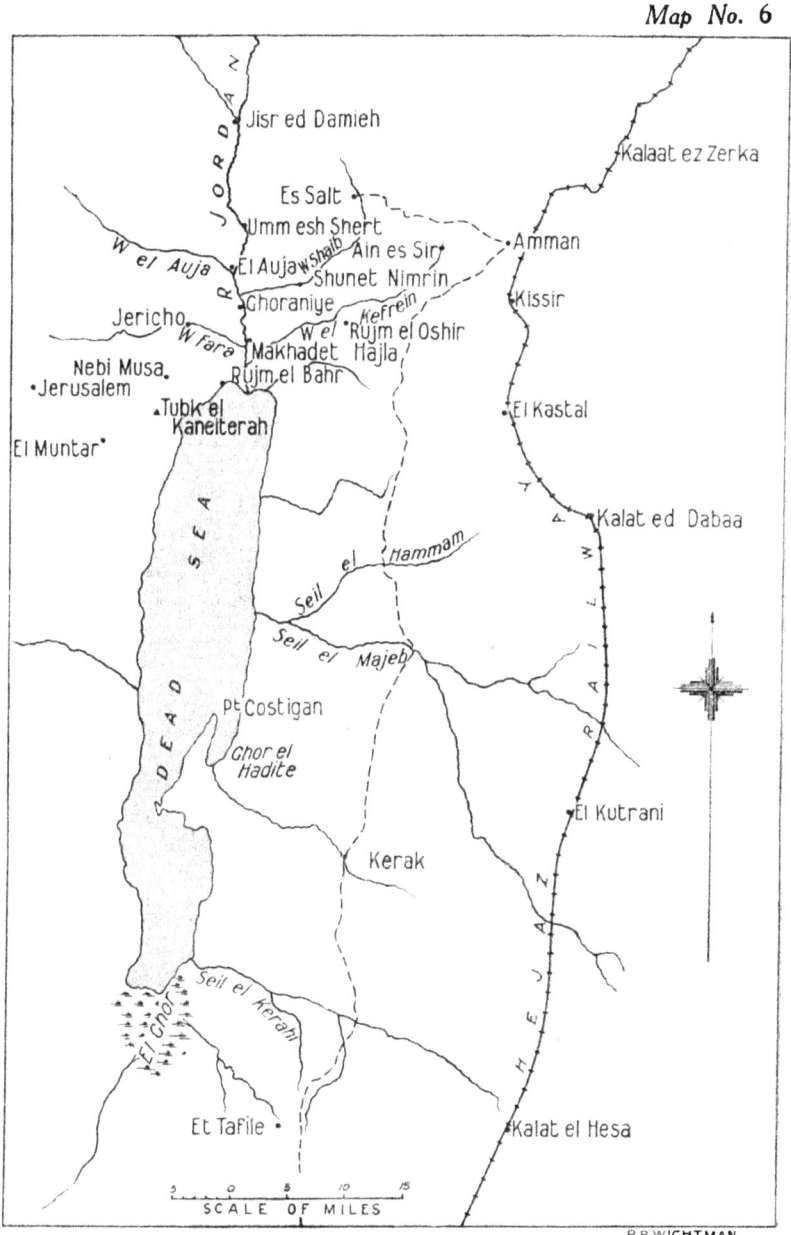

THE COUNTRY EAST OF THE DEAD SEA, SHOWING THE HEJAZ RAILWAY

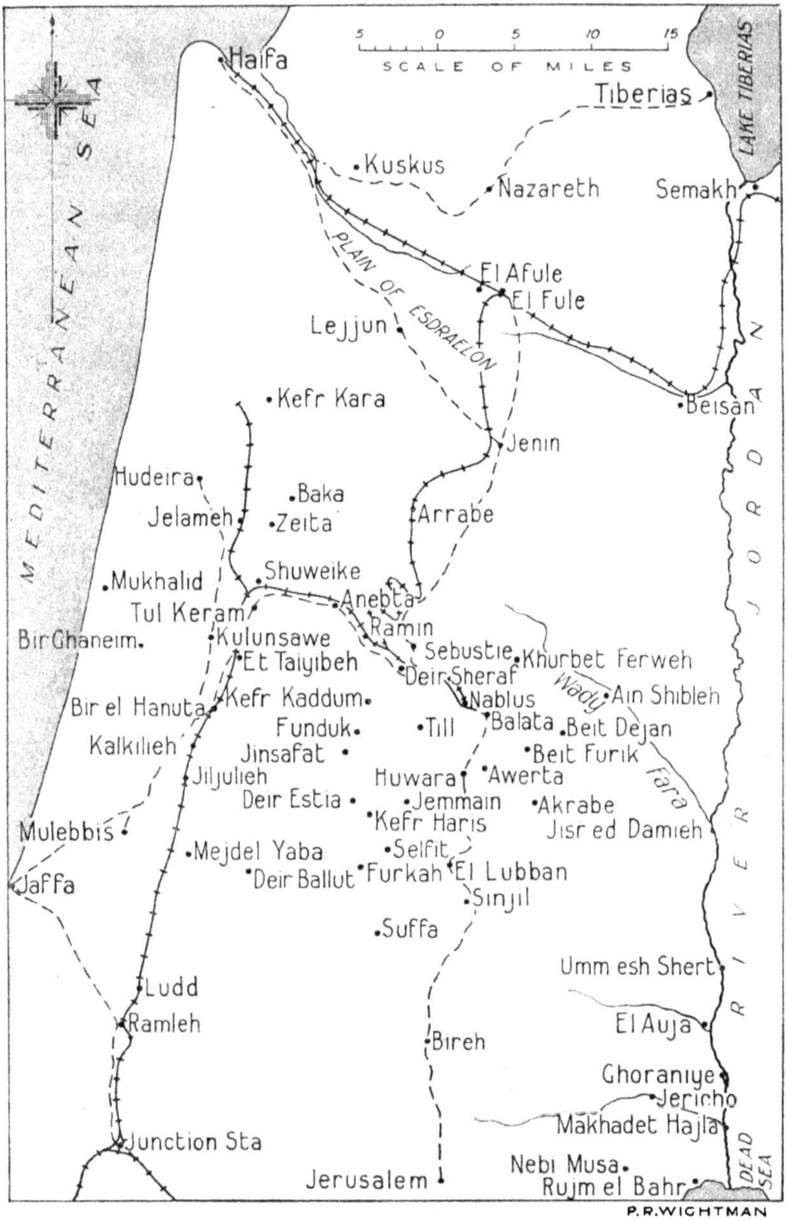

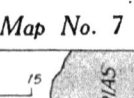

Map No. 7

Central Palestine, the scene of the Battle of Nablus

Map No. 8

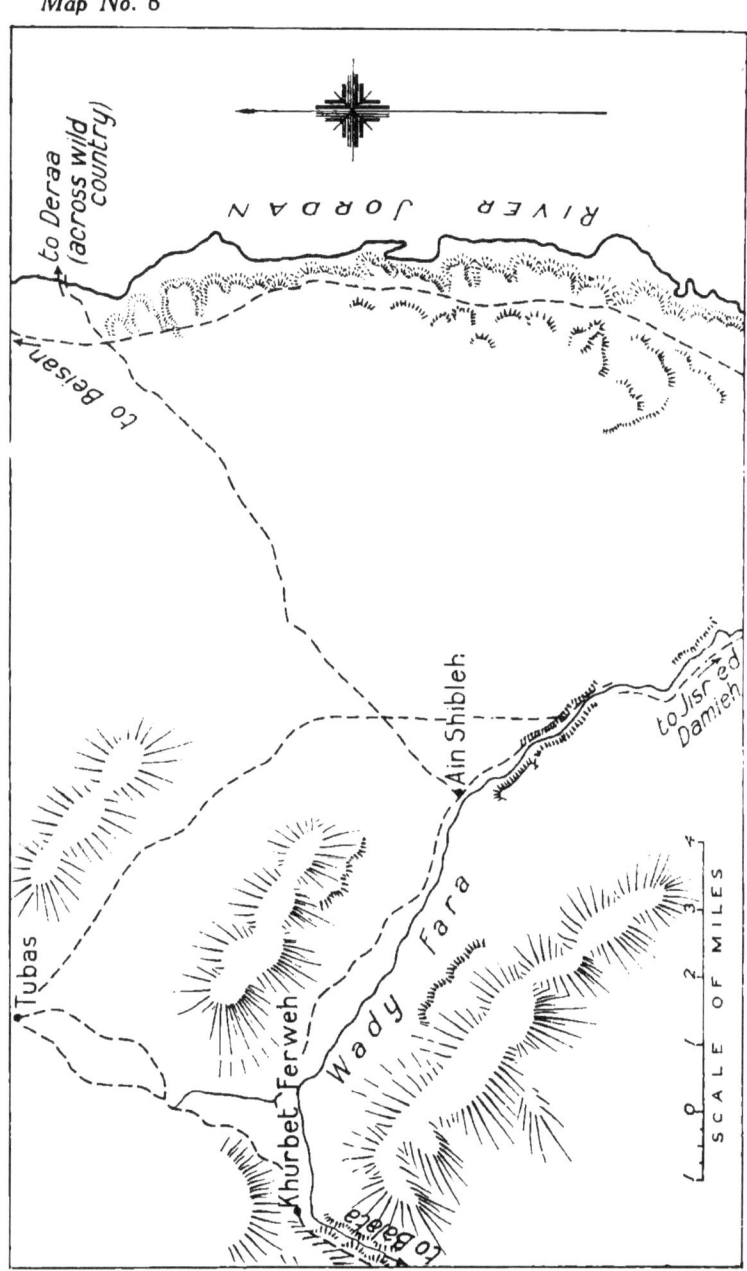

The Wady Fara, in which heavy bombing operations occurred on 21st September, 1918

Map No. 9

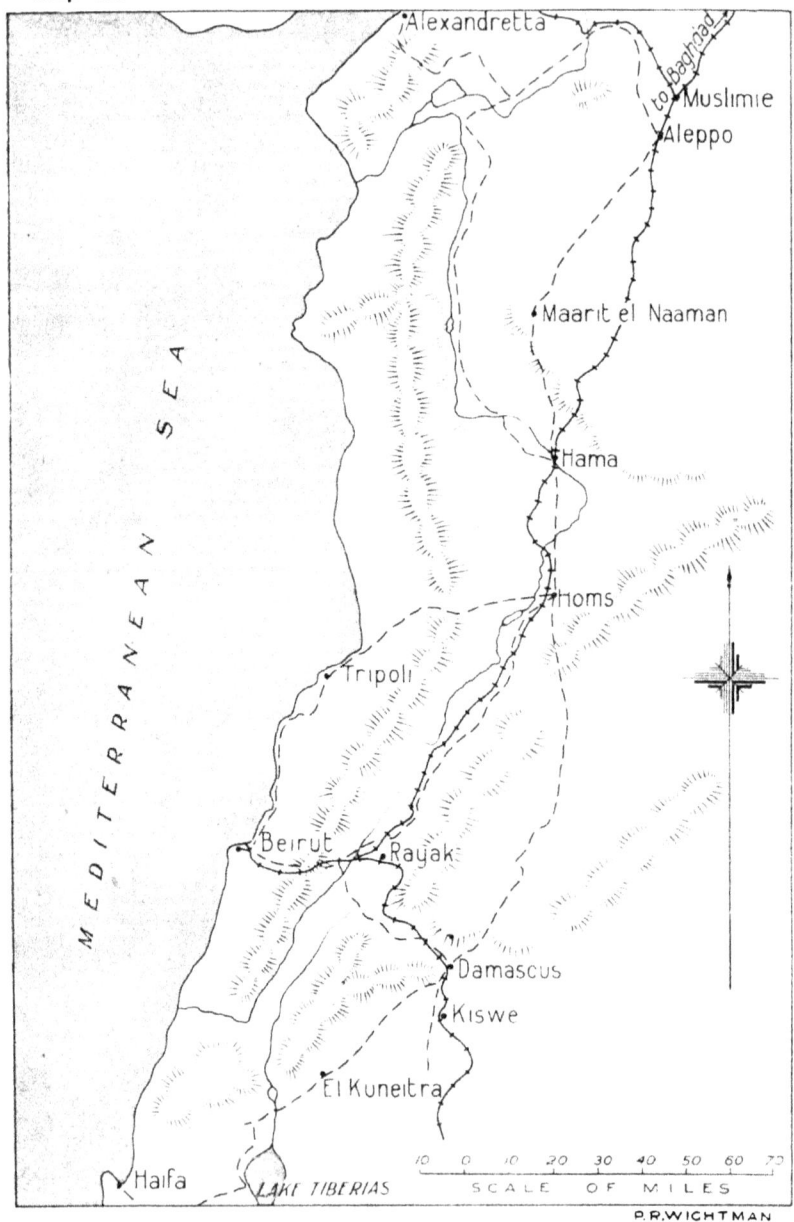

SYRIA, SHOWING THE AREA OF THE LAST STAGES OF THE CAMPAIGN AGAINST THE TURKS

Map No. 10

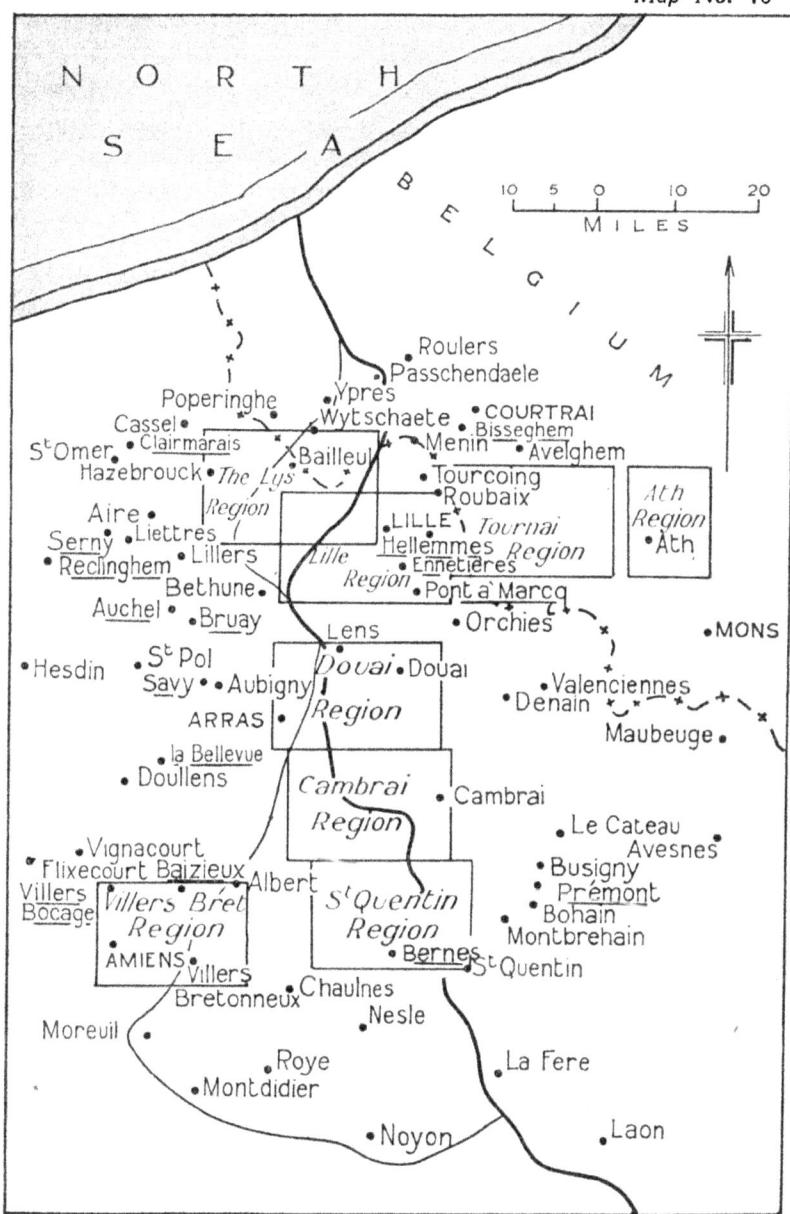

NORTH-EASTERN FRANCE, SHOWING THE AREAS ILLUSTRATED BY OTHER MAPS IN THIS VOLUME. THE DARK LINE MARKED SHOWS THE FRONT HELD BY THE ALLIES IN OCTOBER, 1917, AT THE BEGINNING OF THE A.F.C. OPERATIONS IN FRANCE. THE THIN LINE SHOWS THE LIMITS OF THE GERMAN ADVANCE IN 1918. THE NAMES OF AERODROMES OCCUPIED AT ANY TIME BY AUSTRALIAN SQUADRONS ARE UNDERLINED

Map No. 11

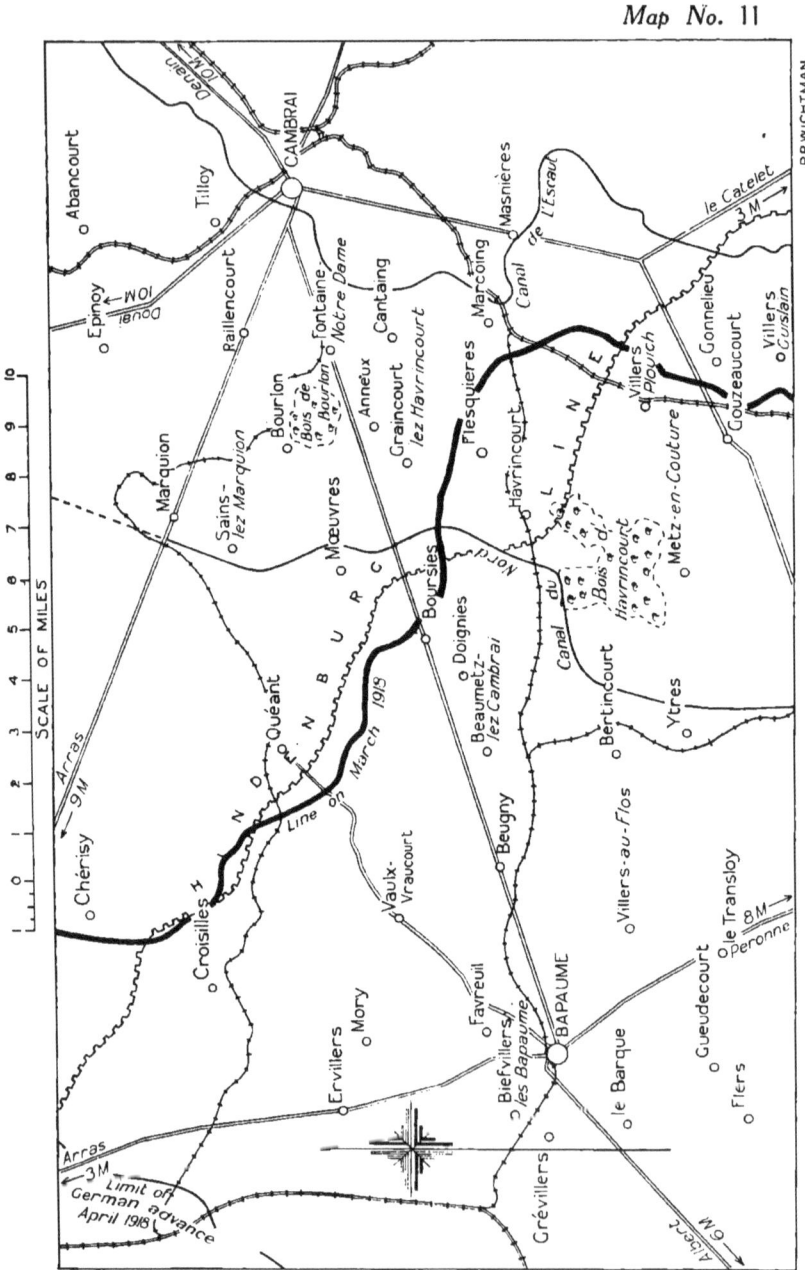

Cambrai Region, showing area of operations of No. 2 Australian Squadron in November and December, 1917, and of No. 2 and No. 4 Australian Squadrons in March, 1918, during the German offensive

Map No. 12

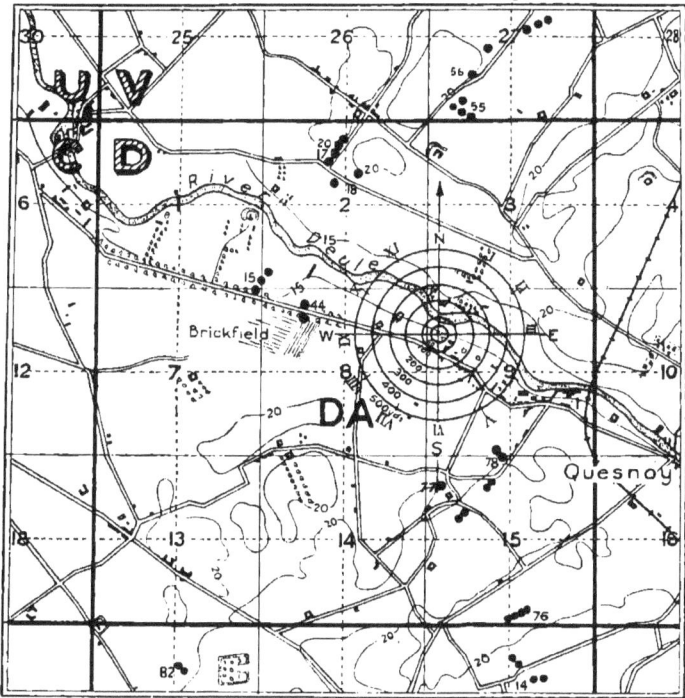

SECTION OF A TYPICAL ARTILLERY MAP, SHOWING METHOD OF RANGING BY REFERENCE TO "CLOCK-FACE." THIS SECTION SHOWS AN AREA IN REGION NORTH-WEST OF LILLE.

● ● ● ENEMY BATTERY POSITIONS

The clock-face diagram is placed, from actual example in the field, with its centre at an enemy battery position. The whole map illustrates the British Army system of placing—or "pin-pointing"—by means of map-squares any position. Military maps were in contiguous sheets, divided into 1,000-yard squares. The main divisions were lettered with capital letters, A, B, C, D, &c., and represented areas measuring 6,000 yards x 6,000 yards, or in some cases for convenience 6,000 x 5,000. The full square D in this example, for instance, contained 36 squares each 1,000 x 1,000, marked from 1 to 36, beginning at the left-hand top corner and ending at the right-hand bottom corner. These 1,000-yard squares, again, were divided into four 500-yard squares, labelled in the same sequence a, b, c, and d. To take an example, the small square farm south-west of the Brickfield is in D7d. To "pin-point" this farm precisely, the method was to imagine each side of the small d square to be divided into ten equal sections. The further calculation by means of these was first horizontally, then vertically—*i.e.*, first east, then north from the left-hand bottom corner of each small square. Thus the farm in the example would be at D7d29. Where it was required to define the point even more precisely these tooth-comb scales were measured to one decimal place: thus the centre of the farm would be set down as D7d2095.

The larger square DA, one quarter of the map square D, was a more general subdivision used by artillery only. One or more British batteries might be allotted the task of dealing with all hostile movement, or guns, in the square DA, that is, in a zone measuring 3,000 yards x 3,000. The targets (enemy batteries) in every such square were numbered as soon as located. Artillery fire could then be called down upon any of them by simply mentioning the letters of the square and the number of the target—*e.g.*, DA76 (which in the map here shown was an enemy battery in the S.E. corner of square DA).

Map No. 13

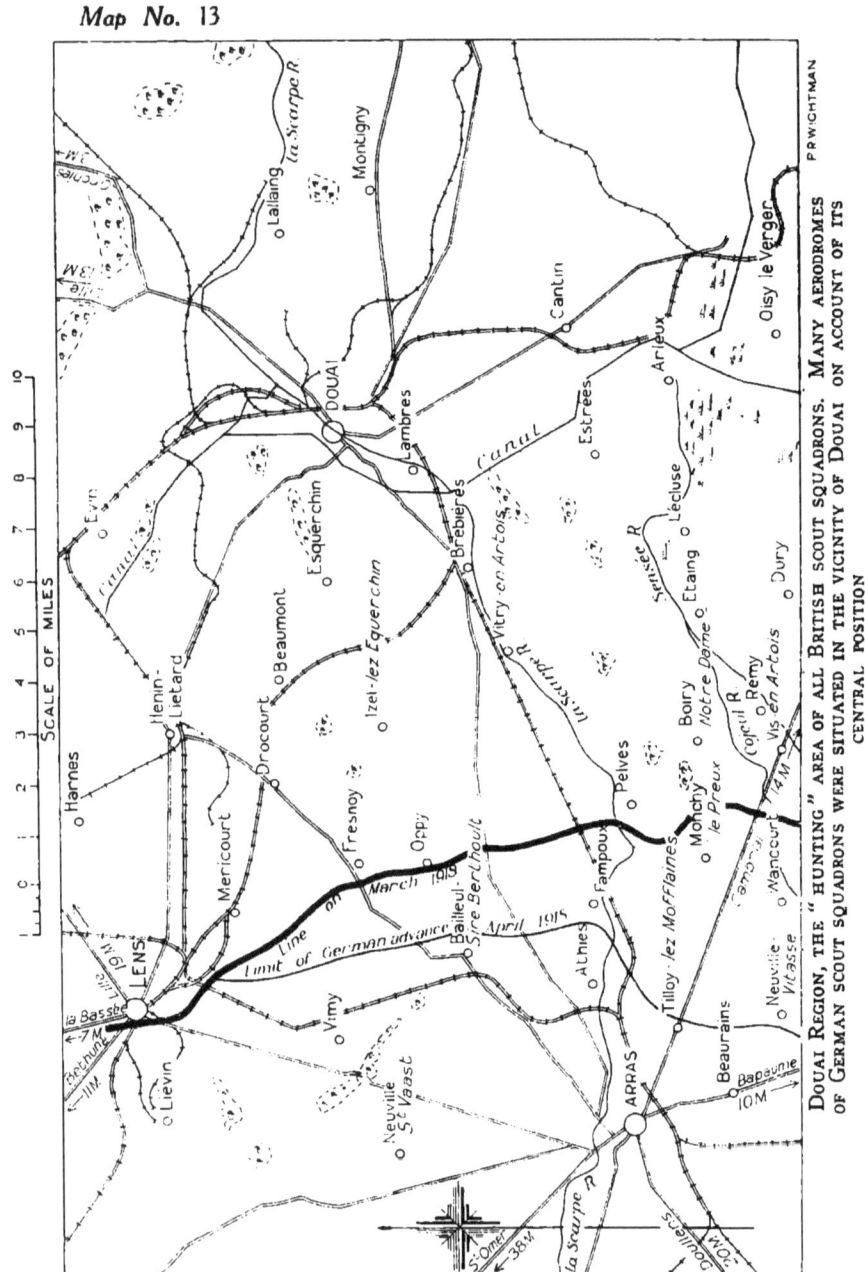

Douai Region, the "hunting" area of all British scout squadrons. Many aerodromes of German scout squadrons were situated in the vicinity of Douai on account of its central position

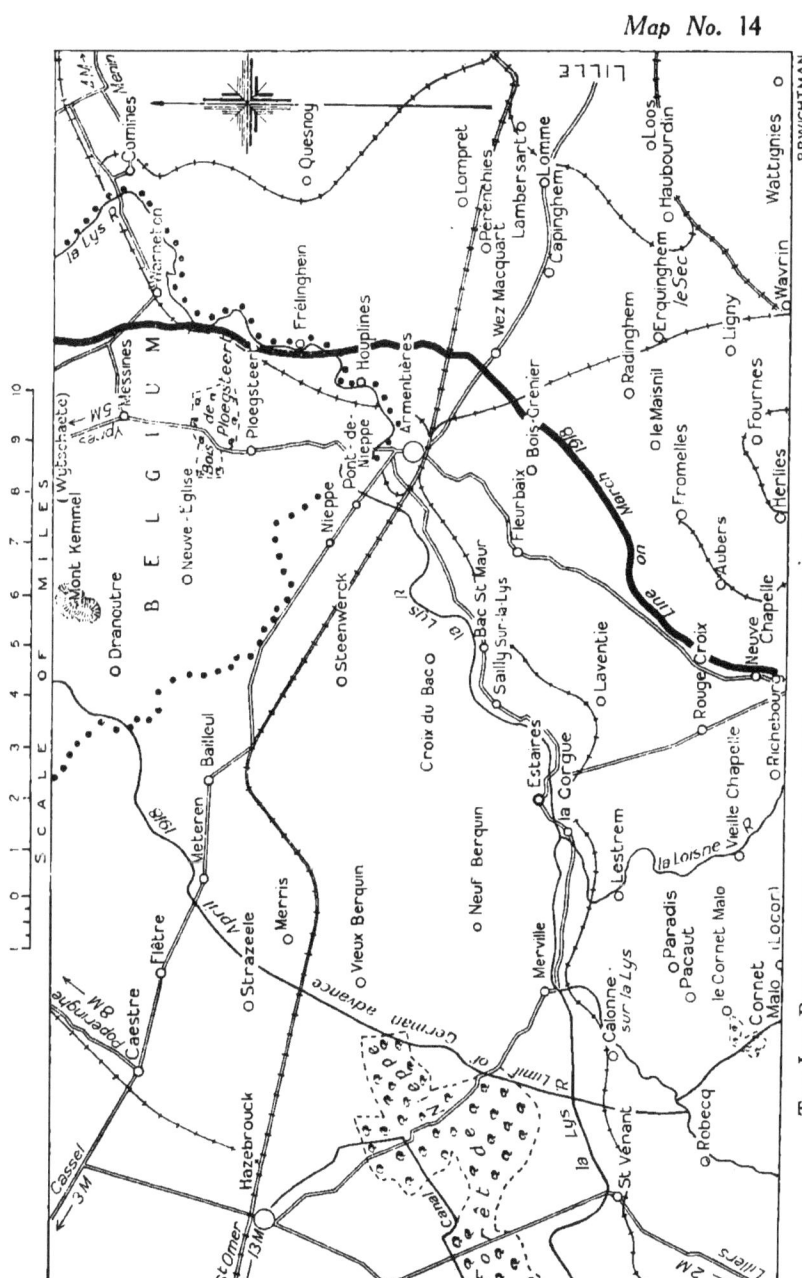

Map No. 14

The Lys Region, showing area of operations of No. 3 Australian Squadron, December, 1917–April, 1918, and of No. 2 and No. 4 Australian Squadrons, May–September, 1918

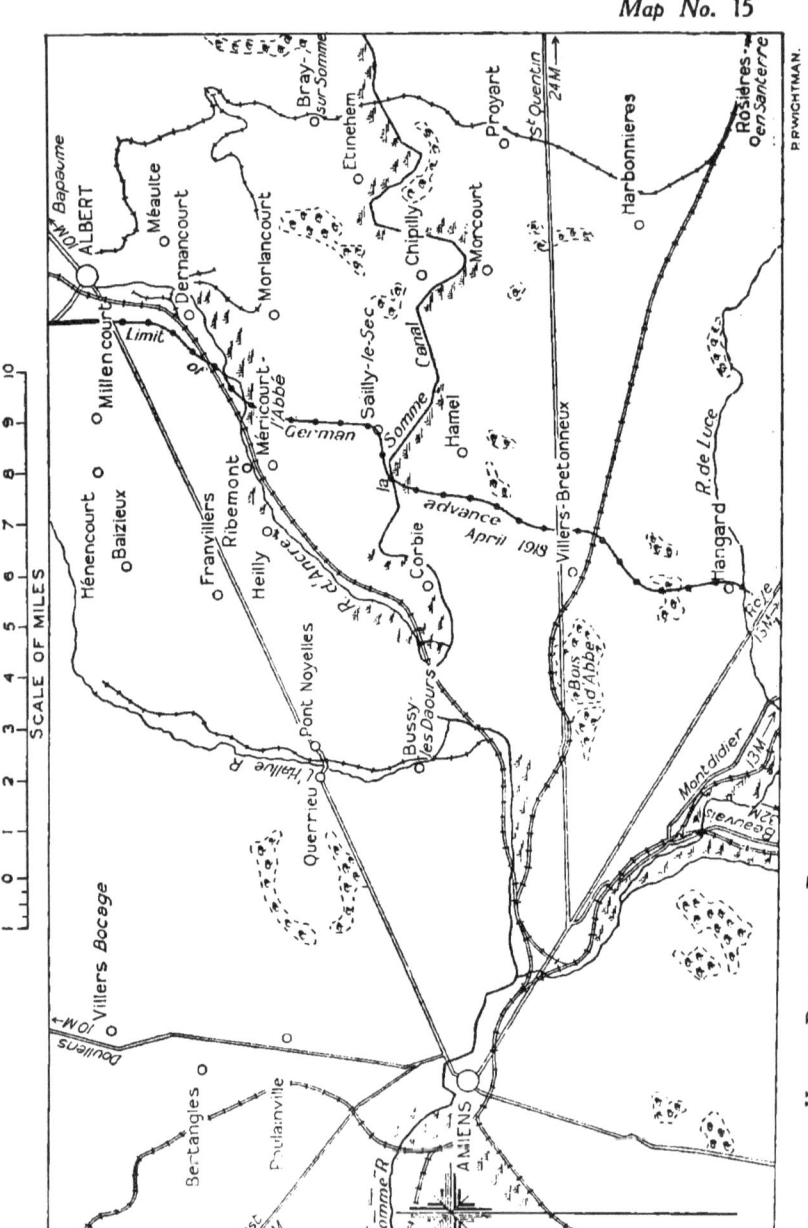

Map No. 15

VILLERS-BRETONNEUX REGION, SHOWING AREA OF OPERATIONS OF No. 3 AUSTRALIAN SQUADRON, APRIL-AUGUST, 1918

Map No. 16

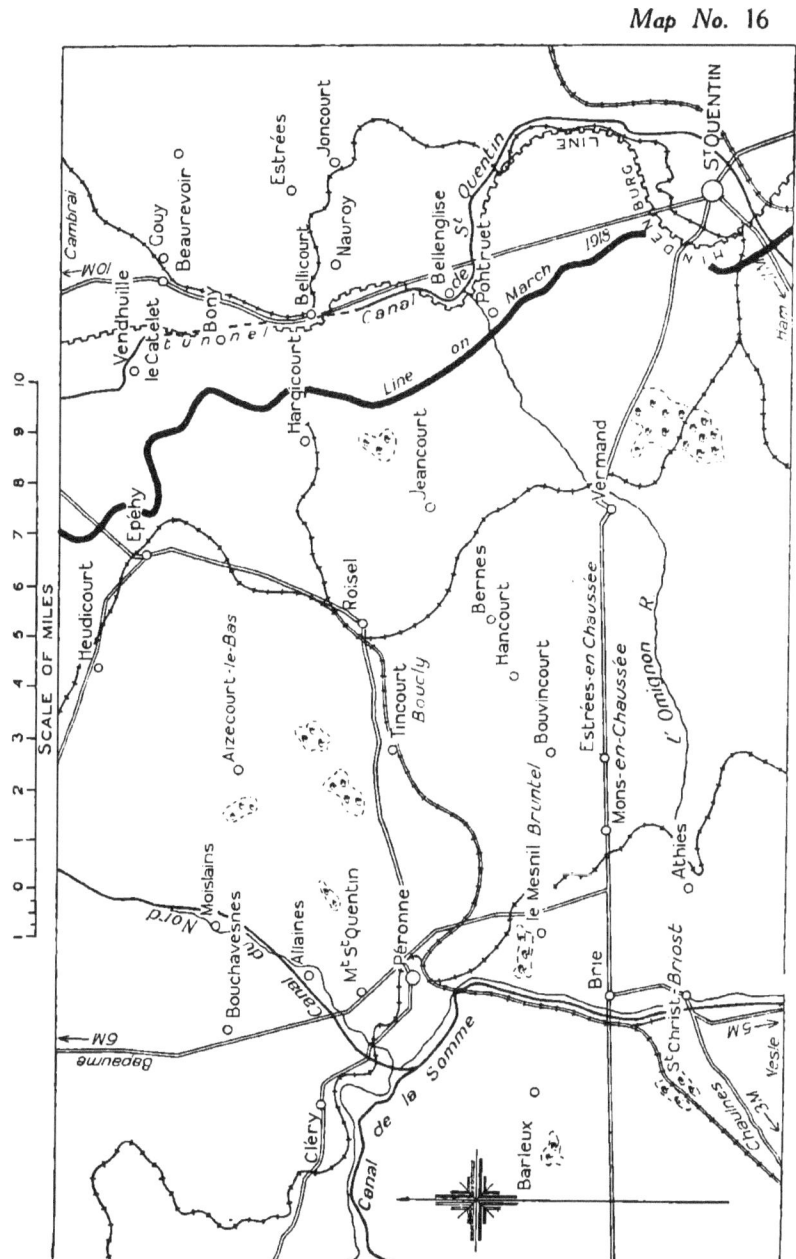

St. Quentin Region, showing area of operations of No. 3 Australian Squadron, September and October, 1918

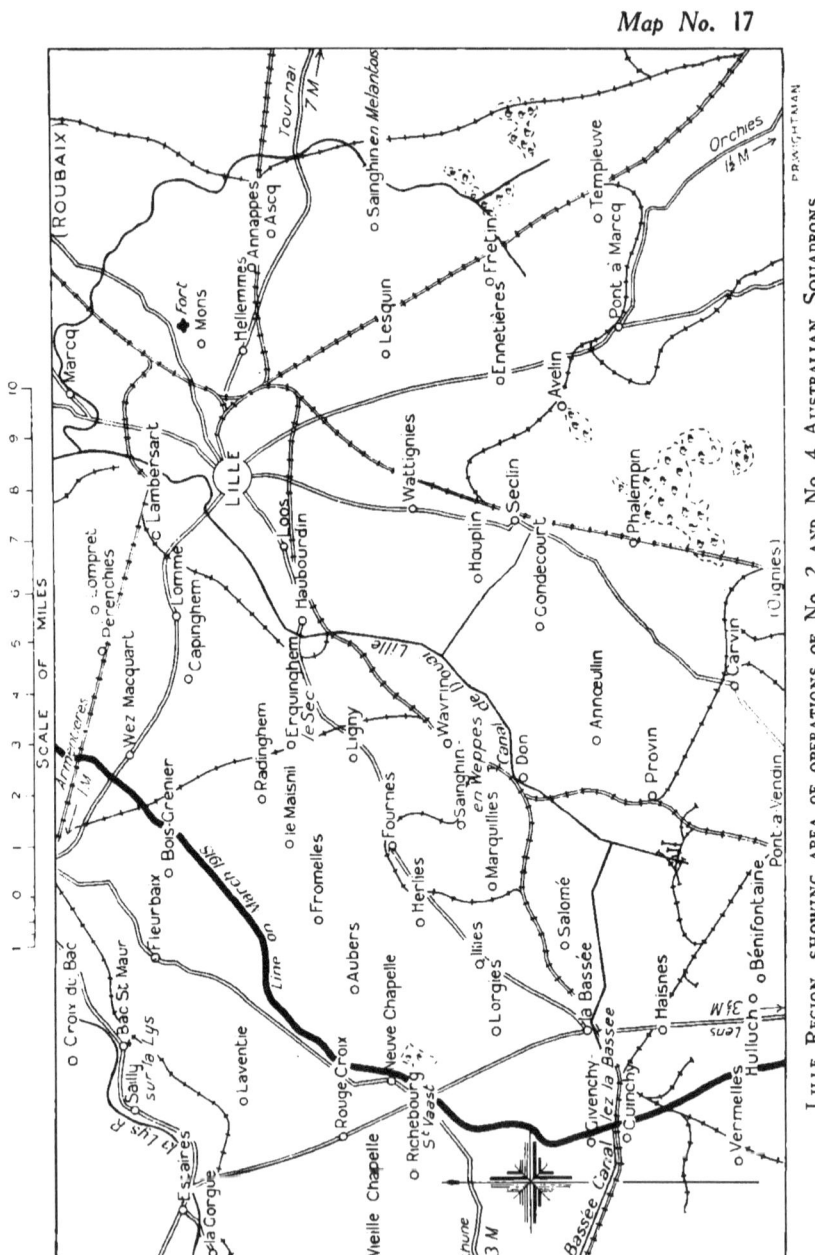

Lille Region, showing area of operations of No. 2 and No. 4 Australian Squadrons, May–October, 1918

Map No. 18

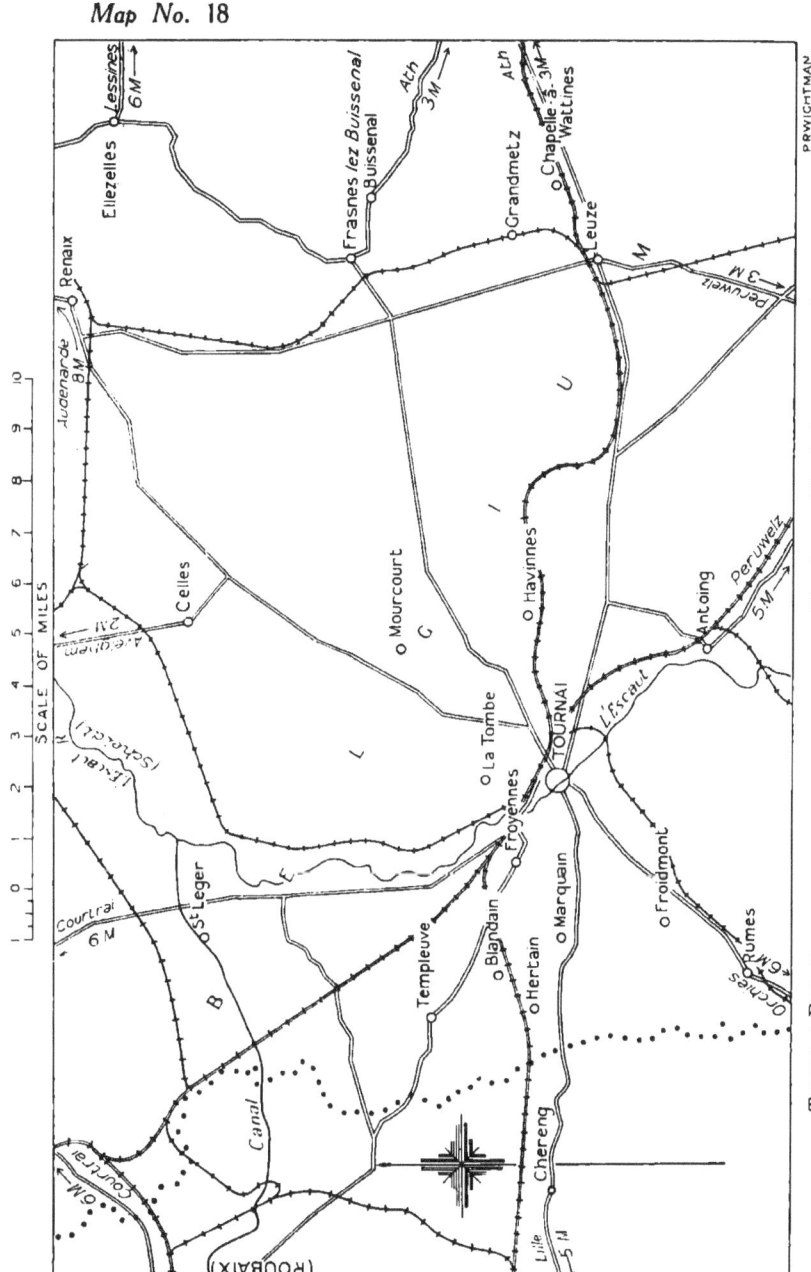

Tournai Region, showing area of operations of No. 2 and No. 4 Australian Squadrons, October and November, 1918

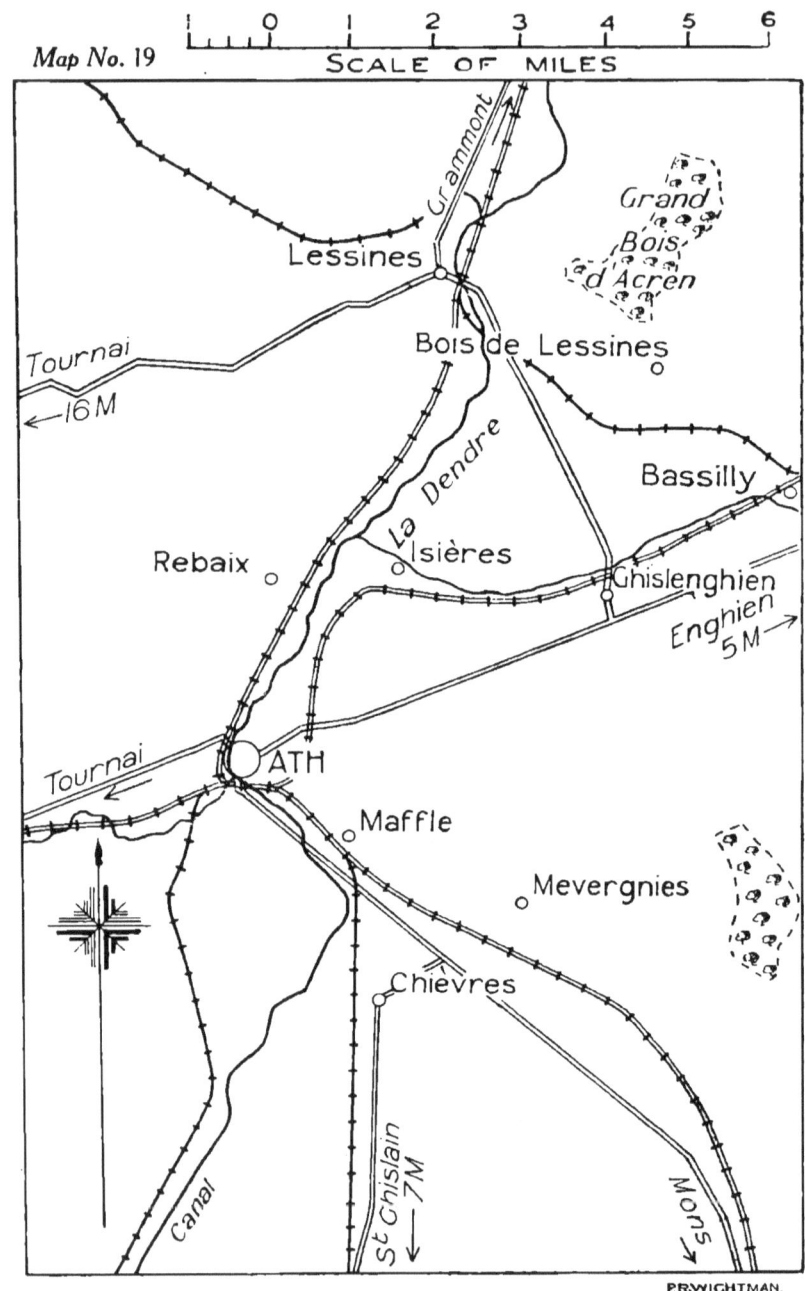

Ath Region, showing area of operations of No. 2 and No. 4 Australian Squadrons, October and November, 1918

THE
ROYAL AUSTRALIAN NAVY
1914-1918

VOLUME IX

LIST OF MAPS

1. The Western Pacific
2. South Pacific Ocean, showing the movements of Admiral von Spee's squadron from 15 July to 8 December 1914
3. Nauru Island
4. Blanche Bay (New Britain) and environs
5. The district around Herbertshöhe
6. The advance towards Bitapaka, showing enemy dispositions at 9 a.m., 11 September 1914
7. The mainland of German New Guinea
8. Movements of the First Convoy round the Australian coast
9. Position of the Australian and New Zealand transports in King George's Sound, October 1914
10. Sailing order of the First Convoy
11. Track of the *Emden* from 1 August to 9 November 1914
12. The *Emden's* raid on Penang
13. The *Sydney-Emden* action
14. The Malay Archipelago
15. Movements of the *AE 2* in the Dardanelles and Sea of Marmora
16. The West Indies
17. The movements of H.M.A.S. *Australia* in the North Sea during 1915
18. The movements of H.M.A.S. *Australia* during 1916
19. The movements of H.M.A.S. *Australia* during 1917
20. The movements of H.M.A.S. *Australia* during 1918
21. The track of H.M.A.S. *Sydney* during her fight with *L 43*, 4 May 1917
22. German submarine campaign—chart showing the danger zones proclaimed by the German Government on 31 January 1917
23. Tracks of the Australian destroyer flotilla on its way to the Mediterranean
24. The Adriatic Sea and adjacent waters, showing the area in which the Australian destroyer flotilla worked in 1917-18
25. Cruise of the German raider *Wolf*
26. Australia, showing coastal precautions
27. Australia and the islands, showing wireless stations working in 1914
28. The Cocos Group and Direction Island

MAP

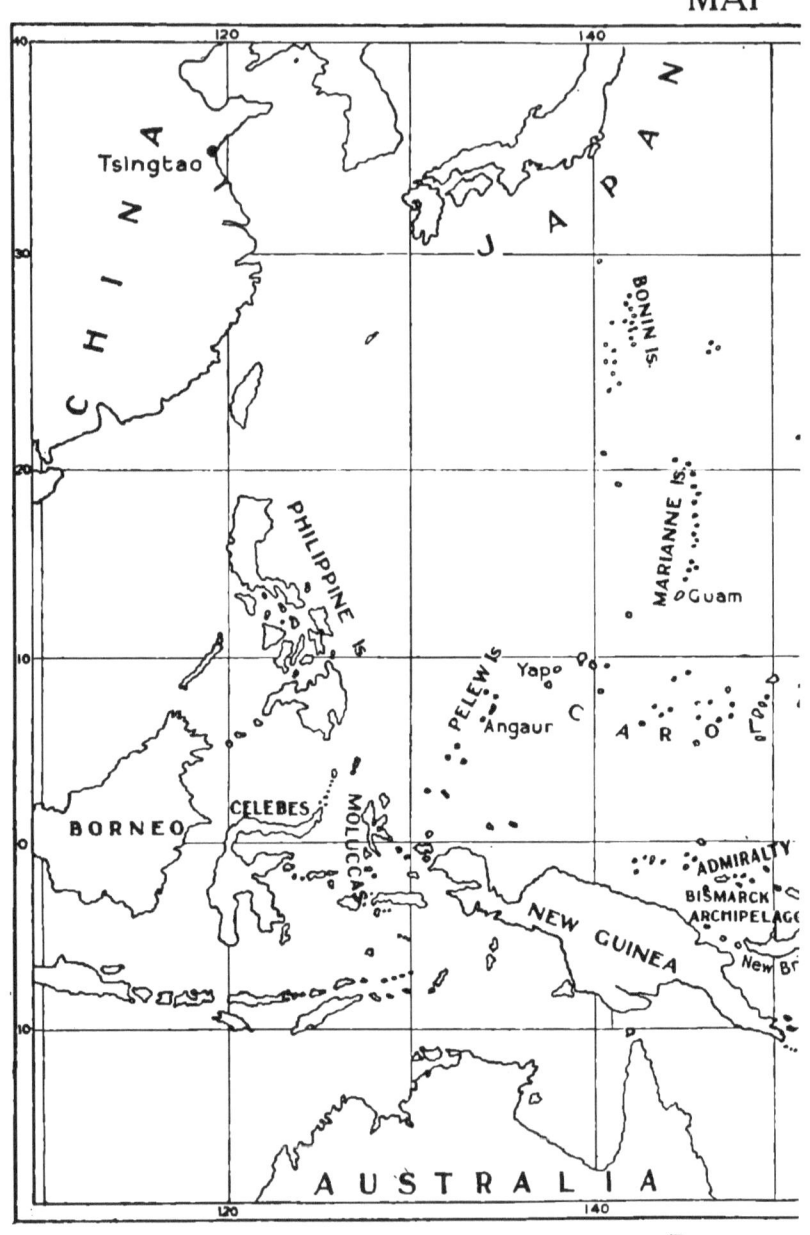

THE WESTERN

No. 1

Map No. 2

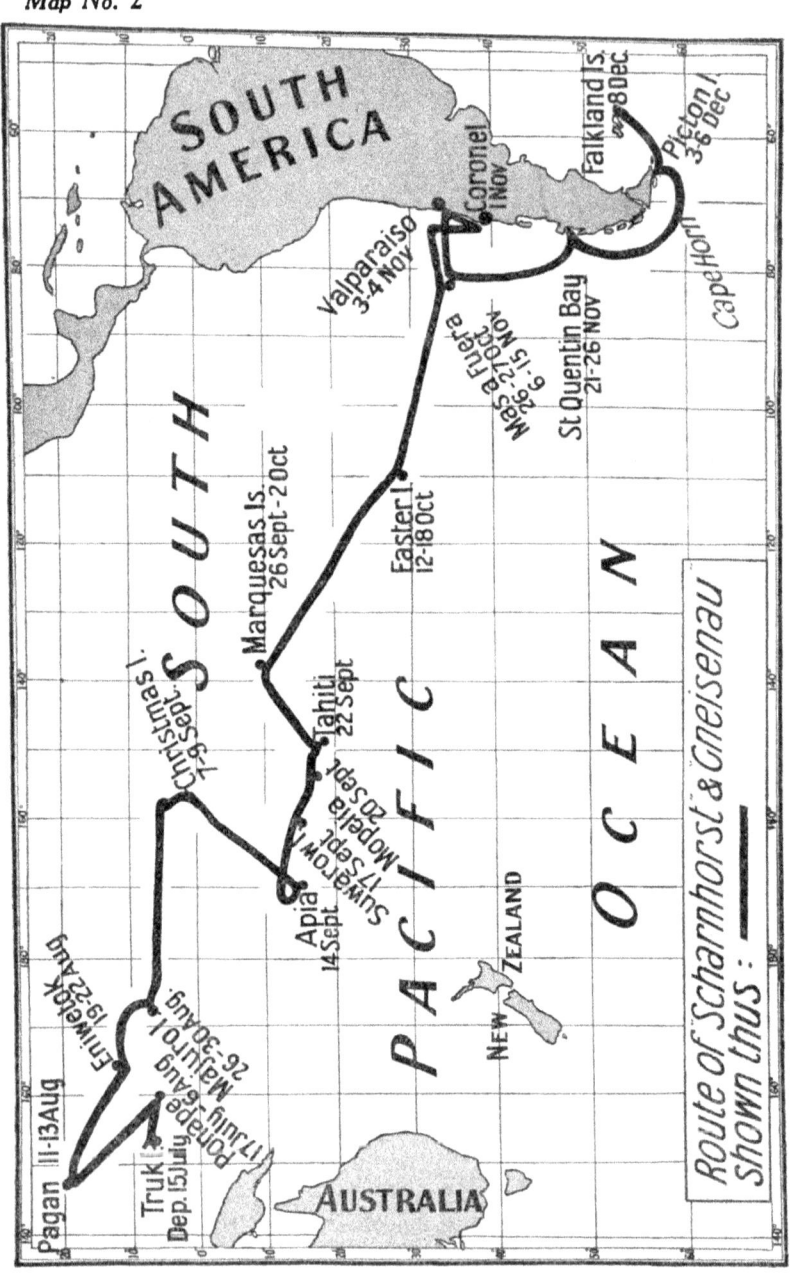

South Pacific Ocean, showing the movements of Admiral von Spee's Squadron from the 15th of July to the 8th of December, 1914

Map No. 3

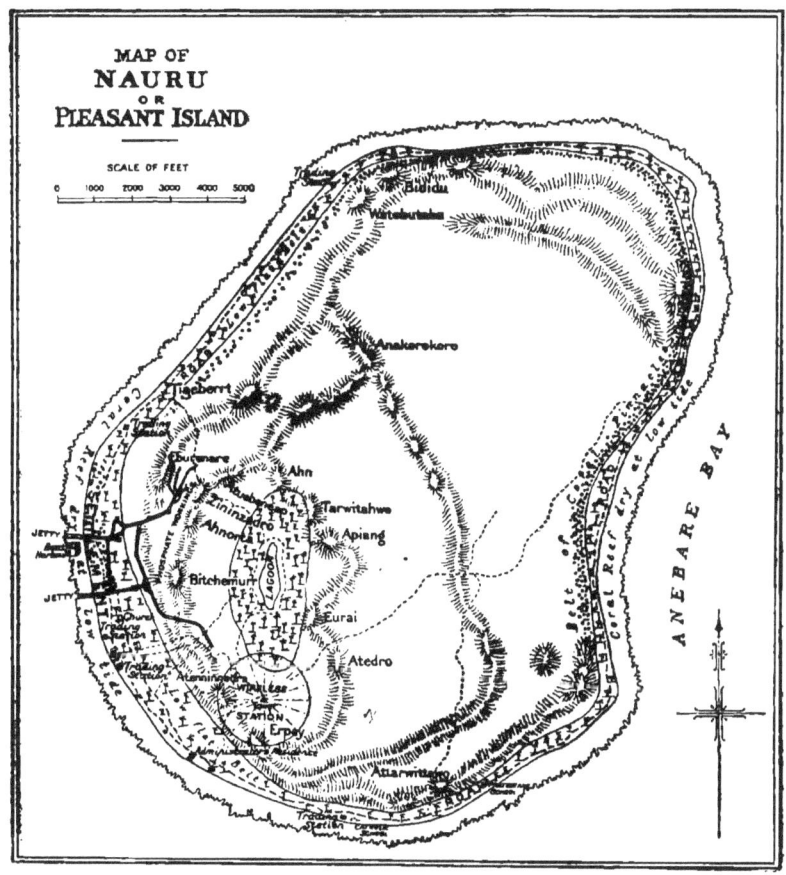

NAURU ISLAND

By courtesy of The British Phosphate Commission.

Map No. 4

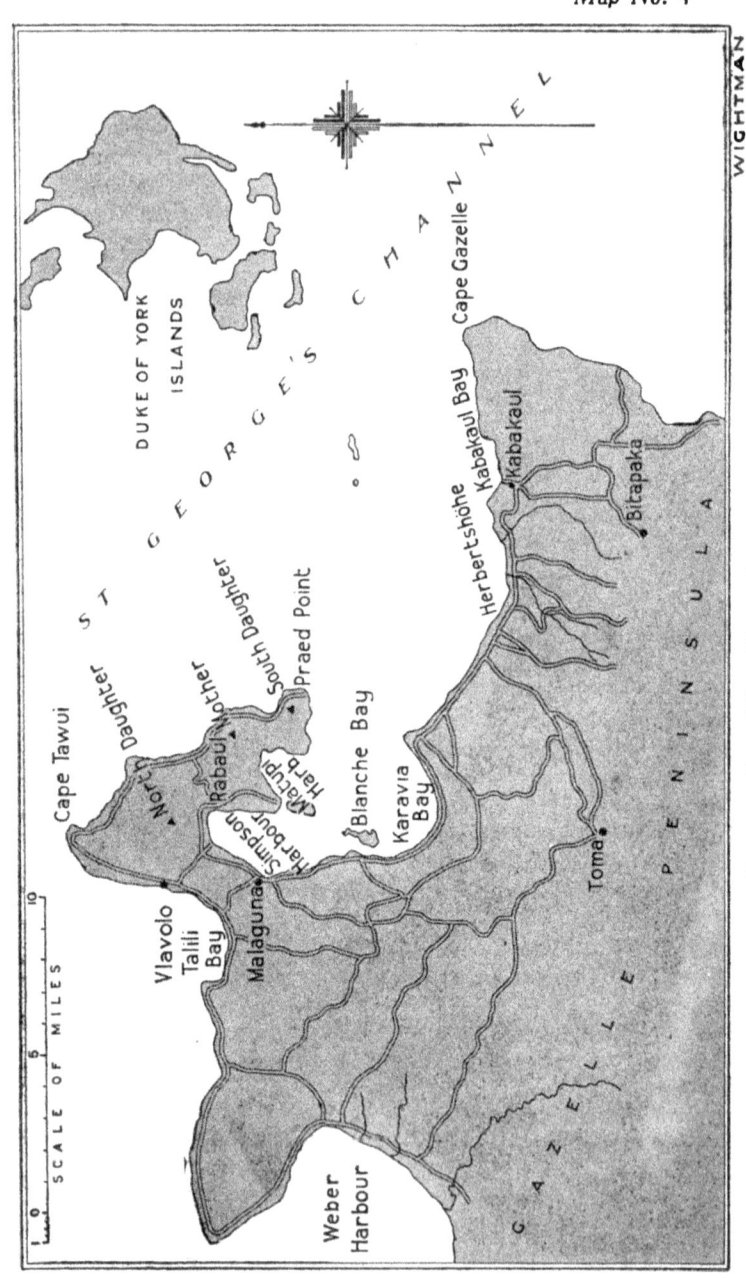

BLANCHE BAY (NEW BRITAIN) AND ENVIRONS

Map No. 5

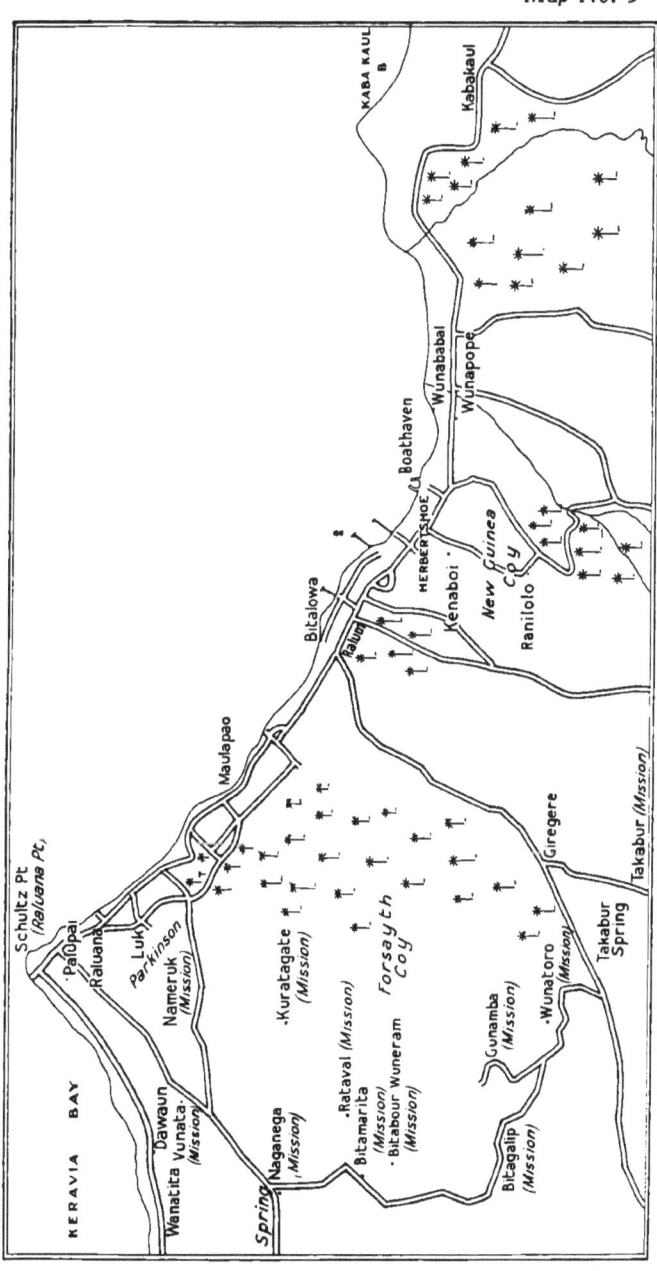

THE DISTRICT AROUND HERBERTSHÖHE

Copied from the only map available at the time of the attack on Bitapaka. The spelling is that of the original.

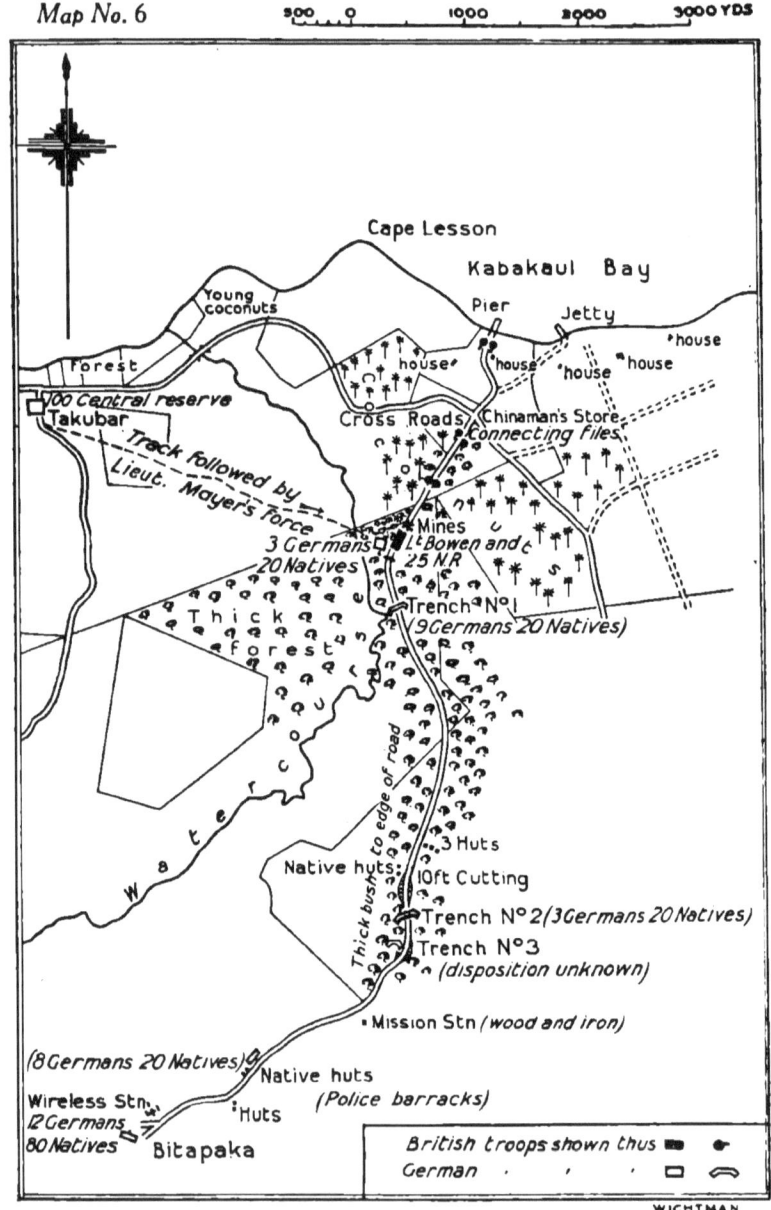

THE ADVANCE TOWARDS BITAPAKA, SHOWING ENEMY DISPOSITIONS AT
9 A.M. ON THE 11TH OF SEPTEMBER, 1914

Map No. 7

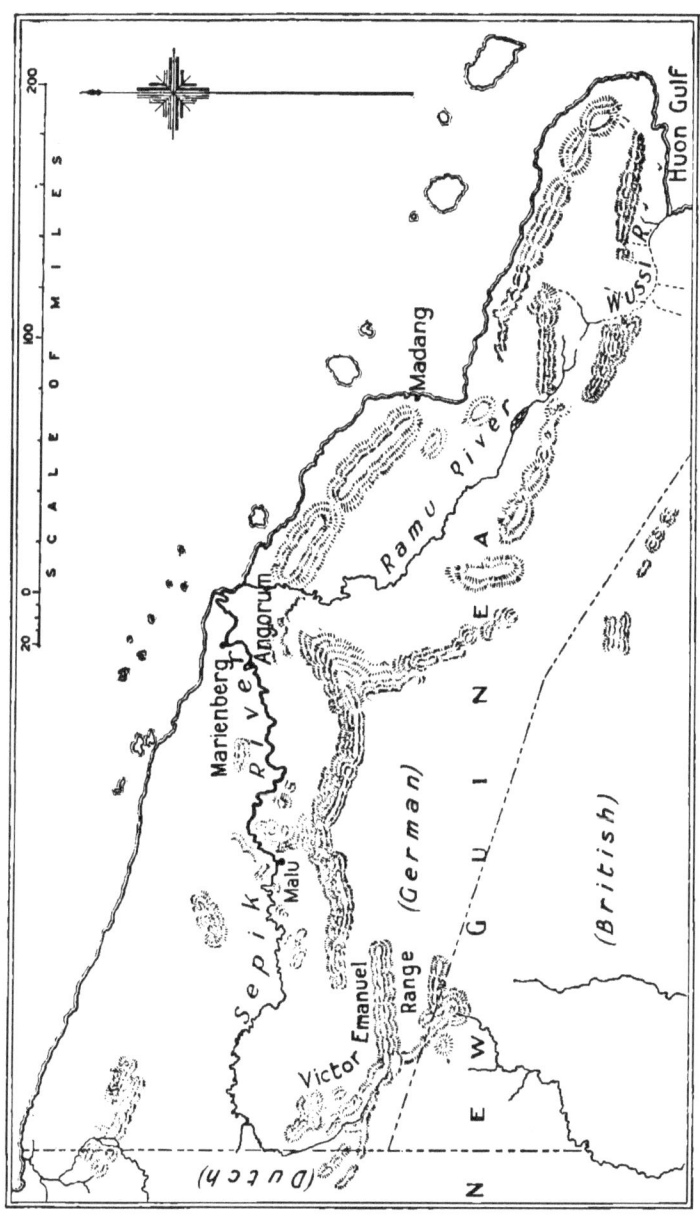

THE MAINLAND OF GERMAN NEW GUINEA

Map No. 8

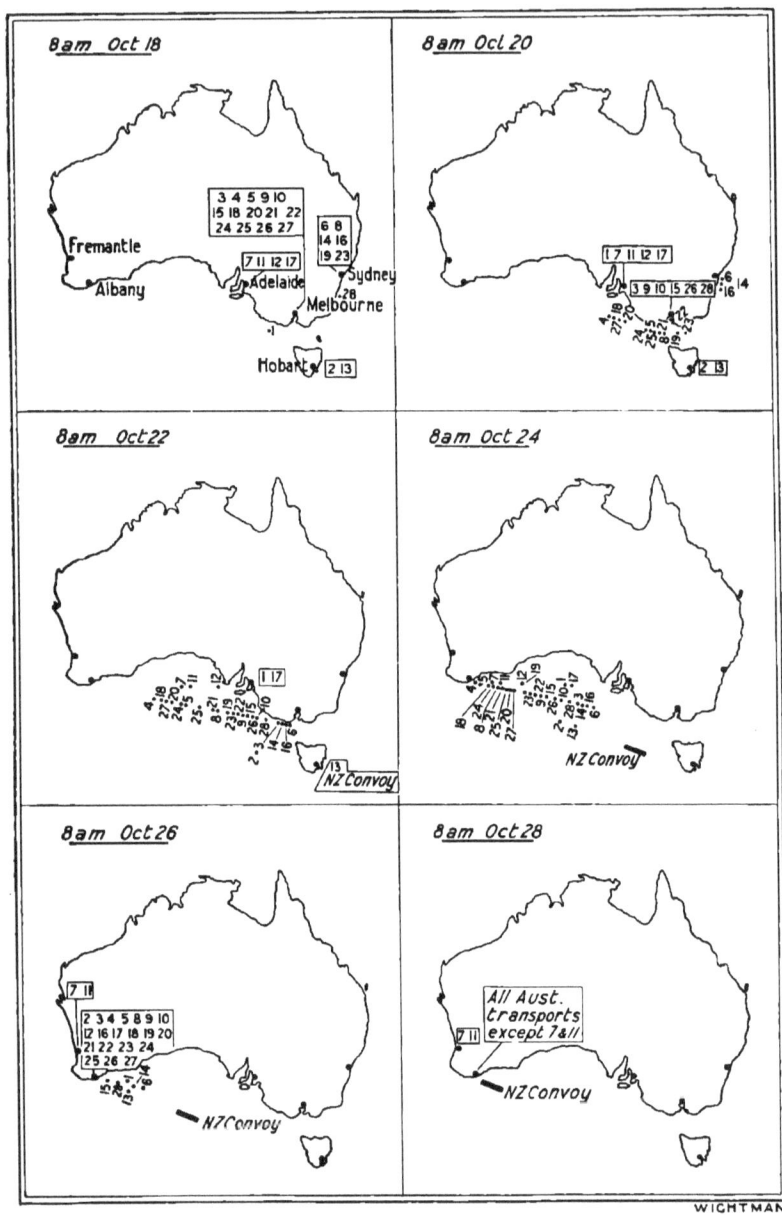

MOVEMENTS OF THE FIRST CONVOY ROUND THE AUSTRALIAN COAST

Map No. 9

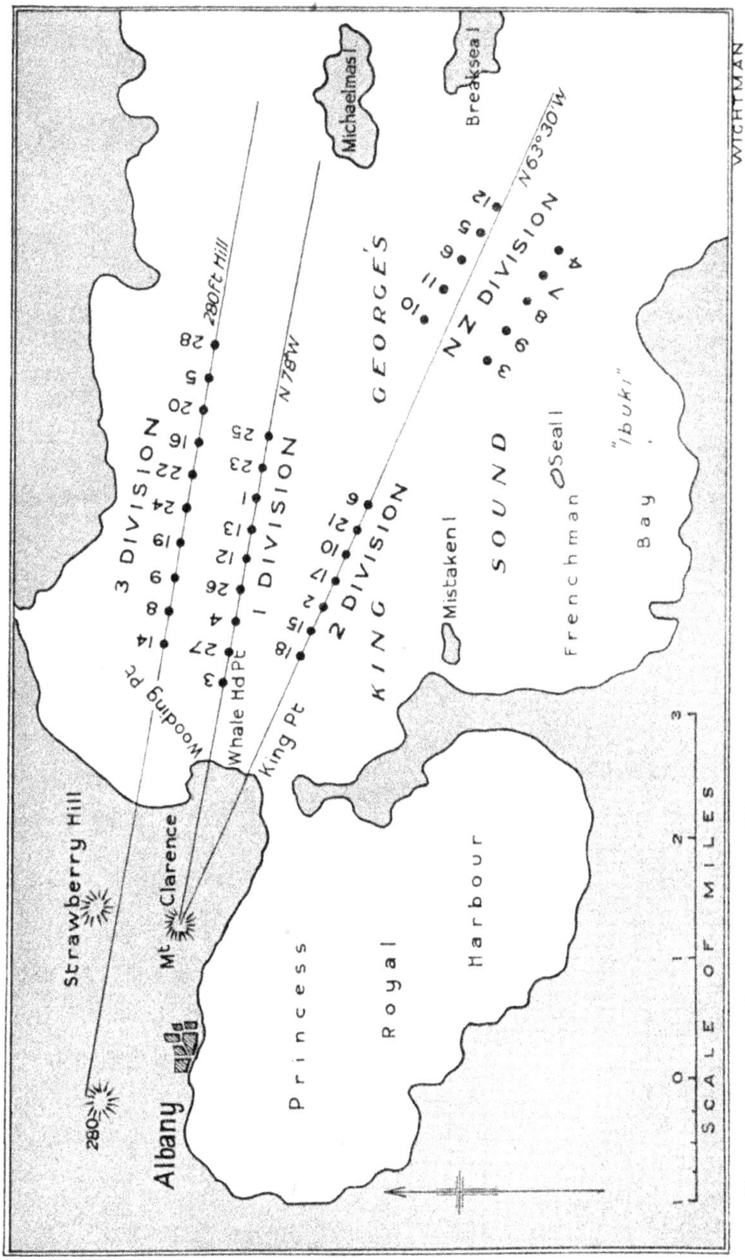

Position of the Australian and New Zealand transports in King George's Sound, October 1914

Map No. 10

```
                        • Minotaur


                      •A18  •A3   •A14
 •Sydney              •A7   •A27  •A8                    Ibuki •
                      •A11  •A4   •A9
                      •A15  •A26  •A19
                      •A2   •A12  •A24
                      •A17  •A13  •A22
                      •A10  •A1   •A16
                      •A21  •A23  •A20
                      •A6   •A25  •A5
                                  •A28
                        •NZ10 •NZ3
                        •NZ11 •NZ9
                        •NZ6  •NZ8
                        •NZ5  •NZ7
                        •NZ12 •NZ4




                        • Melbourne
```

SAILING ORDER OF THE FIRST CONVOY   WIGHTMAN

MAP

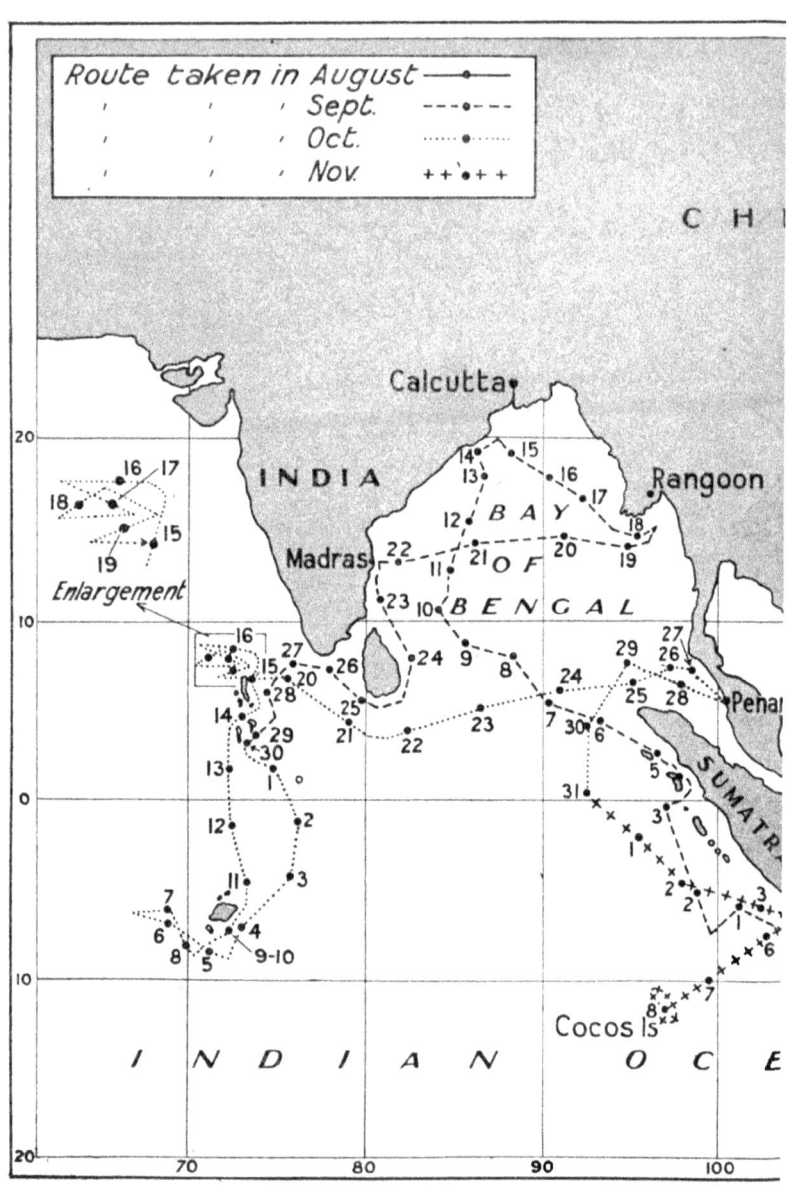

Track of the *Emden* from the 1st

No. 11

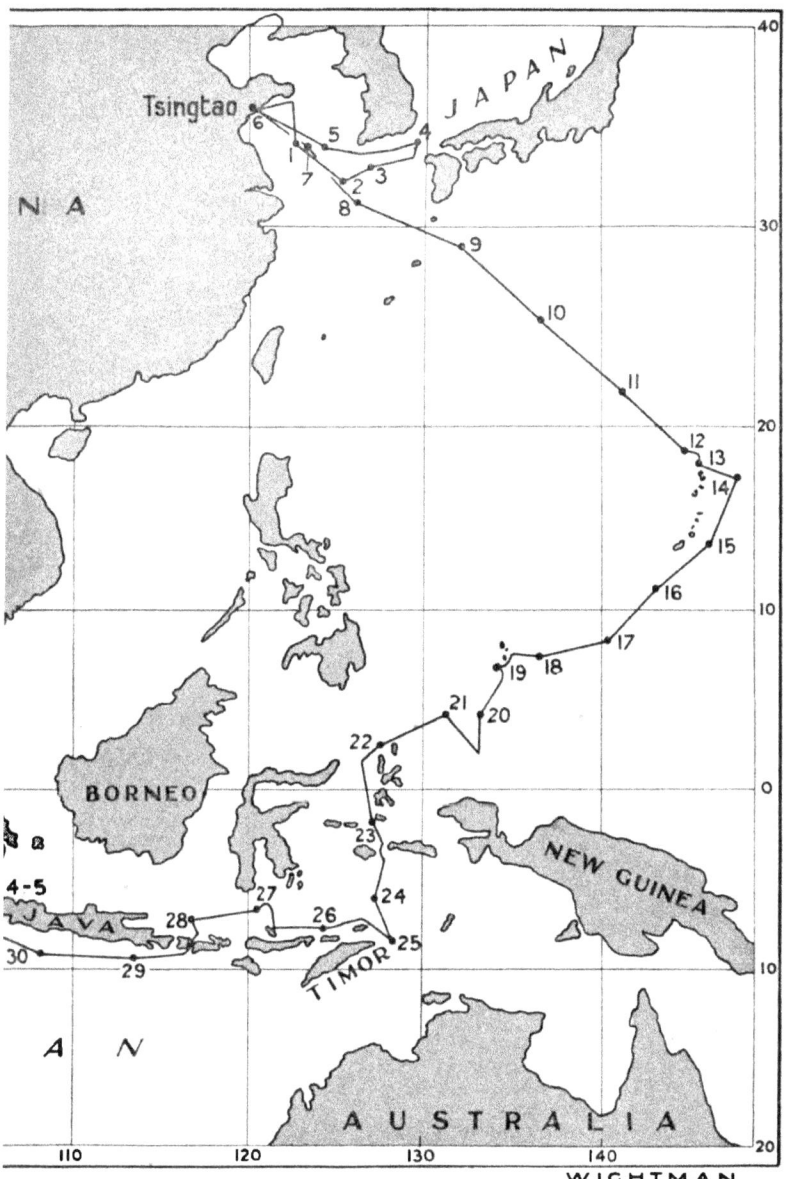

,UGUST TO THE 9TH OF NOVEMBER, 1914

Map No. 12

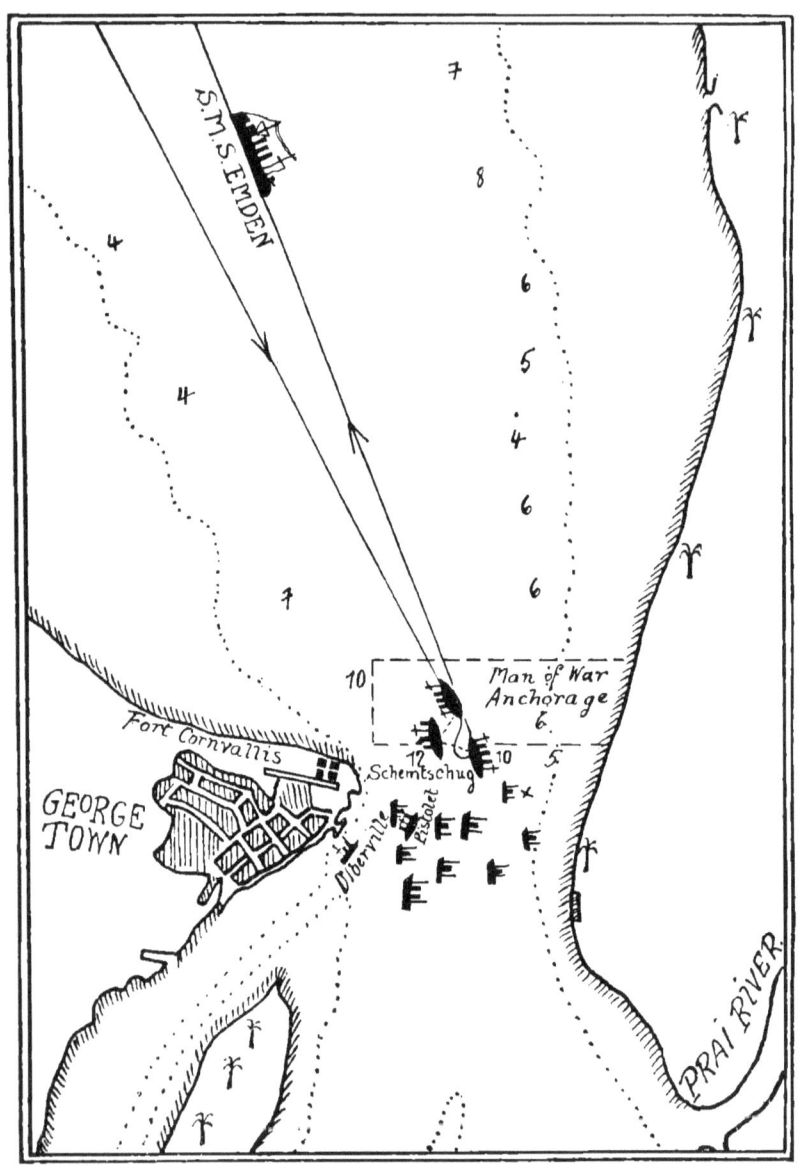

THE *Emden's* RAID ON PENANG
Copy of a sketch by an officer in the *Emden*.

Map No. 13

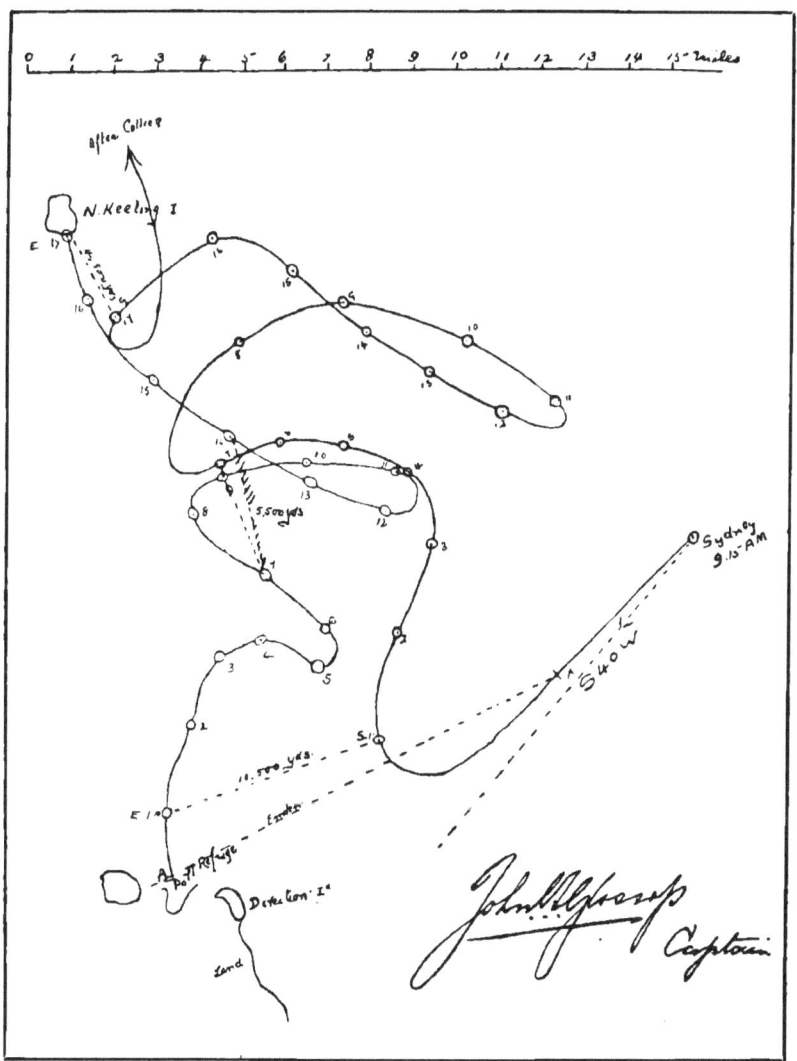

THE *Sydney-Emden* ACTION

Copy of a sketch made by Captain Glossop and Captain von Müller. (It will be observed that one of the two dotted lines, showing the bearing of the two ships from each other at position "7," has been partly erased, having been drawn in error.)

MAP

THE MALAY

The figures indicate the number of enemy vess

No. 14

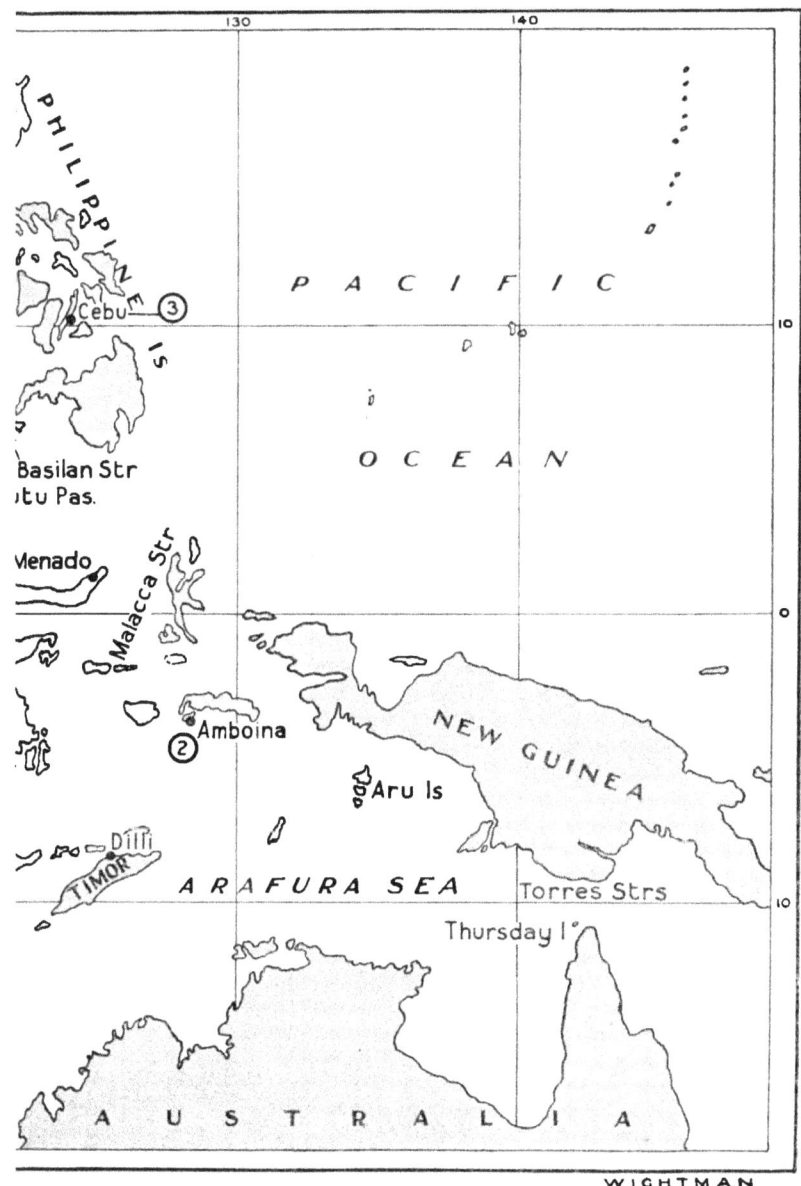

CHIPELAGO

sheltering at one time in certain neutral ports.

Map No. 15

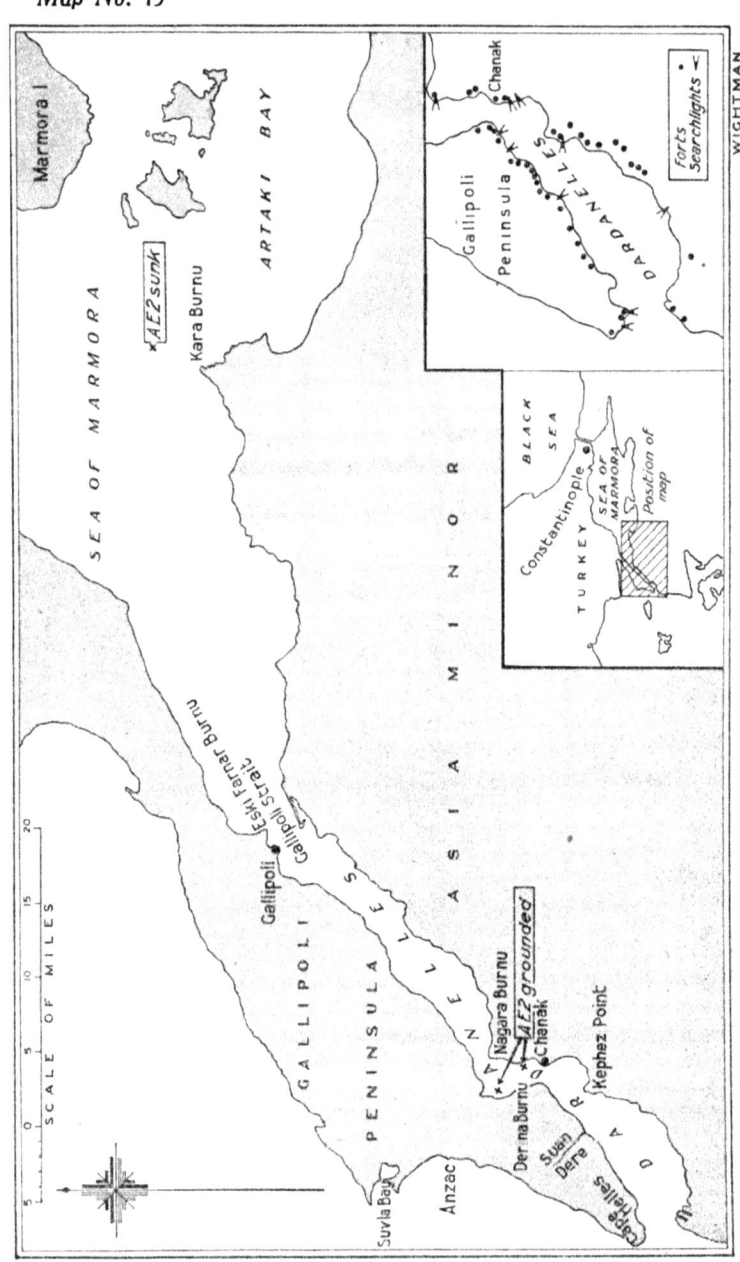

Movements of the *AE 2* in the Dardanelles and Sea of Marmora

MAP

The figures indicate the number of

No. 16

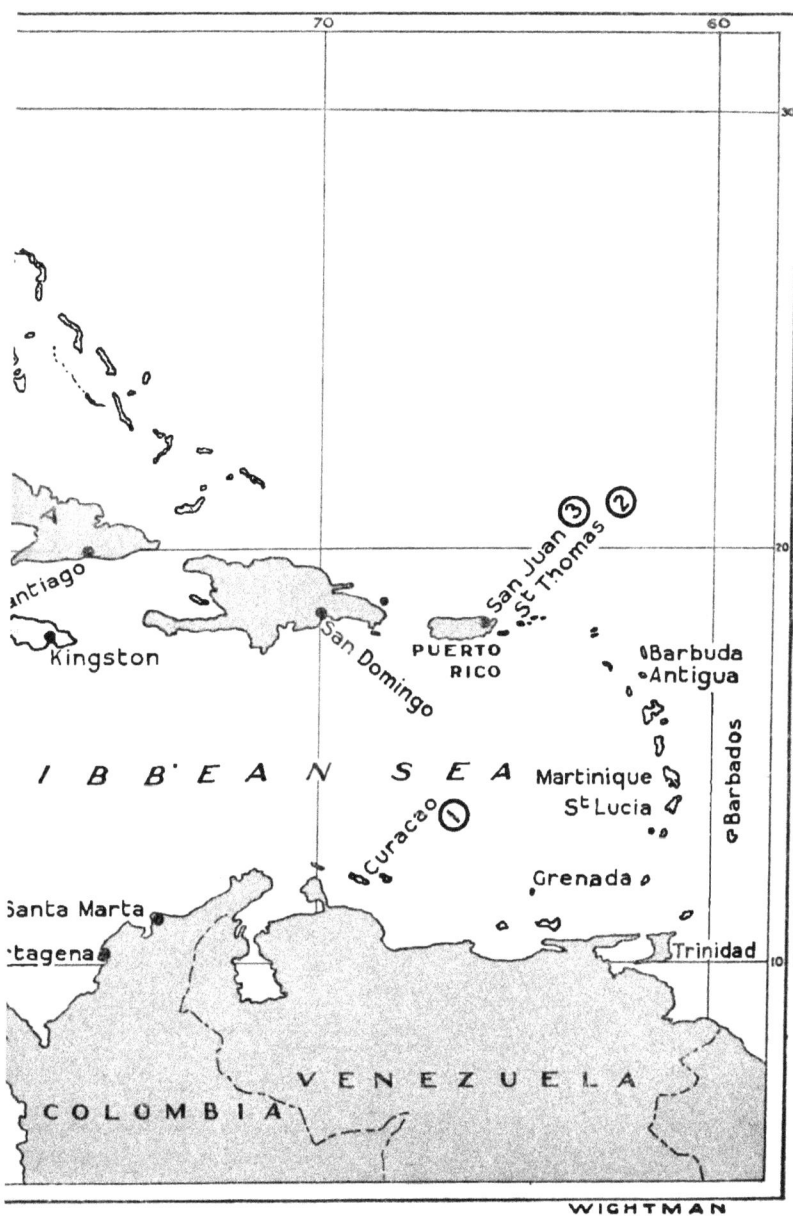

· INDIES

ny vessels sheltering in neutral ports.

Map No. 17

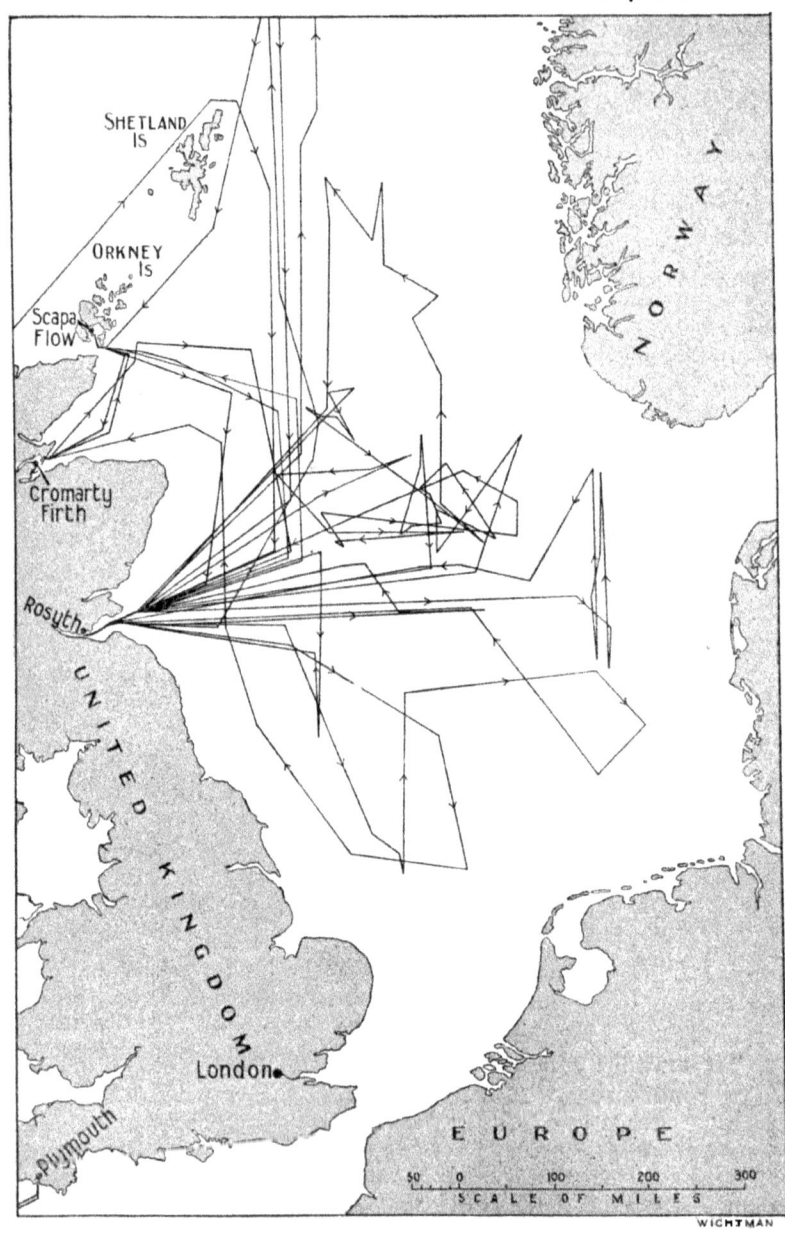

THE MOVEMENTS OF H.M.A.S. *Australia* IN THE NORTH SEA
DURING 1915

Map No. 18

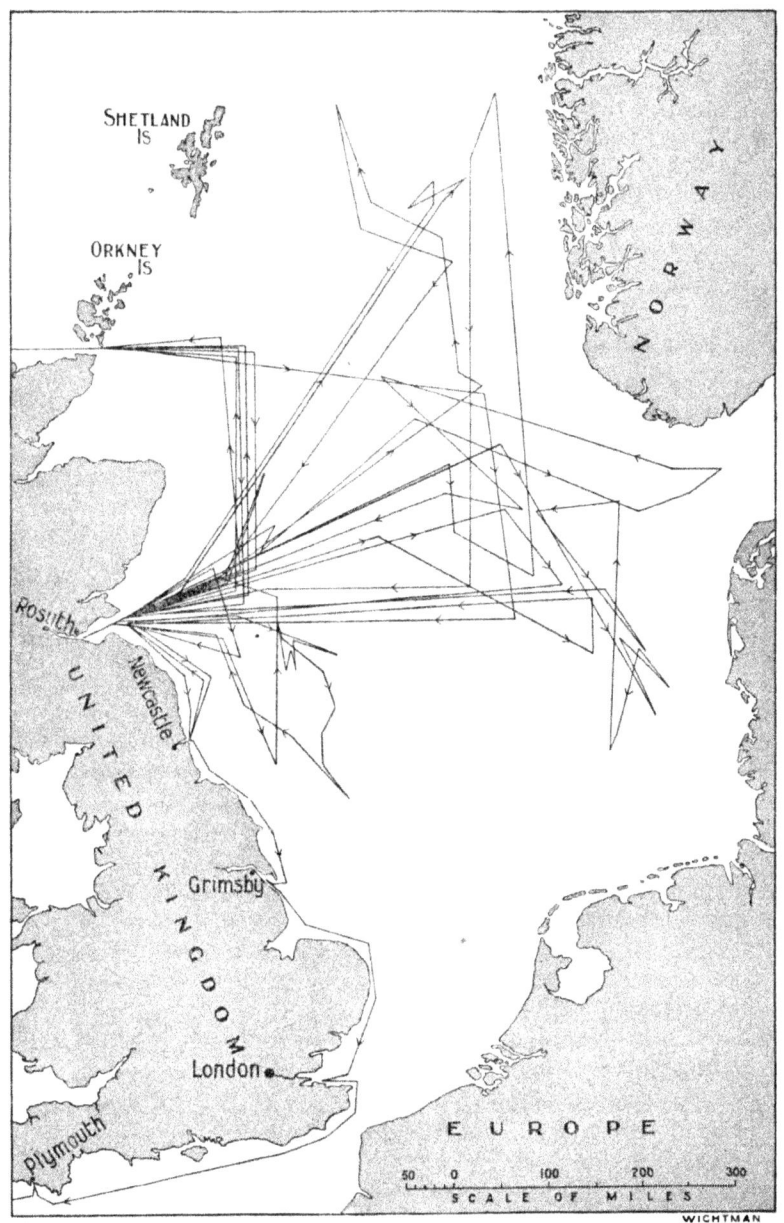

THE MOVEMENTS OF H.M.A.S. *Australia* DURING 1916

Map No. 19

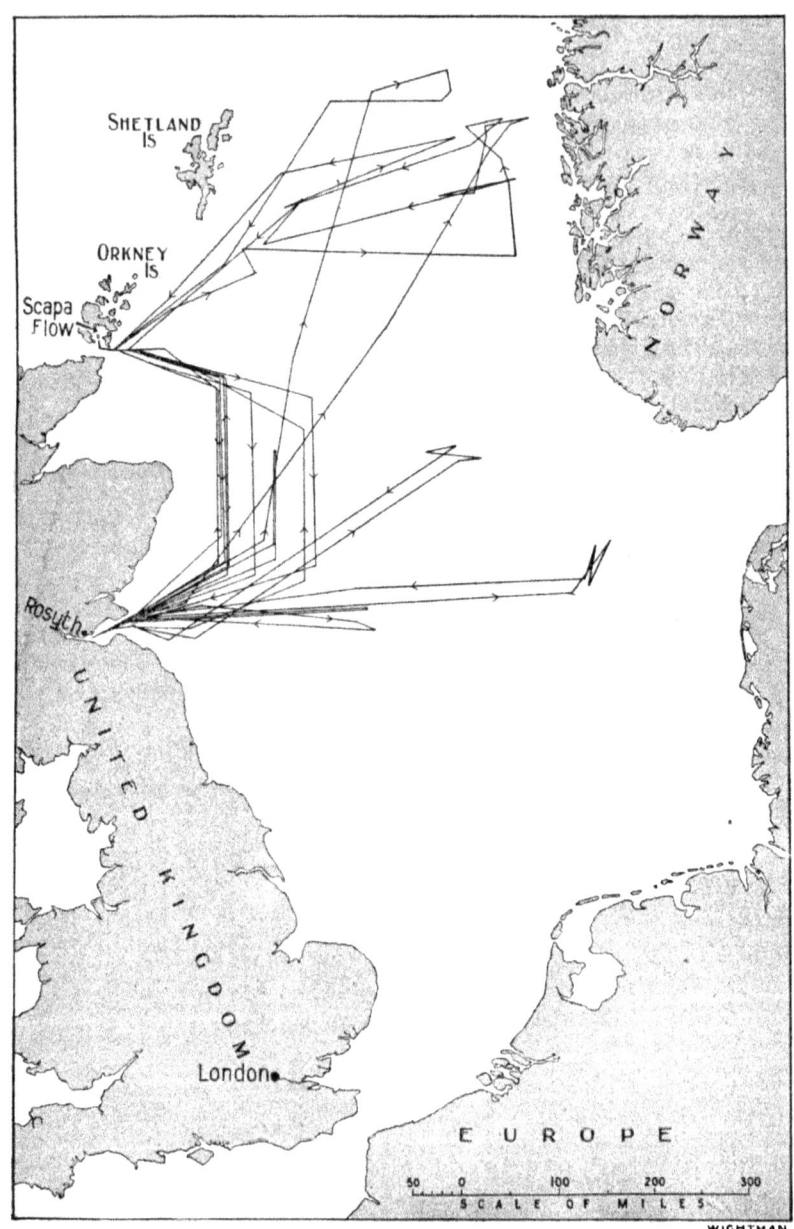

THE MOVEMENTS OF H.M.A.S. *Australia* DURING 1917

Map No. 20

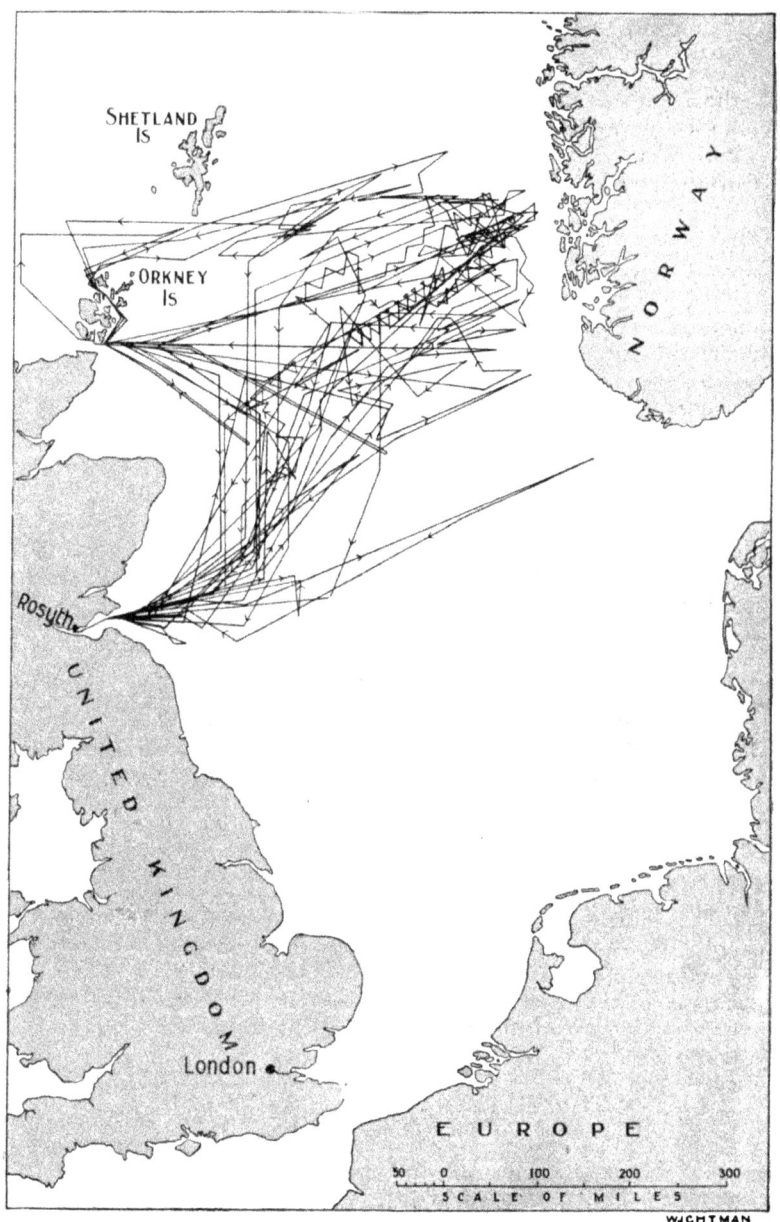

THE MOVEMENTS OF H.M.A.S. *Australia* DURING 1918

Map No. 21

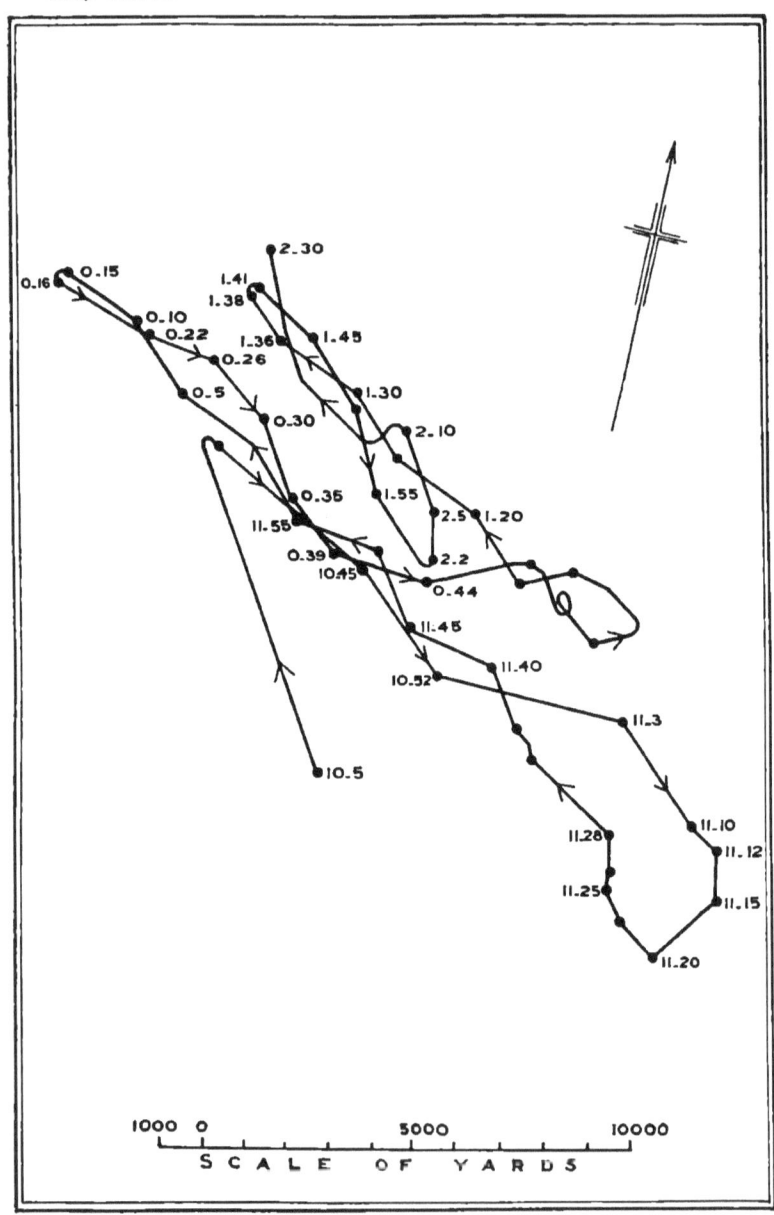

THE TRACK OF H.M.A.S. *Sydney* DURING HER FIGHT WITH *L 43* ON
THE 4TH OF MAY, 1917

The small loop in the *Sydney's* course represents its sudden alteration
when the first bombs were dropped by the airship.

Map No. 22

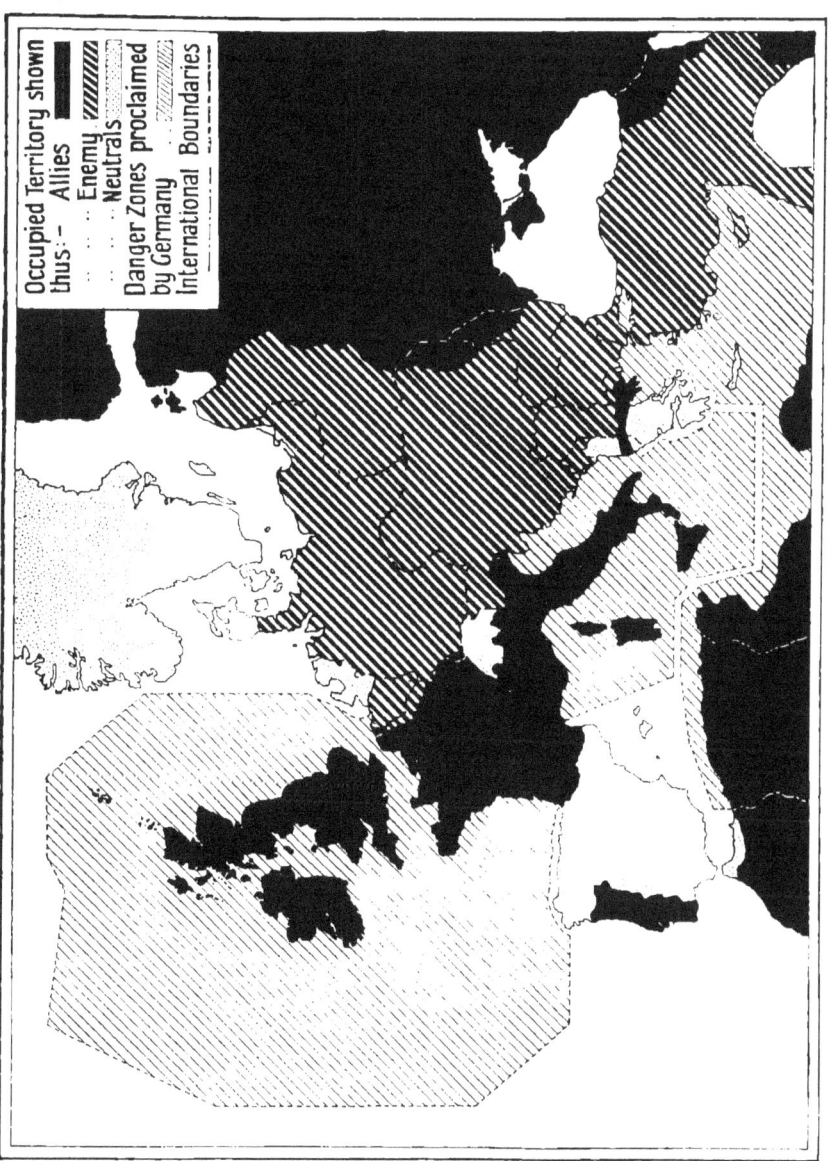

GERMAN SUBMARINE CAMPAIGN—CHART SHOWING THE DANGER ZONES PROCLAIMED BY THE GERMAN GOVERNMENT ON THE 31ST OF JANUARY, 1917

Map No. 23

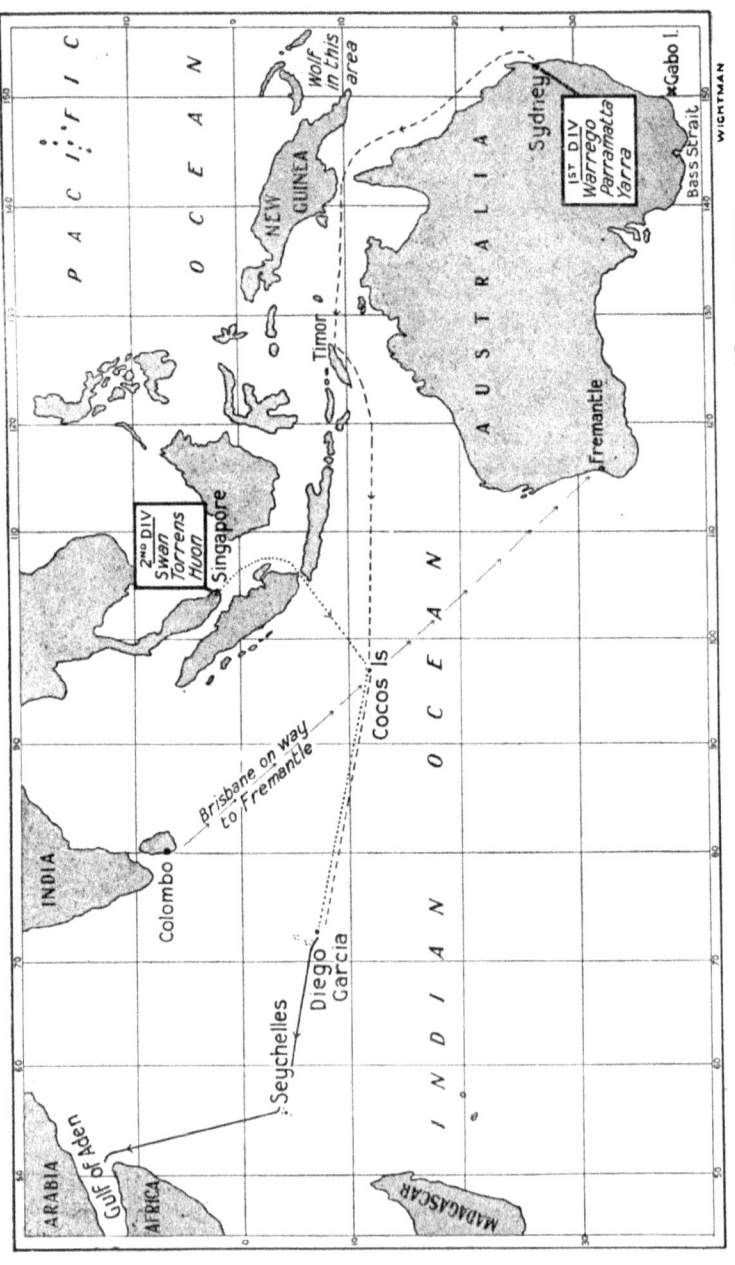

TRACKS OF THE AUSTRALIAN DESTROYER FLOTILLA ON ITS WAY TO THE MEDITERRANEAN

Map No. 24

THE ADRIATIC SEA AND ADJACENT WATERS, SHOWING THE AREA IN
WHICH THE AUSTRALIAN DESTROYER FLOTILLA WORKED IN 1917-18

Map No. 25

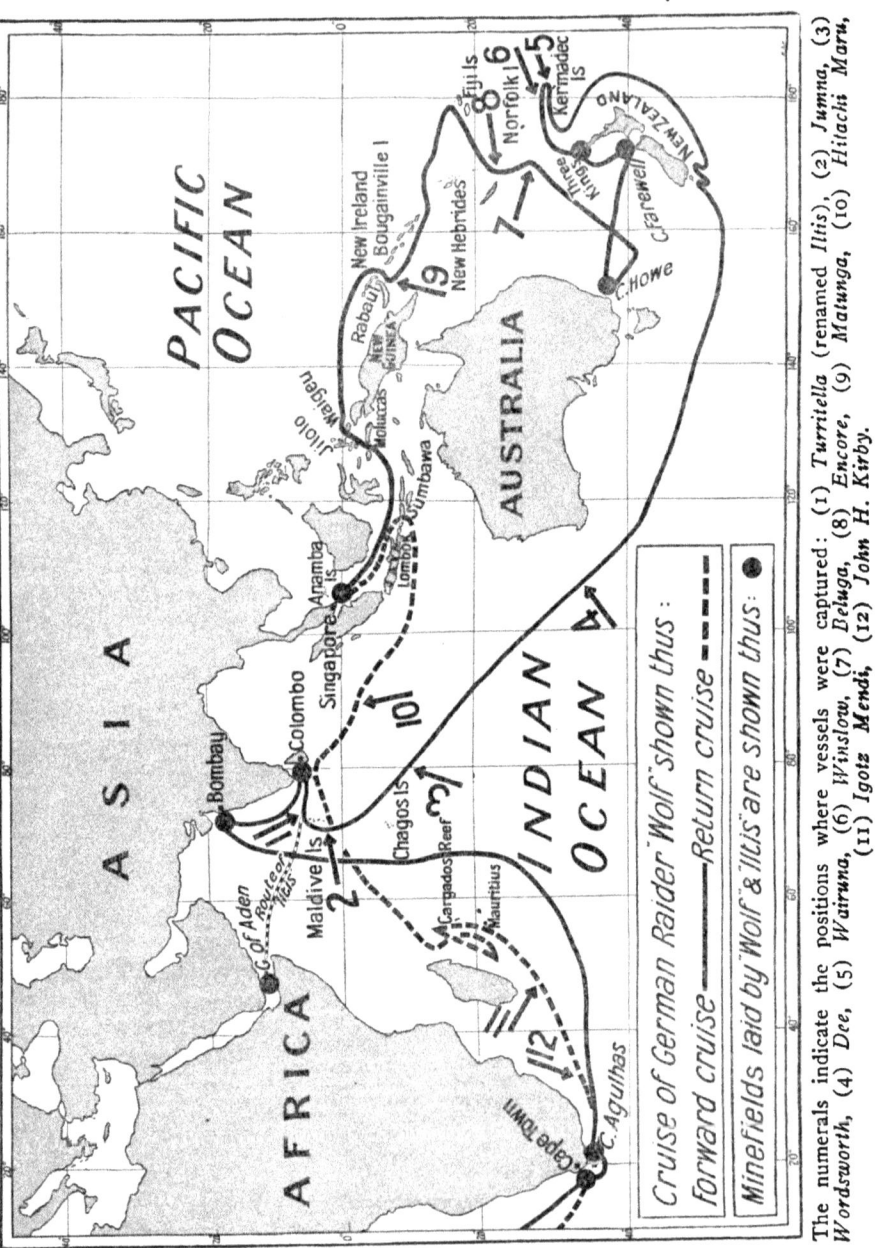

The numerals indicate the positions where vessels were captured: (1) *Turritella* (renamed *Iltis*), (2) *Jumna*, (3) *Wordsworth*, (4) *Dee*, (5) *Wairuna*, (6) *Winslow*, (7) *Beluga*, (8) *Encore*, (9) *Matunga*, (10) *Hitachi Maru*, (11) *Igotz Mendi*, (12) *John H. Kirby*.

Map No. 26

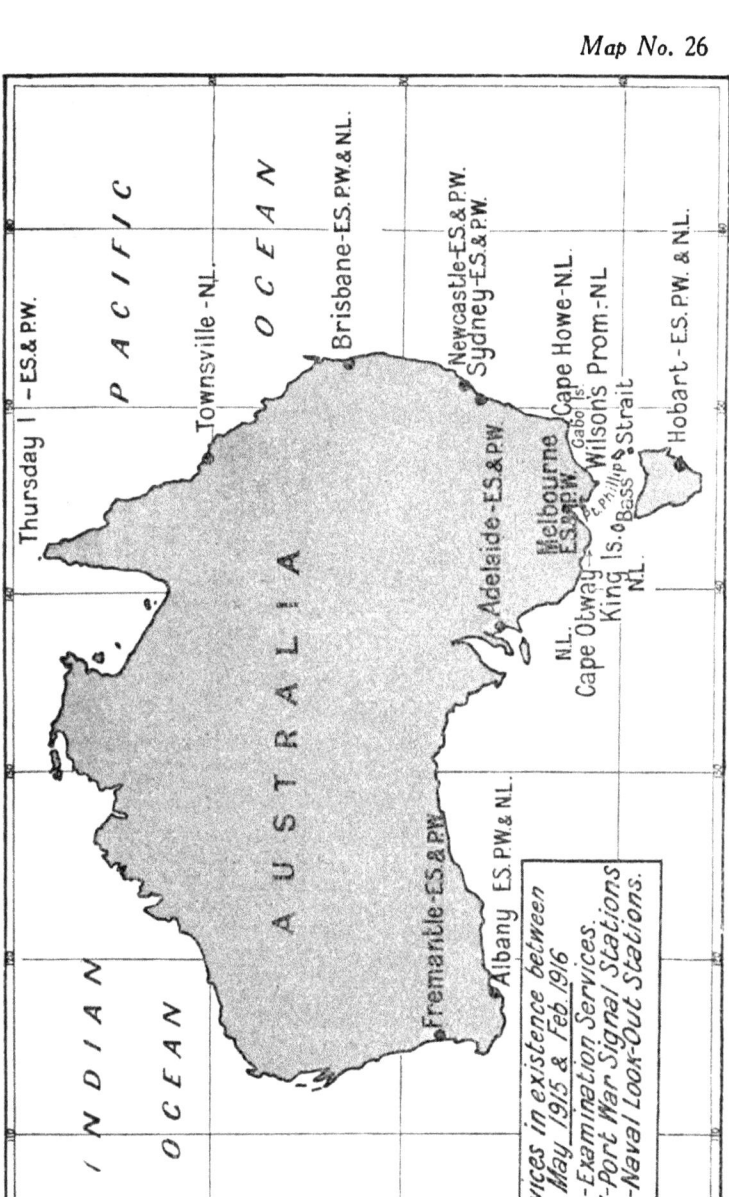

AUSTRALIA, SHOWING COASTAL PRECAUTIONS

During part of 1915 and 1916 the precautions were modified. Except at Thursday Island, Sydney, Melbourne, and Fremantle, only naval lookout stations were maintained; in October, 1916, however, fuller services were reimposed.

MAP

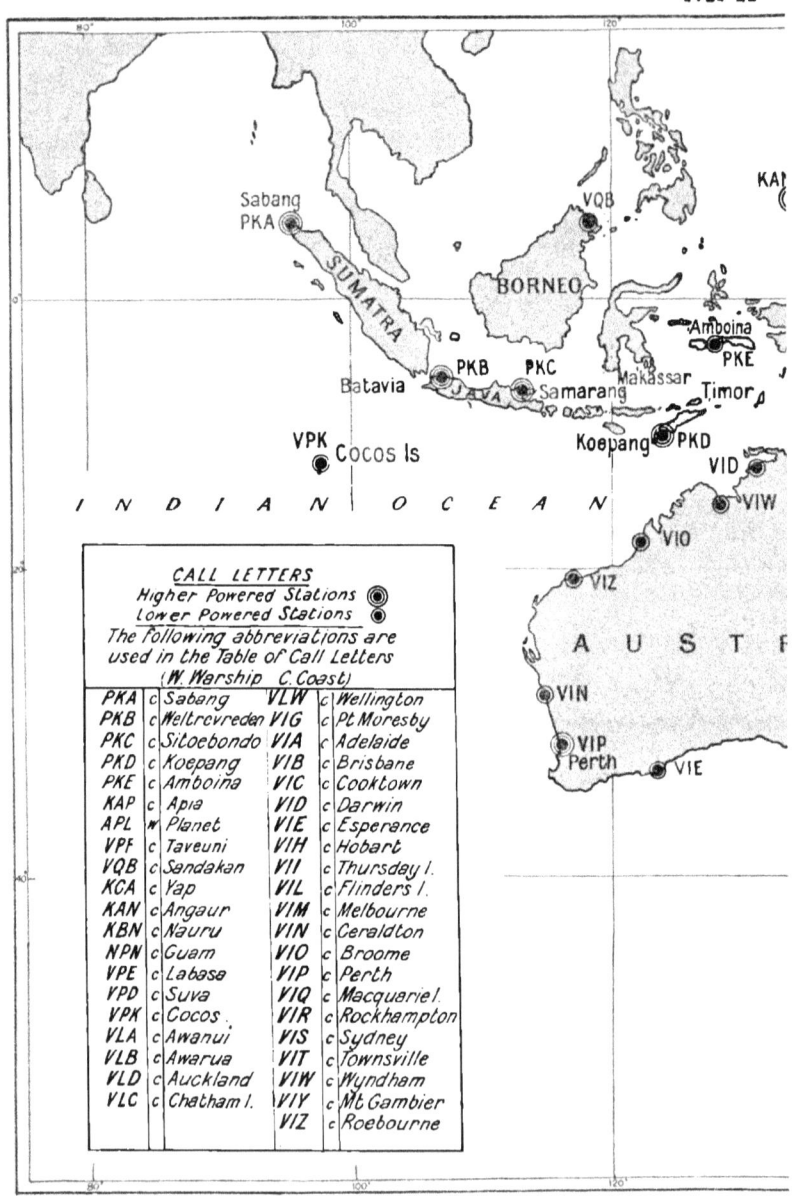

Australia and the Islands, show

No. 27.

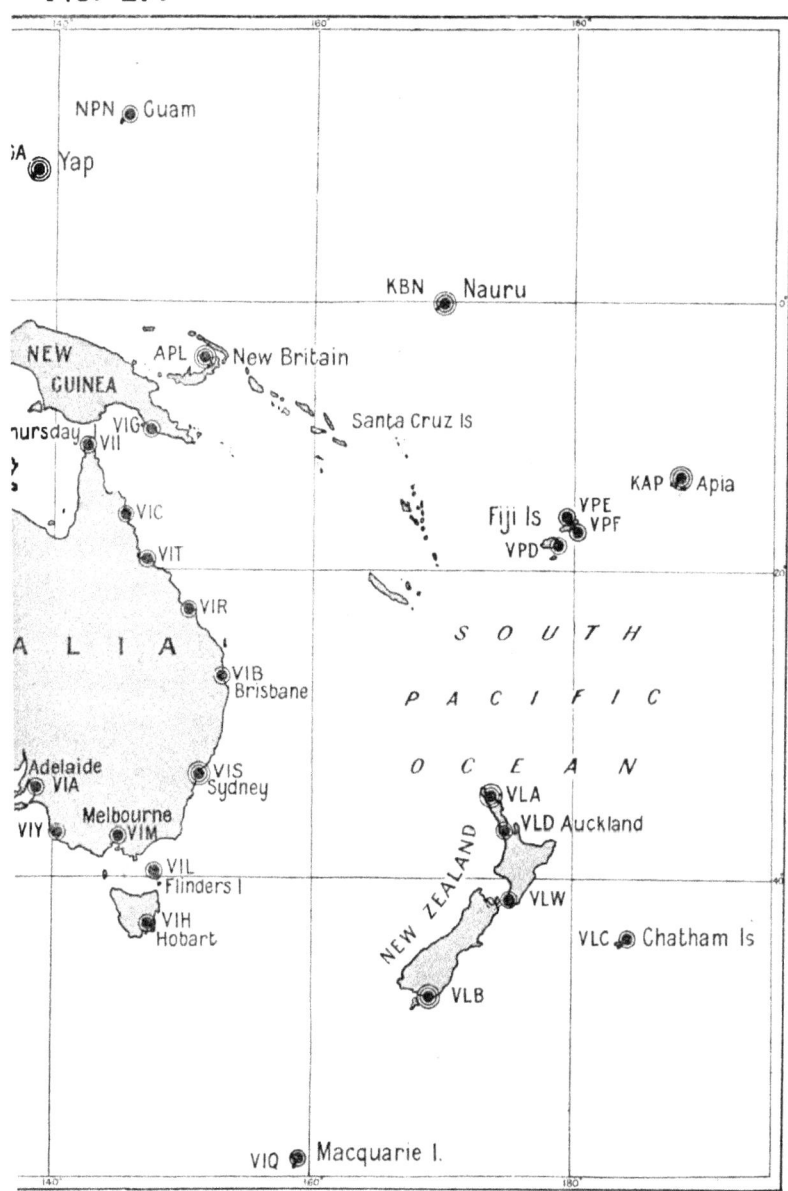

WIRELESS STATIONS WORKING IN 1914

Map No. 28

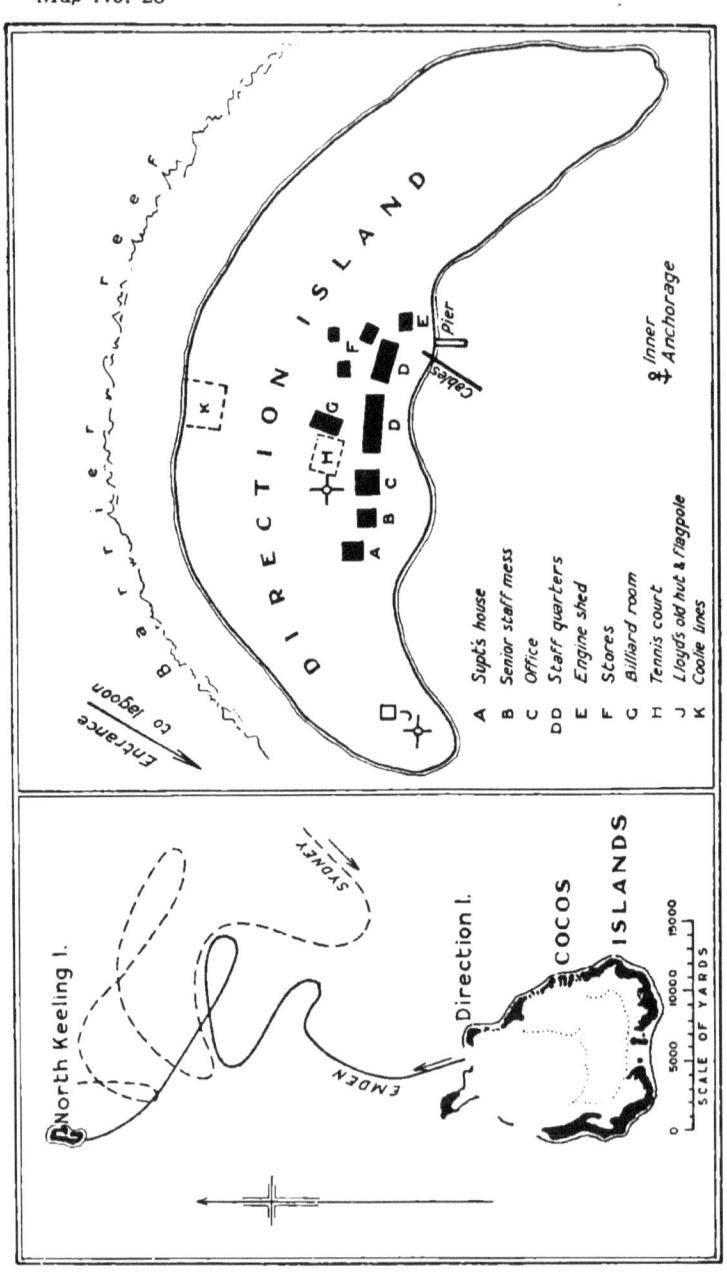

The Cocos Group and Direction Island

THE
AUSTRALIANS AT RABAUL

THE CAPTURE AND ADMINISTRATION OF THE
GERMAN POSSESSIONS IN THE
SOUTHERN PACIFIC

VOLUME X

LIST OF MAPS

1. The Western Pacific
2. The "Old Protectorate" division of German New Guinea
3. Malaysia and adjacent islands
4. New Britain
5. Rabaul and environs
6. The north-east part of the Gazelle Peninsula, New Britain
7. The advance towards Bitapaka, showing enemy dispositions at 9 a.m. on 11th September, 1914
8. Nauru Island

MAP

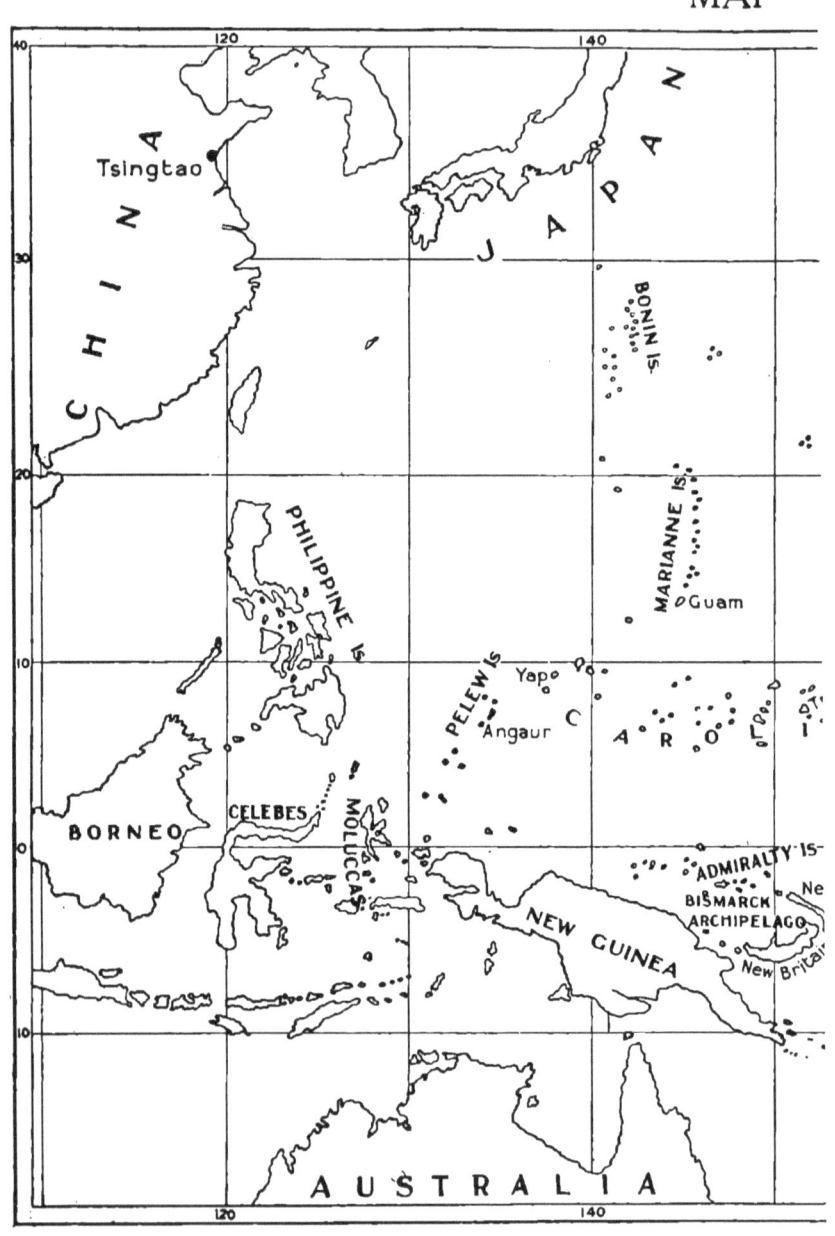

THE WESTERN

No. 1

PACIFIC OCEAN

MAP

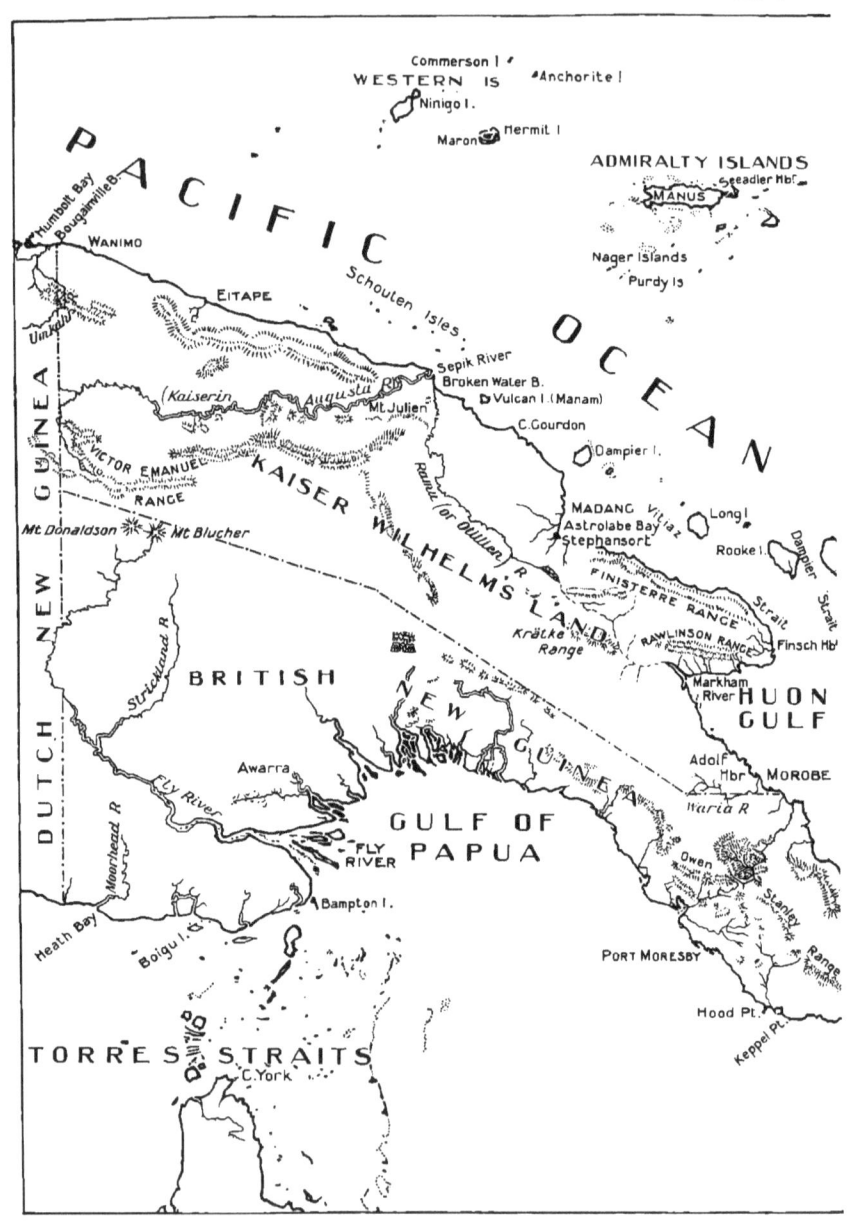

The "Old Protectorate" division

No. 2

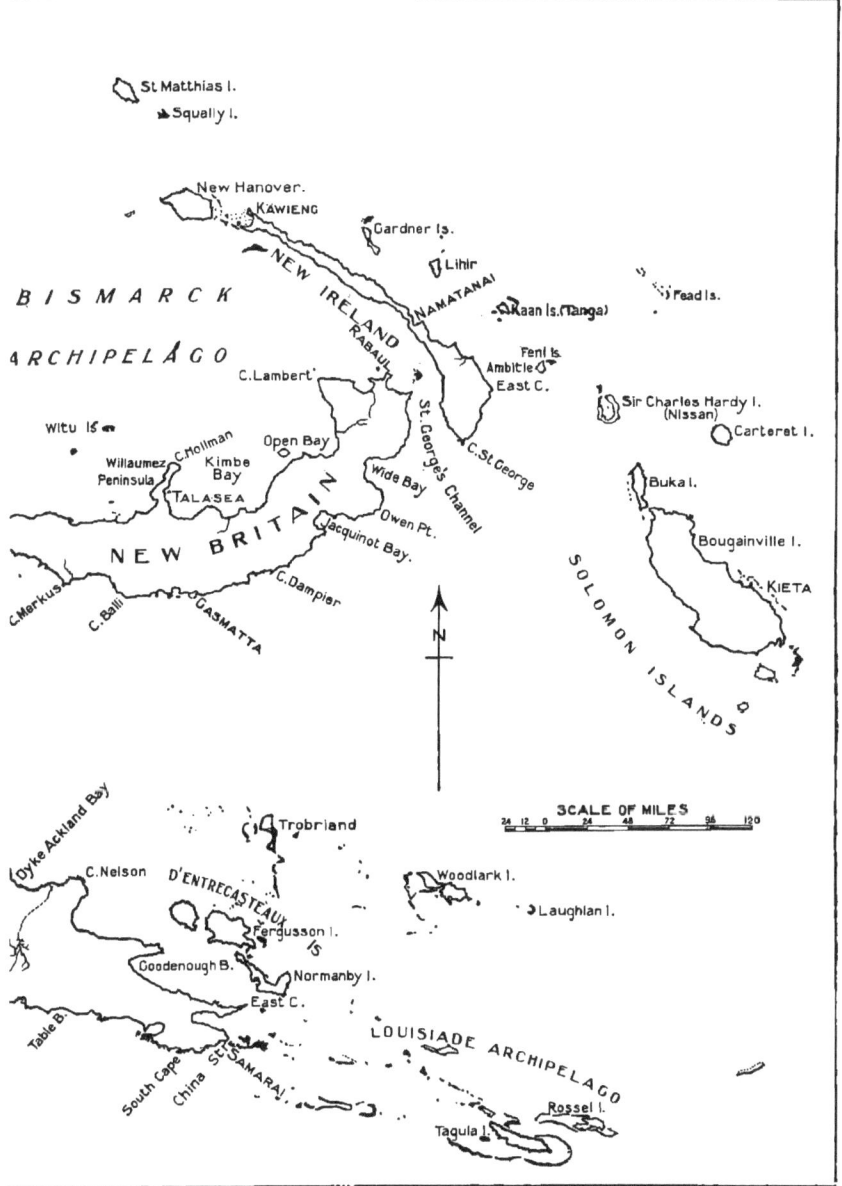

OF GERMAN NEW GUINEA

A. E. Scam.n ell

Map No. 3

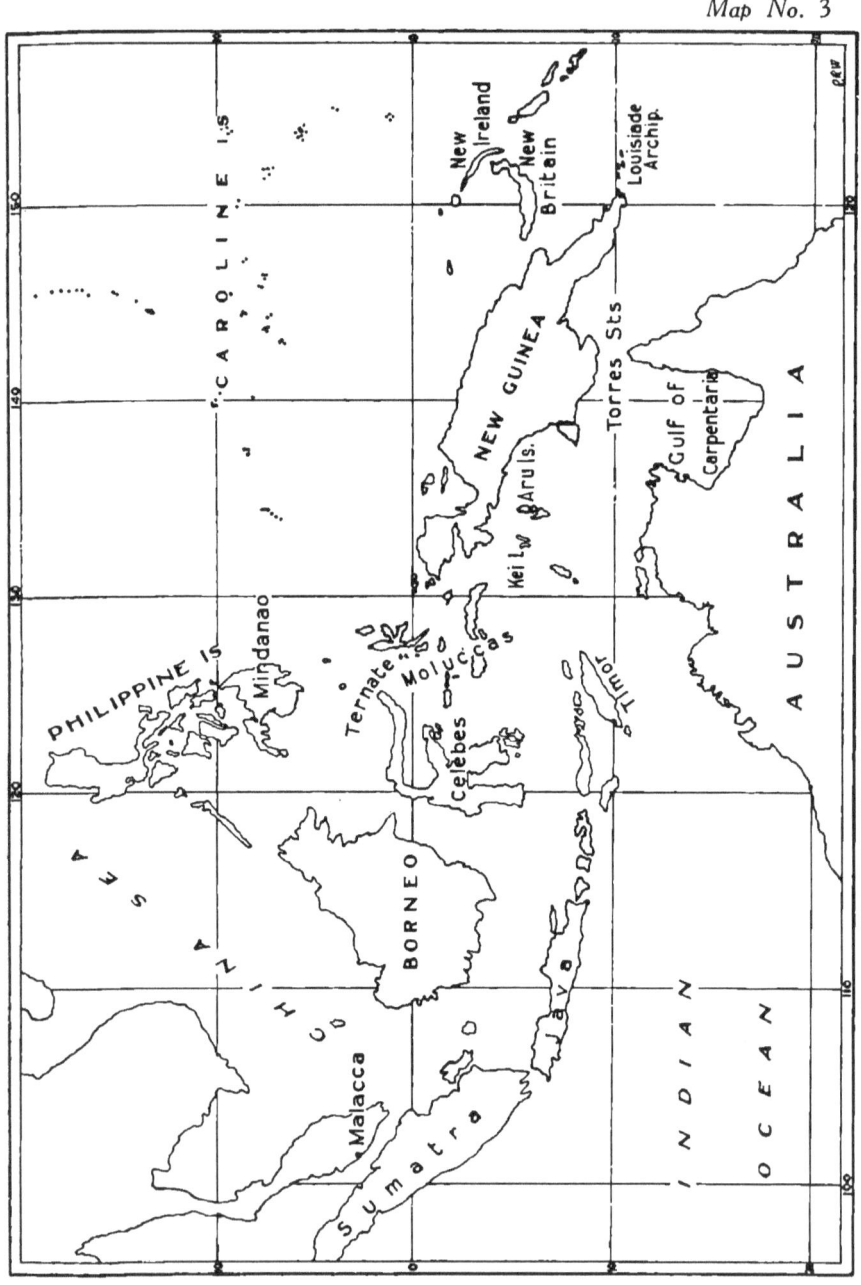

MALAYSIA AND ADJACENT ISLANDS

Map No. 4

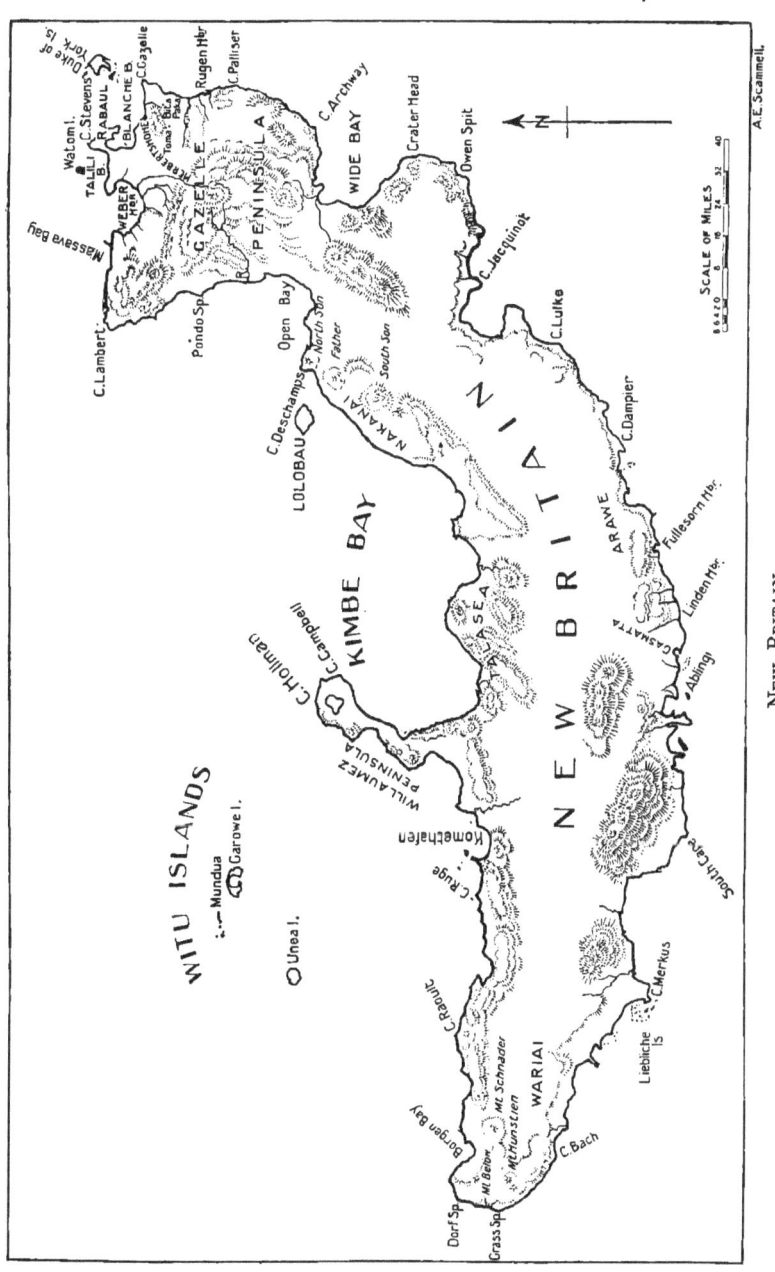

New Britain

Map No. 5

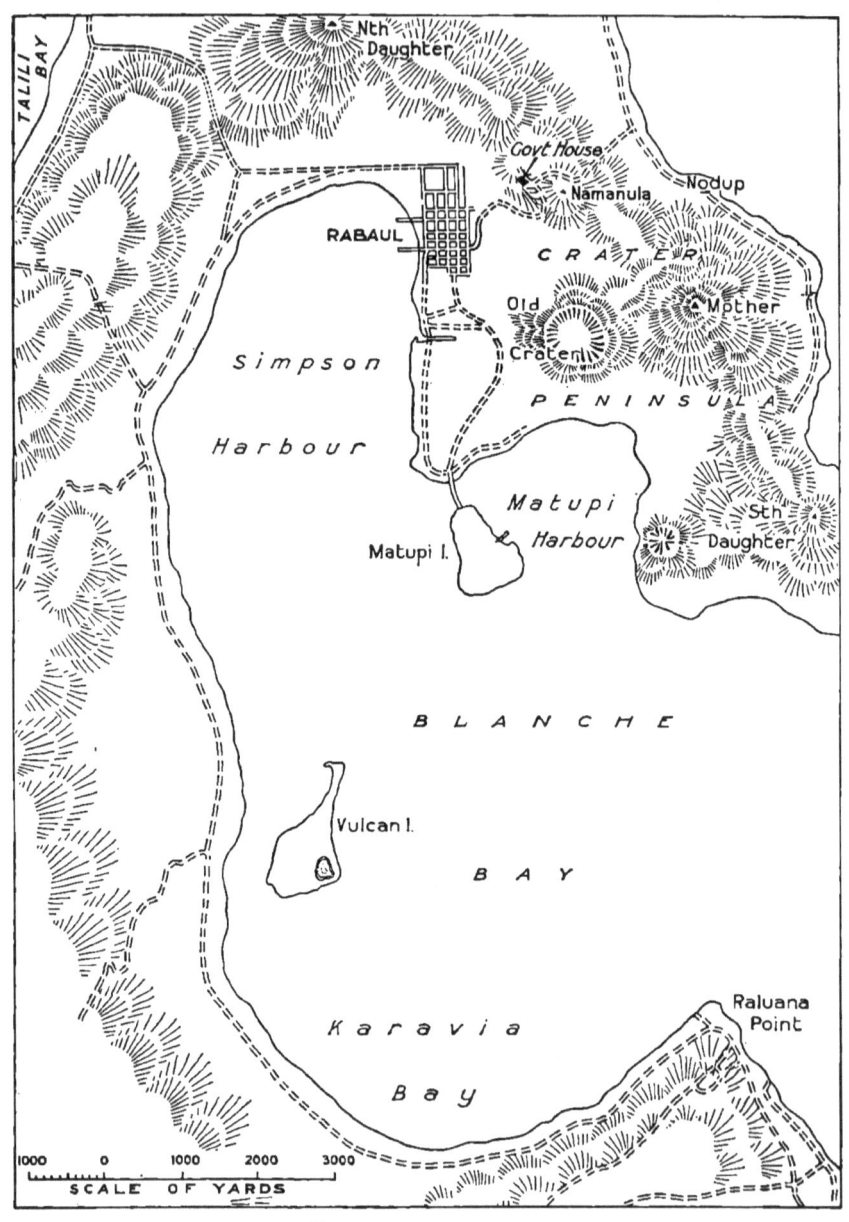

Rabaul and environs

Map No. 6

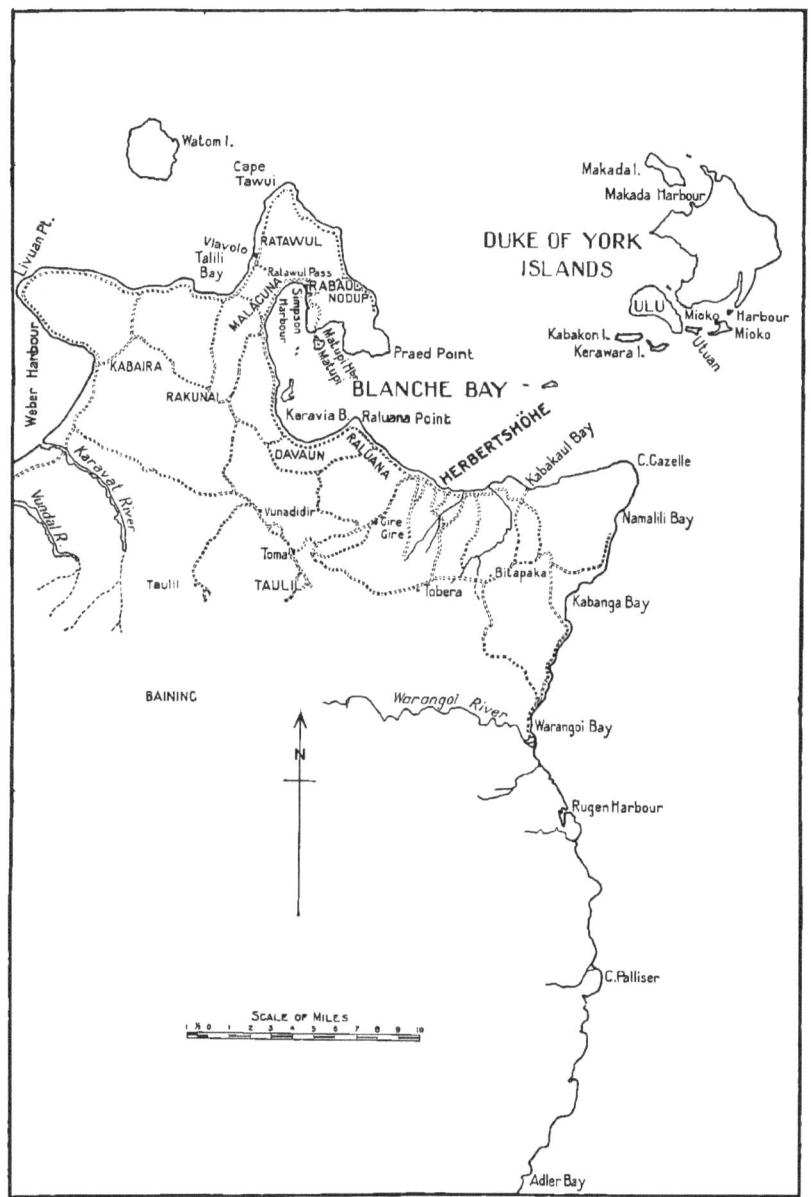

THE NORTH-EAST PART OF THE GAZELLE PENINSULA, NEW BRITAIN

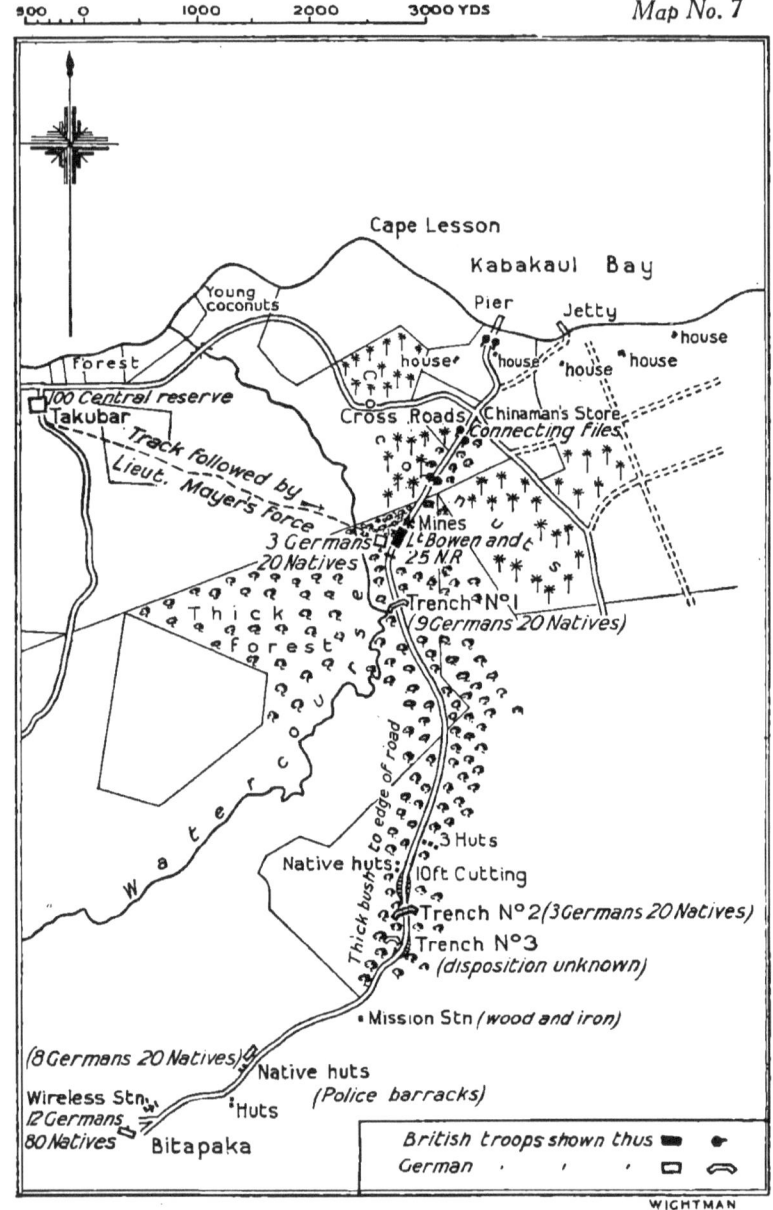

THE ADVANCE TOWARDS BITAPAKA, SHOWING ENEMY DISPOSITIONS AT 9 A.M. ON THE 11TH OF SEPTEMBER, 1914

Map No. 8

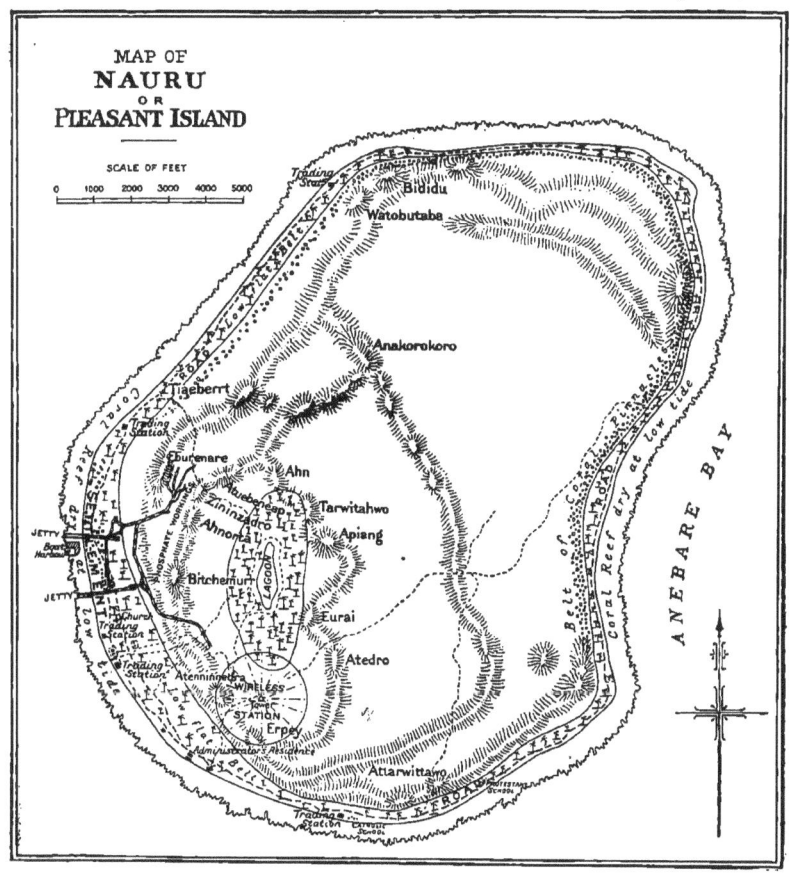

NAURU ISLAND

By courtesy of The British Phosphate Commission.

AUSTRALIA DURING THE WAR

VOLUME XI

MAP

Distribution of Australian Munitions and War Workers in Great Britain and France, 1916-1919

Map No. 1.

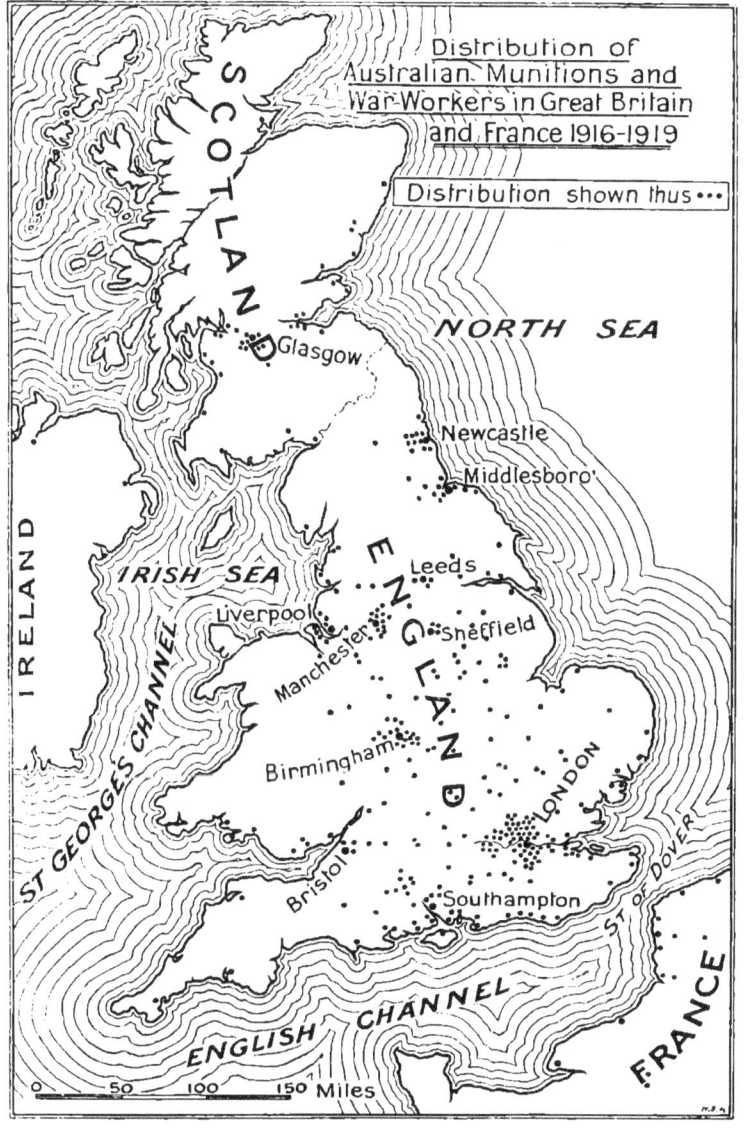

OFFICIAL HISTORY OF AUSTRALIA IN THE WAR OF 1914-1918

Complete 12-volume series

Series edited by C.E.W. Bean, and written by C. E. W. Bean, H.S. Gullett, Frederic Morley Cutlack, Arthur W. Jose, Seaforth Simpson Mackenzie and Ernest Scott.

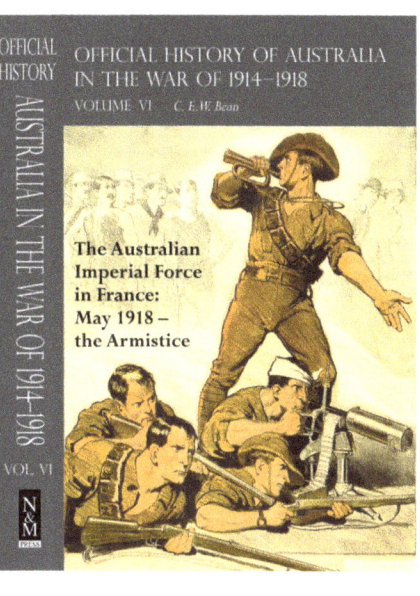

The Official History of Australia in the War of 1914–1918 is a 12-volume series covering Australian involvement in the First World War. The series was edited by C. E. W. Bean, who also wrote six of the volumes, and was published between 1920 and 1942. The first seven volumes deal with the Australian Imperial Force while other volumes cover the Australian Naval and Military Expeditionary Force at Rabaul, the Royal Australian Navy, the Australian Flying Corps and the home front; the final volume is a photographic record. Unlike other official histories that have been aimed at military staff, Bean intended the Australian history to be accessible to a non-military audience. The relatively small size of the Australian forces enabled the history to be presented in great detail, giving accounts of individual actions that would not have been possible when covering a larger force.

www.naval-military-press.com

The contents of the individual volumes are as follows:

Volume I – The Story of Anzac: The First Phase
SB. xlviii + 662 pp with 111 maps (some in colour) & 50 illustrations.
ISBN: 9781783313280

Starting with the outbreak of war and ending on 4 May 1915, just after the Gallipoli landing, this is the first volume in the Official History series. It sets the whole campaign in perspective, starting with the assassination of Archduke Franz Ferdinand of Austria in June of 1914 and the almost inevitable build-up to full-scale war. Quick to respond, the Australians and New Zealanders started recruiting for the AIF six days after the outbreak of war. By early November the first Australian and New Zealand contingent was able to set sail from Australia, arriving in Cairo in early December.

Volume II – The Story of Anzac: From 4 May 1915 to the Evacuation
SB. xviii + 975 pp with 28 maps (some in colour) & 524 illustrations.
ISBN: 9781783313297

The second volume in this series covers the period immediately following the ill-fated Gallipoli landing of 25 April 1915 until January of the following year. It tackles in detail the evacuation of Helles, the struggle for Krithia, the repulse of the Turks, the battles of Lone Pine and Sari Bair, and the landing at Suvla Bay. Kitchener's visit to Anzac and the subsequent British Government order to evacuate Anzac and Suvla are also given good coverage.

Volume III – The Australian Imperial Force in France: 1916
SB. xvi + 1036 pp with 9 maps (some in colour) & 475 illustrations.
ISBN: 9781783313303

After its evacuation from the Gallipoli Peninsula, the AIF was reorganised into two corps: I and II Anzac. By the middle of 1916 both corps had arrived on the Western Front, where operations on the Somme were about to begin. In this third volume of Bean's Official History he describes the Australian contribution to the Somme campaign. The Somme offensive was the worst ordeal of the Great War for the AIF, and the Battle of Fromelles and operations at Pozieres are both among the topics given good coverage.

www.naval-military-press.com

Volume IV – The Australian Imperial Force in France: 1917
SB. x + 1030 pp with 9 maps & 475 illustrations.
ISBN: 9781783313310

Volume four of this momentous Official History opens with the plans for the next twelve months, after the terrible losses at Fromelles and on the Somme in 1916. But these plans were set back after the extensive German evacuation that saw them entrench themselves behind well-prepared defences, which for the rest of 1917 the allies attacked, with very little real success.

Volume V – The Australian Imperial Force in France: December 1917–May 1918
SB. xii + 825 pp with 4 maps (in colour) & 279 illustrations.
ISBN: 9781783313426

In volume five we see Australian troops fighting better and with more telling effect in a decisive period of military history. The great German offensive of March-April 1918 saw important battles for the Australian forces that were fought around Amiens and Hazelbrouck in the spring of 1918. By the end of April, despite huge casualties, the 2nd, 3rd and 5th Divisions were holding half the crucial front from Arras in the north to Amiens in the south-east.

Volume VI – The Australian Imperial Force in France: May 1918 – the Armistice
SB. xi + 1096 + lxxvi pp with 4 maps (in colour) & 530 illustrations.
ISBN: 9781783313433

Volume six covers the last six months of the Great War and gives us the story of how the Australians hit back, showing how they were constantly on the offensive. The successful Battle of Hamel was followed by the great offensive, starting on 8th August, in which the AIF was the main spearhead in a series of smashing victories. Also of interest is the biographical information on General Monash, the corps' Commander, as well as pen sketches of other Generals and heroes of all ranks.

Volume VII – The Australian Imperial Force in Sinai and Palestine
SB. xi + 844 + lxxvi pp with 77 maps (some in colour) & 83 illustrations.
ISBN: 9781783313440

The seventh volume in Bean's history gives coverage to the fighting against the Turks following the Turkish invasion of Egypt, and its various operations including the Gaza engagement, the advance to and capture of Damascus, Aleppo and the Armistice. It comprehensively deals with the Light Horse and also with the foundation of the new Australian Flying Corps.

Volume VIII – The Australian Flying Corps: 1914–1918
SB. xxvii + 485 pp with 32 maps (some in colour) & 54 illustrations.
ISBN: 9781783313457

Volume eight, written by Frederic Cutlack, covers in great detail the first air operations in war undertaken by Australia. These first operations were carried out by the famous "Half Flight" of the Australian Flying Corps, which was despatched to disease-ridden Mesopotamia in 1915 to provide air services for the Anglo-Indian Army. This army was attempting to drive out the Turks and thus protect the Empire's oil resources. The next phase came in early 1916, with the formation of No.1 Squadron, Australian Flying Corps, and its despatch to Egypt where it took part in operations in the Sinai desert and then Palestine. Cutlack places in perspective the role played by the young Australian aviators in helping to win air supremacy against the German Air Force. After that victory, the Australian pilots had a devastating effect in the ground attack role, particularly in the final offensive against the Turkish armies in 1918. Finally, Cutlack describes the achievements of squadrons 2, 3 and 4, which arrived in France at a late, crucial stage of the war. After the briefest introduction to an entirely new way of fighting, they were sent into the thick of the aerial battle, remaining on operations until the war ended.

Volume IX – The Royal Australian Navy: 1914–1918
SB. xli + 649 pp with 28 maps (some in colour) 2 diagrams & 202 illustrations.
ISBN: 9781783313464

The ninth volume in the Official History, written in the 1920s under trying conditions of censorship by the Admiralty (eventually partially overcome), is set out to show that during the Great War the Royal Australian Navy had justified the policy of the pre-war Australian leaders who had inaugurated it. Covered, amongst other topics, is the Capture of the German Colonies, the Sydney-Emden Fight, Overseas Service in East Africa, Dardanelles, North Atlantic and also in European Waters. It confirms that whether fighting in action, in routine patrolling, or working ashore, the young Australian fleet an